Joseph Brodsky: Conversations

Literary Conversations Series

Peggy Whitman Prenshaw
General Editor

Photographed by Richard Avedon
Joseph Brodsky
Poet
New York, New York
June 16, 1991

Joseph Brodsky: Conversations

Edited by
Cynthia L. Haven

University Press of Mississippi
Jackson

www.upress.state.ms.us

The University Press of Mississippi is a member of the Association of American University Presses.

Manufactured in the United States of America

10 09 08 07 06 05 04 03 02 4 3 2 1
∞

Library of Congress Cataloging-in-Publication Data

Brodsky, Joseph, 1940–
Joseph Brodsky : conversations / edited by Cynthia L. Haven.
p. cm.—(Literary conversations series)
Includes index.
ISBN 1-57806-527-5 (cloth : alk. paper)—ISBN 1-57806-528-3 (pbk. : alk. paper)
1. Brodsky, Joseph, 1940—Interviews. 2. Poets, Russian—20th century—Interviews.
I. Haven, Cynthia L. II. Title. III. Series.
PG3479.4.R64 Z468 2003
811′.54—dc21 2002033082

British Library Cataloging-in-Publication Data available

Selected Books by Joseph Brodsky

Stikhotvoreniia i poemy [Short and Long Poems]. Washington D.C. and New York: Inter-Language Literary Associates, 1965. Editors Gleb Struve & Boris Filipoff.

Elegy to John Donne and Other Poems. London: Longmans, 1967. Selected and translated with an introduction by Nicholas Bethell.

Ostanovka v pustyne [A Halt in the Desert]. New York: Izdatel'stvo Imeni Chekhova, 1970. Unnamed co-editor George L. Kline, with Max Hayward. Revised edition, Ardis, 1988; revised edition with co-editor named, NY: Slovo/Word and St. Petersburg: Pushkinskii Fond, 2000.

Joseph Brodsky: Selected Poems. Harmondsworth, U.K.: Penguin Books, 1973; New York: Harper & Row, 1973. Translated by George L. Kline; foreword by W. H. Auden.

Chast' rechi [A Part of Speech]. Ann Arbor, Mich.: Ardis, 1977; reissued, NY: Slovo/Word and St. Petersburg: Pushkinskii Fond, 2000.

V Anglii [In England]. Ann Arbor, Mich.: Ardis, 1977.

Konets prekrasnoi epokhi [The End of a Lovely Era]. Ann Arbor, Mich.: Ardis, 1977; reissued, NY: Slovo/Word and St. Petersburg: Pushkinskii Fond, 2000.

A Part of Speech. New York: Farrar, Straus, & Giroux, 1980, and London: Oxford University Press, 1980. Translated by various hands.

Verses on the Winter Campaign 1980. London: Anvil Press Poetry, 1981. Translated by Alan Myers.

Novyie stansy k Avguste; stikhi k M.B., 1962–1982 [New Stanzas to Augusta; Poems to M.B., 1962–1982]. Ann Arbor, Mich.: Ardis, 1983; reissued, NY: Slovo/Word and St. Petersburg: Pushkinskii Fond, 2000.

Mramor [Marbles]. Ann Arbor, Mich.: Ardis, 1984.

Less Than One; Selected Essays. New York: Farrar, Straus, & Giroux, 1986, and London: Viking Press, 1986.

Uraniia, Ann Arbor, Mich.: Ardis, 1987; reissued, NY: Slovo/Word and St. Petersburg: Pushkinskii Fond, 2000.

To Urania: Selected Poems 1965–1985. New York: Farrar, Straus, & Giroux, 1988, and London: Viking, 1988. Translated by various hands.

Marbles; A Play in Three Acts. Translated by Alan Myers, with the author. New York: Farrar, Straus & Giroux, 1989. London: Penguin, 1990.

Democracy! Act I: *Granta,* Volume 30 (Winter 1990), translated by Alan Myers; Act II: *Partisan Review,* Spring 1993, translated by the author; revised edition: *Performing Arts Journal* (Volume XVIII, 1996).

Chast' rechi; izbrannye stikhi, 1962–1989 [A Part of Speech; Selected Poems, 1962–1989]. Moscow: Khudozhestvennaia literatura, 1990.

Osennii krik iastreba. Stikhotvoreniia 1962–1989 [The Hawk's Autumn Cry: Poems 1962–1989]. Leningrad: LO IMA Press, 1990.

Ballada o Malen'kom Buksire [Ballad of a Small Boat]. Leningrad: Detskaia literatura, 1991. Children's Poems.

Watermark. New York: Farrar, Straus & Giroux, 1992, and London: Hamish Hamilton, 1992.

Kappadokiia [Cappadocia]. Saint Petersburg: Aleksandra, 1993.

On Grief and Reason; Essays. New York: Farrar, Straus & Giroux, 1995, and London: Hamish Hamilton, 1995.

V okrestnostiakh Atlantidy; novye stikhotvoreniia [In the Vicinity of Atlantis: New Poems]. Saint Petersburg: Pushkinskii Fond, 1995.

So Forth. New York: Farrar, Straus & Giroux, 1996; London: Hamish Hamilton, 1996.

Peizazh s Navodneniem [Landscape with Flood]. Dana Point, Calif.: Ardis, 1996; reissued, St. Petersburg, Pushkinskii Fond, 2000. Edited by Alexander Sumerkin.

Sochineniia Iosifa Brodskogo [Works of Joseph Brodsky], Vols. 1–4: Saint Petersburg: Pushkinskii Fond, 1992–96; revised edition, Vols. 1–4, 1997–98; Vol. 5, 1999; Vol. 6, 2000; Vol. 7 and *Kommentarii,* by Viktor Kulle (forthcoming).

Pis'mo Goratsiiu [Letter to Horace]. Moscow: Nash dom-L'Age d'Homme, 1998.

Discovery. New York: Farrar, Straus & Giroux, 1999. Illustrated by Vladimir Radunsky.

Collected Poems in English. New York: Farrar, Straus & Giroux, 2000. Edited by Ann Kjellberg.

Vtoroi vek posl'e nashei ery: Dramaturgiia [The Second Century After Our Times: Plays]. Saint Petersburg: *Zvezda,* 2001.

V ozhidanii varvarov; Mirovaia poeziia v perevodakh [Waiting for the Barbarians: World Poetry in Translation]. Saint Petersburg: *Zvezda*, 2001.

Nativity Poems. New York: Farrar, Straus, & Giroux, 2001. Translated by various hands.

Contents

Introduction

Exiles face the prospect of instant irrelevance when they land on foreign soil. The life-or-death concerns that led to their departure have only peripheral interest in their new milieu; they depend on translators for a voice. It's a recipe for literary impotence. Joseph Brodsky, however, opted for a more unconventional course after his 1972 expulsion from the Soviet Union. He transformed himself from a stunned émigré into, as Brodsky termed it, "a Russian poet, an English essayist, and of course, an American citizen."[1]

The interviews included in this volume, which cover the course of his exile (the last occurs ten weeks before his death), calibrate the process of his remarkable reinvention—from a self-educated, brilliant, brash, but decidedly provincial Leningrad poet to an erudite Nobel laureate and international man of letters. It was a daunting task: in an early interview, Brodsky commented that living under Soviet rule was akin to living under increased gravity, where every word and act had enormous repercussions. Living in the West, by contrast, was like living on the moon—one could bounce and somersault with no effort, but it meant nothing, since everyone else was doing exactly the same. Brodsky had never left Soviet soil and his spoken English was all but incomprehensible. Yet the Leningrad street-fighter quickly reoriented himself, learning fast with each swing, broadening his outlook, expanding his poetic repertoire, and yet, remaining curiously himself.

His first Western interviewers met a man tussling with the sudden irrelevance of exile: "The democracy into which he has arrived provides him with physical safety but renders him socially insignificant. . . . And the reality of it consists of an exiled writer constantly fighting and conspiring to restore his significance, his leading role, his authority." For Brodsky, the higher ground was to recognize that exile is a metaphysical condition, for "[e]xile brings you overnight where it would normally take a lifetime to go." Exile, "famous for its pain," should also be known for its "pain-dulling infinity, for its forgetfulness, detachment, indifference, for its terrifying human and inhuman vistas."[2] This attitude reinforced a preexisting aesthetic bent, as these interviews show.

As he said in the early (1974) *Mosaic* interview: "I think if I can talk about any development, my writing becomes a bit more hard . . . more sober, more dry—less emotional, just more deaf in some sense." Not that his poetry was ever hysterical. Russian poet and colleague Alexander Kushner notes that Brodsky had already established a pre-exile style as classical and restrained as the architecture of Petersburg and a tonal reserve, precision, and intellectualism typical of the Leningrad poets from which he arose.[3] (He was also under a very different influence since the 1960s—that of John Donne and the metaphysical poets—which may have had an even greater impact than his beloved Leningrad.) Brodsky's sobriety was to grow more profound with the years. He revealed his admiration for a minor Alexandrian poet in an interview with Solomon Volkov, then paraphrased the poet: "Try during your life to imitate time. That is, try to be restrained and calm and to avoid extremes. Don't be especially eloquent, but strive for a monotone. . . . But do not be upset if you cannot do this during your life. Because when you die, you will be like time anyway."[4]

Some say Brodsky succeeded all too well. One Russian poet, Larissa Vasileva, cried out that "his poems leave me indifferent because I see how his heart does not beat, how he is cold toward everything that doesn't pertain to himself" (Rich 30). Even a prominent colleague, Yevgeny Rein, found the poems of his last decade "too cerebral," commenting that the poetry "renders itself like a computer and gives the impression that it is operating under the influence of some unbelievably superpowerful intellectual consciousness" (Rich 12). However, he added, "Poetry becomes great in spite of its shortcomings . . . owing to the uniqueness of the creator. . . . And Brodsky was an absolutely unique creator" (Rich 12). In these interviews, one can hear the occasional coldness, the brusqueness, but also his struggle for the perfect sentence, the perfect thought. Typically, one can hear his mind whir restlessly as he plays for a few extra moments to think with an "et cetera, et cetera, et cetera," or as he punctuates a phrase with an inevitable 'ya."

Heraclitis observed that "the dry soul is the wisest and best." Brodsky would have agreed, at least in principle. But no one who reads these interviews will fail to note his passionate engagement with the world—the very world from which, as a poet, he was always trying to detach himself. The development of the poetry and the development of the human animal writing the poetry are often distinct—yet in Brodsky's case, the overlap is poignant. Certainly his psyche turned to darkness as his body betrayed him—another force driving him to seek the absolute lucidity and infallibility of a mathematical axiom in his poetry, another level of his eternal combat between grief and reason. The struggle is evident in this volume.

All these contradictions complicated the task for Brodsky's interviewers, who reported the experience to be everything from epiphanic to unnerving. Christina Daub said Brodsky was the most difficult interview she ever conducted. Noting an earlier interview with Mark Strand, she said, "Strand had the ability of putting one at ease. Brodsky, it seemed, had the opposite." John Woodford, interviewing Brodsky on the familiar turf of the University of Michigan, found that he was "was a pleasure to talk with . . . intensely familiar." Woodford recalled that he was "full of wit, malicious gossip, and quite ready to deliver a laughing insult to anyone around him, whether he knew them or not. . . . He was Restless Intelligence personified with extreme quantities of both qualities."[5]

Brodsky's comments on women, politics, religion, and other sensitive issues often grate and are occasionally offensive and usually controversial ("You liberals should try to solve one problem instead of diffusing your energy all over the world!"[6]). Woodford conceded, "Sure he could be arrogant and swaggering. . . . When someone asked about the sensual impact of various languages on his ear and mind, and included Spanish in the question: 'Spanish?!' he said. 'I don't believe I can consider it a language.'" His *ex cathedra* proclamations about poetry ring with defiance: "[W]e should recognize that only content can be innovative and that formal innovation can occur only within the limits of form. Rejection of form is a rejection of innovation. . . . More than a crime against language or a betrayal of the reader, the rejection of meter is an act of self-castration by the author."[7] Often, time has proved him right. But, in any case, he never pulled a punch, as these interviews show.

Richard Wilbur noted that Brodsky could be "harshly downright at times," but added that "a little scorn can be a precious thing in a slack age."[8] Many of us agreed. I remember him angrily ejecting a student from our small University of Michigan seminar class. Was the student unwilling to invest in the book he recommended? Or protesting the memorization of poetry, a staple of the Brodsky curriculum? I can't recall which, but it was a breathtaking event in a class of less than a dozen, and on a campus so liberal. Journalist James Marcus, while attending Columbia University, heard rumors of a student in the previous term whose work Brodsky had ridiculed so mercilessly that she burst into tears in class. In a short reminiscence posted on amazon.com, Marcus recalls Brodsky's first day of class: Brodsky, wearing a corduroy jacket, had "thinning reddish hair and the sort of pale skin, stippled with freckles, that seemed never to have been out in the sun. . . ." He lit a cigarette—the first of many. "Throughout the semester he would bum cigarettes from the few addicts in the class, tearing the filters off with his teeth before applying a match." Brodsky explained his worldview to his students: "Poetry, in his estimation, was the glue of civilization, and language the repository of time itself." Later in the semester, after assigning a short paper for class, he warned them, "Assume that this may be the last thing you write. . . . Don't forget, you could get hit by a car after you hand it in. Keep that thought in mind." While it may have been "grandiose nuttiness" from anyone else, Marcus concludes that Brodsky was merely extending his own "high seriousness about writing to his students"—few of whom deserved it. High seriousness and, yes, even grand nuttiness abound in his encounters with journalists, writers, poets, and other interviewers.

Brodsky's interviews reflect as much about the Western sensibility as they do about him, often painfully so. Their frequent repetitiveness shows the monomania of Western journalism—its voyeurism, its vulgar fascination with suffering not its own. As a journalist, I can testify to the difficulty of selling a poetry story without a real-world "hook"—yet for most, it's admittedly easier to ask all-purpose questions about Soviet injustices and lurid details of persecution than to zero in on the more obscure and difficult issues of poetics and aesthetics. The corny CBS "voiceover" sound of typewriter keys clicking—or Morley Safer joining Brodsky as they gaze soulfully out to the Hudson—provide distressing illustration, exemplifying Brodsky's declared enemy, "poshlust."[9]

Brodsky called it the vulgarity of the human heart. It is dangerous to invoke it and accuse others of it—for to do so is to imply one's superiority to it, and thus fall prey to all its manifestations. As Brodsky said, "Evil takes root when one man starts to think that he is better than another." But for Brodsky also, there was another operating principle, at least when journalists persistently asked him about his trial, interrogations, incarcerations, and internal exile. Speaking of "those who would make your life miserable," he admonished a University of Michigan audience: "Above all, try to avoid telling stories about the unjust treatment you received at their hands; avoid it no matter how receptive your audience may be. Tales of this sort extend the existence of your antagonists."[10] His credo was to blame nobody. And if he didn't always live up to it, certainly it marks the level of his vision.

What was Brodsky's attitude towards interviewers? At best, the interviews veer towards conversations with himself, as he so typically plays with an idea, attenuates it, or reverses an opinion—sometimes in mid-sentence, sometimes all in the same sentence. On the other hand, sometimes the conversations tumble towards bellicosity and peppery contempt. The interviews were, after all, prose. "And what does the poet learn from prose?" he asked. "Not much . . . theoretically—but only theoretically—a poet can get along without prose."[11] In the *Plum Review* interview, this attitude is even blunter: "I hate prose," he said, qualifying later in the interview, "As for prose, I don't like it very much. Not at all in fact. It's mostly out of necessity. It's prostituting yourself." Perhaps, but it is ironic, then, to note that Brodsky's essays have influenced Western literature and thought more than his poetry, which has been unevenly translated. In prose, Brodsky emerges even more forcefully as a provocative thinker as well as a poet, another aspect of Brodsky that is reinforced in these interviews.

To those who would argue that some of these interviews seem tossed off, that he didn't seem to take them seriously—well, one could argue that we are perhaps most ourselves in our unconsidered moments. That argument underpins much of today's journalism and psychology. Nevertheless, while his impromptu remarks may not have the durability of his poetry or essays, they do have outstanding merit of their own. He always gave good value for the dollar. His comments are punchy, pithy, provocative, and epigrammatic.

His later interviews were harrowing for reasons linked with his own mortality, and the experience left some shaken. Friends and colleagues remember his chain-smoking, even as he took capsules of nitroglycerine. Elizabeth Roth, an instructor at Southwest Texas State University, said, "I had no idea how sick he was until we met." Neither had the university, she recalls. Staff had not known to make provisions for his illness and boarded him at a bed-and-breakfast with no elevator. At the airport, he surprised Roth and two graduate students by asking for a motorized cart for the long trek to the car and, when one wasn't readily available, waived her offer to find him one and walked on. As soon as he reached the lobby, instead of sitting down, he chose to stand outside and smoke while the car was brought around. "Southwest Texas is built on hills, so there was much breathless trekking to do there, too," she said.[12]

He collapsed at his desk ten weeks later, prematurely dead at age fifty-five from heart disease. "I saw him five days before he died, and he was the color of ashes," said Ardis publisher Ellendea Proffer, whose efforts with her husband, the late Professor Carl Proffer, brought Brodsky to the United States.

"But I'd seen him that way before and he had lived." For Brodsky, smoking and writing were tragically linked. Proffer told me he insisted, after his many heart surgeries, "If I can't smoke, I can't write."[13] His choice was staggeringly characteristic, arguably heroic, ultimately fatal.

In preparing this volume, there were some heartbreaking choices—for every interview included, several were dropped. I aimed to republish not only the more polished, landmark interviews in the *Paris Review* and the *Partisan Review,* the interviews that consolidated his reputation, but also interviews from small publications, many now defunct. Without republication, these interviews are likely to disappear forever. I favored such interviews, even when it meant overlooking an article by a more eminent interviewer. I have also tried to make the interviews chronologically representative of his life. Interviews originally held in Russian, then translated into a second language for publication, then retranslated into English for this volume seemed a dicey proposition. Hence, some of these foreign language interviews remain at large for future volumes to republish. Although there is some repetitiveness in the interview questions, Brodsky's ingenious replies often changed over the years and in different situations.

As always with the University Press of Mississippi's Literary Conversations Series, the interviews are unedited, with only overt typographical and spelling errors corrected. I have corrected some factual errors with notes. Preserving the interviews "as is" enhances their value for scholars, although it often leads to inconsistencies (and idiosyncrasies) in style, usage, and spelling. I have altered some Russian spellings to accommodate what has, in the intervening decades, become the accepted rendering of names (e.g., today's reader might have trouble finding a book by Marina Tsvetaeva using the earlier "Tzvetayeva"). I have preserved Brodsky's tangled and occasionally fractured English, although I have, on occasion, altered punctuation where I thought it might help the reader follow his thought.

My gratitude extends to many. First and foremost, to Professor George Kline, who gave unstintingly of his time, experience, and advice; his support was inestimable. I also owe thanks to Anatoly Naiman, Ellendea Proffer, Ann Kjellberg, Alexander Sumerkin, Lev Loseff, and my friend Inna Soroka. Many thanks to the journals, magazines, books, and other media for allowing me to reprint these interviews, and to the interviewers who shared their recollections of Brodsky as well. Richard Avedon generously allowed the inclusion of his superb photo, which captures the Brodsky that Americans and New Yorkers, in particular, will remember. The staff at the London Library and

Stanford University Libraries were extremely helpful. At the University Press of Mississippi, Seetha Srinivasan and Anne Stascavage extended patience and help. Not least of all, I am grateful to my husband for his unflagging support.

It's been a privilege to ponder this life, so often transposed into a minor key by the media, although it is clearly a life of extraordinary genius, inventiveness, and finally—to risk a cliché—triumph. For me, this book is a personal *omaggio,* in appreciation and memory . . . *quando nel monod li alti versi scrisse.*

This book is dedicated to the memory of Carl R. Proffer (1938–1984), who in the words of Joseph Brodsky, "was simply an incarnation of all the best things that humanity and being American represent."[14]

CLH
March 2002

Notes

1. Anna Husarka, "I Was Simply A-Soviet: A Talk with Joseph Brodsky," *New Leader* 70 (December 14, 1987), 11.

2. Joseph Brodsky, "The Condition We Call Exile," *On Grief and Reason* (New York: Farrar, Straus & Giroux, 1995), 24, 26, 33.

3. Quoted in Elizabeth Rich, "Joseph Brodsky in Memoriam: The Russian Perspective," *South Central Review* 14 (Spring 1997), 15.

4. Solomon Volkov, *Conversations with Joseph Brodsky* (New York: Free Press, 1998), 141.

5. Christina Daub, email communication, 9 October 2001; John Woodford, email communication, 19 December 2000.

6. Helen Benedict, "Flight from Predictability: Joseph Brodsky," *Antioch Review* 43 (Winter 1985), 10.

7. J. Kates, ed., *In the Grip of Strange Thoughts* (Brookline, Mass: Zephyr Press, 1999), 417.

8. Peter Dale, *Richard Wilbur in Conversation with Peter Dale* (London: Between the Lines, 2000), 49.

9. Gogol's "poshlust" was defined and extended by Nabokov to include "corny trash, vulgar clichés, Philistinism in all its phases, imitations of imitations, bogus profundities," and, in contemporary writing, "moth-eaten mythologies, social comment, humanistic messages, political allegories, over-concern with class or race, and the journalistic generalities we all know." Poshlust "is especially vigorous and vicious when the sham is not obvious and when the values it mimics are considered, rightly or wrongly, to belong to the very highest level of art, thought or emotion."

Vladimir Nabokov, chapter 3, "Our Minister Chichikov," *Nikolai Gogol* (Norfolk: New Directions, 1944).

10. Joseph Brodsky, "A Commencement Address," *Less Than One* (New York: Farrar, Straus & Giroux, 1986), 387; "Speech at the Stadium," *On Grief and Reason* (New York: Farrar, Straus & Giroux, 1995), 146.

11. Joseph Brodsky, "A Poet and Prose," *Less Than One* (New York: Farrar, Straus & Giroux, 1986), 177.

12. Elizabeth Roth, email communication, 28 August, 2001.

13. Ellendea Proffer, telephone conversation, 6 January, 2002.

14. *Detroit Free Press*, September 26, 1984.

Chronology

1940 May 24. JB is born to Maria Moiseevna Volpert Brodsky, who works as a German-Russian interpreter dealing with POWs during the war and later as a clerk and bookkeeper, and Alexander Ivanovich Brodsky, naval officer who rises to highest rank allowed to Jews (his rank, major, was comparable to U.S. Navy rank of lieutenant commander) and is then dismissed. He becomes a photographer in Leningrad. JB is an only child.

1941 September 8. The Germans begin a 900-day siege of Leningrad, during which at least 641,000 people die of cold, starvation, disease, or military attack. It is the worst siege ever seen in one city, causing the largest famine ever in the industrialized world. JB is largely in the care of grandparents.

1953 March 5. Death of Stalin saves the Brodsky family from deportation from Leningrad with other Jews, which is rumored to be imminent but never actually confirmed.

1955–56 Winter. JB drops out of school in eighth grade, at age fifteen. Over the subsequent years, he works at an armaments factory, a morgue, a ship's boiler room, and elsewhere as a stoker, a metal worker, and a milling-machine operator, and as an assistant in a crystallography lab at Leningrad University's Department of Geology.

1956 JB begins to study Polish, a language that will give him access to leading Polish poets, such as Cyprian Norwid, Zbigniew Herbert, Czeslaw Milosz, Konstanty Galczynski, as well as to many Western works translated into Polish, but not Russian. It will also allow him to work as a translator.

1957 JB joins geological expedition to Far North (White Sea region).

1958 JB joins geological expedition to the Far East. After finding a volume of Baratynsky in Yakutsk, he begins to write poetry.

1959 January. First poetry reading. Over the next few years, JB completes a number of translations from the Polish, Spanish, and Serbo-Croatian. JB is arrested and jailed without formal charges—the first of many such occurrences in the years before his exile.

1960 February 14. Public performance at the "Tournament of Poets" at the Gorky Palace of Culture. Summer. JB joins geological expedition to South (Caspian Sea region).

1961 August 7. Yevgeny Rein takes JB for his first meeting with Akhmatova at her dacha in Komarovo.

1963 JB reads the Bible for the first time and writes "Isaac and Abraham" within the first few days after finishing Genesis. November 29. Article in the *Vechernii Leningrad (Evening Leningrad)* attacks JB for poetry that is considered pessimistic, half-educated, and decadent. December. Akhmatova inscribes a volume of her poetry to JB with the words, "To Joseph Brodsky, whose poems seem to me to be magical." December 13. The Secretariat of the Union of Writers decides unanimously to turn JB over to the court as a parasite. Shortly before Christmas, JB is surrounded by KGB men and wrestled into the back of a car. He is interrogated, his journals and papers seized.

1964 February 14 and March 13. JB's trial is conducted in two segments. He is charged with about two dozen points, among them vagrancy, the distribution of works by forbidden authors (e.g., Akhmatova and Tsvetaeva), and corruption of the youth. Moreover, JB is accused of "having a worldview damaging to the state, decadence and modernism, failure to finish school, and social parasitism . . . except for the writing of awful poems." JB sentenced to five years' internal exile in a *sovkhoz*. During this period, he is held at Kashchenko psychiatric hospital in Moscow, Na Priazhke psychiatric hospital in Leningrad, and Kresty ("Crosses"), a huge prison complex in Leningrad. He writes several poems, most notable the long philosophical poem, "Gorbunov and Gorchakov." In the psychiatric hospitals, JB is given "tranquilizing" shots, wakened in the middle of the night, plunged into a cold bath, wrapped in a wet towel, and placed next to a heater so that the towel would cut into his flesh as it dries. March 25. JB is sent to the village of Norenskaya, close to the Arctic Circle, where he shovels manure, cleans stables, cuts wood, shifts large stones and grain, and performs other hard labor. During this period, JB masters literary English, using Louis Untermeyer's anthology of English and American poetry.

1965 4 January. T. S. Eliot dies. JB hears the news within a week, and within a few days completes his "Verses on the Death of T. S. Eliot." Early April. First collection of poems, *Stikhotvoreniia i poemy,* published via smuggled manuscript collected by Konstantin Kuzminsky and Grigory Kovalev. In the U.S., editors Gleb Struve and Boris Filippov publish the book. November. JB's sentence is commuted, after international protests, spearheaded by Akhmatova, and includes the participation of Efim Etkind, Kornei Chukovsky, and Dmitri Shostakovich.

1966 March 5. Death of Anna Akhmatova. JB assumes much of the responsibility for her funeral and burial. June 22. Yevgeny Yevtushenko invites JB to join Bella Akhmadulina and Bulat Okudzhava in a public reading at Moscow University to commemorate the 25th anniversary of the USSR entering World War II.

1966–67 Four of JB's poems appear in Leningrad anthologies: *Molodoi Leningrad* (1966) and *Den' poezii* (1967).

1967 *Elegy to John Donne and Other Poems,* translated by Nicholas Bethell, is published in London. October 9. Birth of JB's son, Andrei Basmanov (he has since taken the name Brodsky), by Marina Basmanova, the "M.B." of *New Stanzas to Augusta.*

1969 Robert Lowell invites JB to participate in the Poetry International Festival in London. Soviet authorities refuse permission.

1970 U.S. publication of *Ostanovka v pustyne (A Halt in the Wilderness),* the first book of poetry in which JB is actively involved.

1971–74 Russian writer Vladimir Maramzin attempts a complete *samizdat* edition of JB's poems. He painstakingly searches for texts, establishes the correct dates, and writes scholarly commentaries. Before his exile, JB selects and corrects the approximately 2,000 pages of text. Mikhail Kheifets, another Russian writer and literary critic, wrote an introductory essay to the collection entitled "Joseph Brodsky and Our Generation."

1971 December 31. JB receives an "official" invitation to emigrate from the fictitious Ivri Yakov ("Jacob the Jew") in Rekhovot, Israel.

1972 May 10. JB is ordered to report to agency of visas and immigration; receives notification from the authorities that he is being issued an exit visa for emigration to Israel. When he replies that he does not wish to leave his native land and culture, he is warned that the coming winter could be "very cold." Carl Proffer, visiting Leningrad at the time, invites JB to become poet-in-residence in Ann Arbor, which JB accepts. June 4. Expulsion. Moscow airport customs confiscate and impound manuscripts. Proffer contacts Benjamin Stolz, chair of the Department of Slavic Languages & Literatures, to get authorization to hire JB. Stolz obtains an immigration visa personally approved by William Rogers, U.S. secretary of state. June 6. JB and Proffer, stopping in Vienna, meet Auden in Kirchstetten, outside Vienna. It is the first of several visits for JB, who flies to London with Auden. July 9. JB arrives at Ann Arbor's University of Michigan to assume teaching position. With Proffer's support, he begins post as poet-in-residence and special lecturer at U of M. He is the first poet-in-residence at the university since Robert Frost, five decades earlier; Auden also had a short appointment at the university in the 1940s.

1974 April. The homes of both Maramzin and Kheifets are searched, and manuscripts and *samizdat* documents are confiscated, including the attempted Brodsky volumes. Maramzin and Kheifets are accused of anti-Soviet propaganda and agitation and tried by the Leningrad City Court. Maramzin is sentenced to five years in a labor camp, although the sentence is commuted in July 1975 and he is allowed to emigrate from the Soviet Union. Kheifets serves four years in a labor camp and two years in internal exile.

1974–75 JB becomes the first Five College Distinguished Visiting Professor, based at Smith, during the academic year.

1976 December 13. JB has first heart attack and is hospitalized in New York City. Over the subsequent years, JB undergoes a number of heart surgeries and procedures, including double- and triple-bypass surgery.

1977 JB receives John Simon Guggenheim Memorial Foundation Fellowship in poetry. October 11. JB becomes U.S. citizen in Detroit.

1978 JB receives honorary doctorate of letters from Yale University. JB assumes teaching appointment in the Faculty of the Arts at Columbia University.

1979 JB is inducted as a member of the American Academy and Institute of Arts and Letters and the Bavarian Academy of Fine Arts. He receives Feltrinelli Prize for Poetry and Mondello Literary Prize. He receives a tenured appointment as professor of Slavic Languages and Literature at the University of Michigan, beginning September 1.

1981 JB receives the John D. and Catherine T. MacArthur Foundation's "genius" award. JB is named Five College Professor of Literature, based at Mount Holyoke, for a five-year appointment. He leaves Ann Arbor, dividing his time between New York City and Mount Holyoke in Massachusetts.

1986 *Less Than One* is awarded National Book Critics' Circle prize. Mount Holyoke names him its Andrew W. Mellon Professor of Literature, an appointment he held until his death.

1987 JB receives the Nobel Prize for literature. Award given for "all-embracing authorship, imbued with clarity of thought and poetic intensity," calling his writing "rich and intensely vital," characterized by "great breadth in time and space." JB resigns membership in American Academy of Arts and Letters, which has extended honorary membership to Yevgeny Yevtushenko: "I cannot in good conscience sustain membership in an organization which has thus so compromised its integrity." December. *Novyi mir,* under editorship of Oleg Chukhontsev, publishes JB's first poems to appear officially in Russia since his exile.

1988 *Neva* publishes JB poems. JB is awarded an honorary doctorate of letters from the University of Michigan.

1990 September 1. JB marries Maria Sozzani in the Stockholm City Hall.

1991 JB is named U.S. poet laureate, the first foreign-language poet to be so honored, serving in 1991–92. JB receives honorary degree from Oxford University—the second Russian poet to be so honored, after Akhmatova in 1965. JB receives France's Order of the Legion of Honor at the French Consulate in New York.

1992 *Sochineniia Iosifa Brodskogo* (Works of Joseph Brodsky), vols. 1 and 2, appears in St. Petersburg, based on Maramzin's collection.

1993 JB joins Andrew Carroll to found the American Poetry & Literacy Project, a not-for-profit organization devoted to making poetry a more central part of American culture. The APL Project has distributed more than nearly a million free poetry books in public places.

1996 January 28. JB has a fatal heart attack at night, at his desk in his Brooklyn apartment.

Joseph Brodsky: Conversations

A Conversation with Joseph Brodsky

Lynette Labinger / 1970

From *Agni,* 51 (April 2000), 16–20. Reprinted by permission of Lynette Labinger.

In 1970 Ms. Labinger was a brilliant student and utterly reliable researcher at Mount Holyoke College, where I continue to teach Russian history in the history department. Today in 1996 she is a leading lawyer in Providence, Rhode Island. Between these two dates (twenty-six years) I've been totally out of touch with her. In July 1970 she interviewed Brodsky inside Russia, and in October 1970 she sent me the attached interview notes.

In the 1970s I had absolutely vetoed publishing the notes. This is because our first priority was to protect Brodsky. He would have been damaged by the interview in the eyes of his Soviet persecutors (he'd been in their gulag*) because he spoke of me favorably; I was *non grata* to them; my books were banned (for having exposed Soviet anti-Semitism); indeed I'd been expelled from Russia after one of my visits. As Brodsky says in the interview, he never thought he'd be able to get out of the Soviet Union. Also food for thought is his mention that his heart condition, which destroyed him a quarter of a century later, was caused by his gulag labors.*

Since 1970, the interview lay lost (needle in haystack) on my big shelf of Brodsky letters, poems, and articles. The interview was found only in January 1996 when the tragic news of his death sent me back through this vast material. Ms. Labinger sees no harm in now at last publishing the manuscript.

—Peter Viereck

Informal notes by Mount Holyoke graduate Lynette Labinger, who visited Brodsky to deliver [messages] between him and Peter Viereck, who'd had long talks with Brodsky in 1962 and 1969. In 1969 Brodsky gave Viereck some unpublished new lyric poetry for him to bring to the United States and translate. They were unable to correspond because Soviet censorship intercepted letters both to and from Brodsky.

---

*JB was never in a labor camp, or *gulag,* although he served 20 months of a five-year sentence for hard labor in the Archangelsk region. See the chronology at the beginning of this volume.—*ED*

3 Oct. 1970
Dear Mr. Viereck:

The following is copied straight from a journal I kept—irregularly—during my trip. Sorry for the lapses of grammar and sentences, and sorry for the delay—I'm still working on incompletes from last spring.

14 July 1970

Now to try to piece together meeting with JB last night—Finally got a hold of him by phone, around 7:40 p.m. Was supposed to go out with friends at 9, but Brodsky said, Come tonight?—Right. We tried directions in English, then again in Russian: *tramvai,* not train—almost left city instead of taking 15-minute ride to his apartment.

Brodskys'—they share a flat with 2 or 3 other families—about 12 people in all. Building built in 1903 or 1905—so very high ceilings, interior decorations with classic orders, etc. Brodsky's room—great creation. First through a hallway (very short), into a dark room (a real one—his father's a photographer), over a step—head down, low overhang—and here you are. Bed against big window in front of you, desk and bookshelves filled with books to right, bookshelves to left above table, chair with fur covering. Phonograph in bookshelf—during the evening he played Bach, French jazz trio that plays Bach, Mozart, Purcell's *Dido and Aeneas*—didn't like the last—he told me I was young. Does that mean I'll like it when I'm older?—maybe; no, maybe not at all.

We spoke mostly in English—my Russian was a failure—no confidence on my part.

Other wall of room—the best part: two wardrobes with mirrored doors formed the wall and made the space between them an entranceway. The low overhang was produced by an empty box for Chinese tea (brought back from China by his father—there during WWII—Chinese characters on the side meant something like "this side up") spanning wardrobes. Height of wall increased by a number of old suitcases which lined the tops of the wardrobes, but there was still a great space between the top of Brodsky's wall and the ceiling.

Came in—sat on bed. Brodsky took chair. Pulled phone jack out—whenever phone rang, plugged it in after someone else answered, and then forgot to pull it out till it rang again. He was wearing blue jeans and sweater, side burns, hair curling in back, receding in front; not fat, but slightly overweight. I didn't know what to say, how long to stay—in short, anything. I can't remember what we talked about first, but no matter—I'll just jot down the things he said that interested me, and not in any particular order.

We talked a bit about poetry. I know nothing about poetry—why not? what have I read?—very little. "Bad. I am a patriot, but I must say that English poetry is the richest in the world. English-speaking people who avoid study of their own poetry to take up ours—though it is good—are lazy." Told me I must take it up. Gave me John Donne's "The Ecstasy" to read while he made a phone call.

He talked about his poetry—jokingly—but at the same time he said it was good. His first book (gray cover)—no good. His second—just out—much better. Penguin edition of Kline's translations to be out next fall. No one living who JB respects more.

Much later—talked about Viereck. "Liked him very much." I told him PV wanted picture—JB looked through album, found two—which one?—I liked the one with the cat better. He wrote on the back—on top—quote from PV's poem—in book which I just brought him. Thinks PV's poetry is best in America today. He is translating him for a Soviet anthology to appear next year.

We spoke about Leningrad. I had said the rivers and trees made it seem peaceful, though I hated the architecture. Brodsky laughed—he hated Leningrad—superficial quiet, madness breath. Admitted he probably disliked it so because he had lived there all his life and foresaw no chance of leaving. Later asked him—did he want to leave the country?—Yes, probably not forever, but for a while.—Where?—Not Israel (we had been speaking about anti-Semitism), but Ireland. Yes, and Venice in the winter. Not France, I hate France and the French. The only two Frenchmen I ever respected, Pascal and (can't remember), are dead.—Anywhere else?—Italy too. He didn't want to leave Russia forever, he explained, since he wrote poetry in Russia,—he was writing for Russians. . . .

Is anti-Semitism a constant element?—"Yes, only sometimes the government makes use of it—like now—so it's worse. Doesn't affect me so much—my problems stem from my personal position, not from being Jewish. Never happier to be a Jew than during the Six-Day War."

Prison for 2 years—11 different camps.* Bad heart from it. Now—*persona*

---

*See footnote on first page of this interview. JB spent some time in prison (though not 2 years) while awaiting his 1964 trial. See the chronology at the beginning of this volume.—*ED* *non grata*—never got PV's postcard from Germany. Did Viereck know Brodsky wrote to him in West Germany? I said I doubted it. He said he would try to write him in the States.

Altogether—a very warm person—from the first call. He didn't know me, anything about me, but immediately invited me over. Joked a lot, would get serious and then cut it sometimes—he didn't want to get into long discussions on some metaphysical questions. I discerned—I think—an approach to examining life—two aspects to life—one deals with the "whys" of events and attempts to find solutions, applications; the second—his—and the more absolute aspects (more abstract)—deals with Life itself—*za chem*? for what goal; *v chëm imeni*? Earlier he had distinguished between two types of intellectuals. But then he broke off the discussion—first time—coffee?, second—something to eat? His English was surprisingly good for someone who taught himself.* Good not in its grammatical exactness but in his ability to express so many of his ideas. He joked about how bad his English was, but I think he was proud of it and his own accomplishment nevertheless.

He walked me back to the Moskovskaya Hotel at 1:30 a.m. We talked more about his time in prison and other things. He said *Portnoy's Complaint* was very good—not pornography.

15 July

Just remembered: when Brodsky autographed picture for PV he asked the date—the 13th—"No, I don't like it"—So I said put down the 14th then. Superstitious, or what?—don't know.

He had told me to call him. If he had time perhaps he would be able to show me some of Leningrad. Called this morning, gone for day; asked father to say good-bye for me.

---

*JB studied English for 4 years in Leningrad secondary schools, though the instruction was ineffectual. He later taught himself literary English by reading Auden, Eliot, and others while in Norenskaya, near the Arctic Circle, in 1964–65.—*ED*

Interview with Iosif Brodsky

Michael Scammell / 1972

From *Index on Censorship,* 1 (Autumn/Winter 1972), 149–54. Reprinted by permission of *Index on Censorship,* London (www.indexoncensorship.org).

Iosif Brodsky, despite his youth (he is thirty-two years old), is widely considered today to be the best living Russian poet. He began writing in 1958 and was quickly recognised by the doyenne of Russian poets, Anna Akhmatova, to have exceptional promise. Brodsky found it virtually impossible, however, to get his work into print, particularly since he was not a member of the Writers' Union. In 1963 he was arrested and in 1964 was sentenced to five years' exile for 'parasitism', the judge maintaining that it was impossible for Brodsky to be a writer without being a member of the Union—therefore he must be unemployed and a parasite. Fortunately, after eighteen months of being employed on physical labour, Brodsky was allowed to return to his native city of Leningrad and resume work as a poet and translator. In subsequent years he found it equally difficult to have his original work published (only four of his poems were printed in the Soviet Union), but continued to write prolifically and to be translated and published abroad. Last June he suddenly left the Soviet Union under the dispensation granted to many Soviet Jews to emigrate to Israel. Having been already offered a post at Michigan University in the USA, and having been invited to take part in the London Poetry Festival of 1972, he came first to England, where he gave the following interview to *Index.*

Michael Scammell: Iosif, when did you start writing poetry?

Iosif Brodsky: When I was 18.

MS: Was your work ever published in the Soviet Union?

IB: Yes, when I was 26 I had two poems published in the Literary Almanac, 'Young Leningrad'. That was in 1966.

MS: And how many poems have you had published since then in the Soviet Union?

IB: Two.

MS: When did it become clear to you that your poems were not going to be published generally in the Soviet Union and what was the effect of this realisation upon you?

IB: I must say that it was never really clear to me. I always thought that they would be published one day and so this idea has had no effect on me at all—not for the last ten years or so, at any rate.

MS: Why do you think that your poems were not published while you were in the Soviet Union?

IB: It is difficult to say. Maybe because they were too aggressive to begin with and then later my name became a sort of taboo, it was a forbidden word.

MS: What sort of a taboo?

IB: Well, I was someone who had been to prison and so on and so forth.

MS: Why do you think they sent you to prison?

IB: I don't really know. In any case that seems to me, if you don't mind my saying so, a typically western approach to the problem: every event has to have a cause and every phenomenon has to have something standing behind it. It is very complex. Sometimes there is a cause, perhaps. But as to why they put me in prison, all I can do is repeat to you the items in the indictment. My own answer perhaps won't satisfy you, but it is very simple. A man who sets out to create his own independent world within himself is bound sooner or later to become a foreign body in society and then he becomes subject to all the physical laws of pressure, compression and extrusion.

MS: Why do you think that you were released so quickly?

IB: I don't know, I honestly don't know. Just as I have no idea why I was sent to prison in the first place. In general I am very confused about these things, the point is that I always tried to be—and was—a separate private person. I suppose it was just that my life somehow acquired an external political dimension. In one sense, I think, it was done to separate me from my audience. That, I am afraid, is the best answer I can find.

MS: How did trial and prison affect your work?

IB: You know, I think it was even good for me, because the two years I spent in the country were from my point of view one of the best times of my life. I did more work then than at any other time. During the day I had to do physical work, but since it was agricultural labour, it wasn't like in a factory and there were lots of periods of rest when we had nothing to do.

MS: You came out of prison in 1965. Did you return to being a private person and have you been working just on your own ever since that time?

IB: Oh no. I worked as a translator. I am a professional translator and I was a member of the Translators' Group at the Leningrad Writers' Union. That is how I earned my living.

MS: And in the meantime your poetry began to be distributed in *samizdat*?

IB: Well, yes, but the point is that *samizdat* is an extremely flexible concept. If by *samizdat* you mean the passing of manuscripts from hand to hand and the copying of them on typewriters in a systematic way, then my poems started to circulate before *samizdat* began. Someone who liked them would simply copy them and take them away to read, and then someone else would borrow them from that person. *Samizdat* came into being only about four or five years ago.

MS: But what about student *samizdat* journals such as *Phoenix* and *Syntax*? They printed your verse, didn't they?

IB: Well, yes and no. It would be stretching a point considerably to call them 'journals'. *Syntax* ran to only about 100 copies in all, and there may even have been less. It was difficult to find people to do the work in those days. In any case I don't think *Phoenix* published me. The *Syntax* did, I can remember that very well.

MS: You were put on trial in 1964 and you were one of the first people in the Soviet Union to be tried specifically as a writer. You were followed by Sinyavsky and Daniel and then, on another plane, Pasternak and Solzhenitsyn have had their difficulties. In contrast to them, however, you have never taken up a position of overt opposition and have never publicly, so far as I know, criticised the authorities, literary or otherwise, in the way that, say, even Pasternak did. What is your attitude to people who take a stand and why have you personally never done so yourself?

IB: It is all very simple, really. The point is that the person who seriously devotes himself to some sort of work—and in my case *belles lettres*—has in any case plenty of problems and difficulties that arise from the work itself, for instance doubts, fears and worries, and this in itself taxes the brain pretty powerfully. And then again I must say that any kind of civic activity simply bores me to death. While the brain is thinking in political terms and thinks of itself as getting somewhere, it is all very interesting, attractive and exciting, and everything seems fine. But when these thoughts reach their logical conclusion, that is when they result in some sort of action, then they give rise to a terrible sense of disillusionment, and then the whole thing is boring.

MS: But do you think that, say, the position that Solzhenitsyn has taken up *vis-à-vis* the authorities, and the literary authorities, in particular, has any sort of positive value, or do you regard it as a distraction from the writer's true work?

IB: In order to answer that question, of course, I would have to look at things from Solzhenitsyn's point of view, something I can't and don't intend to do. From my point of view, I think it would be better if he simply got on with writing his own works instead of spending time on these other activities. On the other hand, it does seem to have some sort of positive value for him and indeed a general value. But I think that for the writer who first of all concerns himself with his own work, the deeper he plunges into it, the greater will be the consequences—literary, aesthetic and of course political as well.

MS: Yes, but is this possible? What is your attitude to such writers as Okudzhava, Viktor Nekrasov, Voinovich and Maximov, who started out by not expressing any sort of open opposition but were forced by their work, or rather by the official attitude to their work, to take up more extreme positions. Is it possible at all to be a true writer in the Soviet Union without being forced into such a position?

IB: I think it is, although it is true that circumstances there do force you more or less to take up such a position. But from my point of view this is extremely unfortunate, first of all because the problems you are then forced to occupy yourself with and the position you are forced to take up by the situation—all these, that is to say any protest you make and the level of that protest, are determined by the nature, the quality and the level of what it is that you are protesting against. If you are faced with an idiot and you say to him 'you are an idiot', well, maybe it is fun but it is not much else . . .

MS: Yes, of course, but let us take the examples of Voinovich and Maximov. They both wrote novels that they wanted to publish in the Soviet Union, but publication was refused. Nobody knows how these novels subsequently found their way to the west, but they did arrive there and then attempts were made to force these writers to denounce their publication over here. On the one hand they had not wished to go into open opposition to the authorities, but on the other hand they didn't want to make statements that were false and untrue. Don't you find that a difficult position for a writer to be in?

IB: Yes, it is a rotten position to be in. But if you have the courage to write something, then you have to have the courage to stick up for it.

MS: And you can find yourself in such a position against your will?

IB: Yes, you can find yourself in such a position without the least intent or desire. It is disgusting, of course, since the writer finds himself in a weird trap: he has a concept of life, he has a background and an upbringing and a point of view and his own ideas about life, all of which are what started him writing in the first place. But the situation develops in such a way that he finds himself forced to occupy himself with completely different activities. It is stupid and degrading, in my opinion it is a complete nonsense when the writer is forced to become a political activist.

MS: You said on BBC Television that in your opinion nothing could be done in the west to help Soviet writers. What do you have in mind when you said that?

IB: I had a number of things in mind. In the first place you can't help a writer to write, can you? You can't help him to live, nor can you help him to die, and so on. A man has to do everything for himself. Everyone does this naturally. On top of this, literary work, like all work in the Arts, is a very individual and lonely business. There is nothing you can do about this. All you can do is help people get published. But I am not sure how helpful this is. I suppose it gives one a pleasant sensation, a sense of not being without hope: up or down, you still exist and you still haven't perished. It gives a certain psychological relief to a man living in rather uncomfortable circumstances. But here again you get all sorts of problems arising, because all forms of comfort are in a way a sort of escapism.

MS: Don't you think that it was a great help to you to have your verse published and to know that you had a public? For example, your poems were first read in the west by Russian literature specialists, students and so on, then were translated into other languages. Did this not influence your writing in the Soviet Union?

IB: In my opinion it had no effect at all. Just as it equally had no effect before it happened, that is to say there was a time when I was writing verses that few read and nobody translated—of course they also weren't very good, which is something I realise now. But still, we are not talking about whether the verses are good or bad, but about what happens to them after they are written. What interested me most of all, and still does, is the process of writing itself. Nothing influenced this, and what is more, I tried to cut myself off and get away from anything that might influence me. I can quite clearly remember my reaction to my first book, which was published in Russian in New York. I had a sensation of something completely ridiculous having happened. I couldn't grasp what had happened or what this book was exactly.

MS: Didn't this book and the support it represented help you to maintain your position of independence? Isn't it possible that otherwise you would have been accused of parasitism again?

IB: It is very difficult to form an opinion about something that didn't happen. Maybe it did help in some way, but I must confess that I doubt it very much. You see, I am not representative in any way, I cannot stand for anything or anybody except myself.

MS: But don't you think that your reputation and the knowledge of your work helped you in coming to the west?

IB: Certainly it had a role to play and it did influence the situation as a whole. But really the question ought to be turned around a bit: is it a good thing that I have come to the west? If it is, then it is fair to use the verb 'helped'. If not, we will have to phrase it in quite a different way.

The Muse in Exile: Conversations with the Russian Poet, Joseph Brodsky

Anne-Marie Brumm / 1973

From *A Journal for the Comparative Study of Literature,* 8 (Fall 1974), 229–46 (now known as *Mosaic, a journal for the interdisciplinary study of literature*). Reprinted by permission of *Mosaic.*

The interview took place in the interviewer's apartment situated very near the main campus of the University of Michigan. It occurred primarily during the cool early days of summer '73 with additions and revisions in January, 1974.

Mr. Brodsky was cheerful and in good spirits. He was casually dressed, with a large airlines tote bag giving him the air of an eternal wanderer. He seemed eager to talk and volunteered information willingly at all times. The poet spoke freely, especially when the questions centered on a general topic or one dealing with poetry as a genre. However, he was somewhat more hesitant when asked to comment on his own poems specifically.

His speaking voice is thoughtful, careful—quite unlike the rich, rhythmic incantatory quality of his poetry readings in Russian. The latter are often almost hypnotic in effect. He speaks English with a unique blend that is partially textbook and partially colloquial. Yet, what is always apparent is Mr. Brodsky's seemingly endless knowledge of world literature, art, music and other related areas of interest to him.

It is not an exaggeration to say that he is fiercely intense about anything related to poetry. His approach is sincere and straightforward—a whole-hearted openness. Unlike many poets, his is not a self-centered absorption but an unusually selfless one. He himself seems to be a mere vehicle for the final distilled product of poetry. It is his entire "essence." And yet, despite his seriousness, he has a definite sense of humor and occasionally exhibits an impish note of glee—at, for example, the idea of lines in free verse walking naked.

The serving of dinner provided a break and period of relaxation. The poet expressed a preference for hamburgers over steaks and Coca-Cola over cocktails. He browsed through my bookcases commenting on a variety of authors he found there. Noticing a University of Michigan gradebook similar to his own, he also glanced at it, observing that I have a "lot" of "different" grades and that so few students had names that were "real American."

He was quickly "at home" as he began to answer the questions. In general his diction and accent have been preserved in the following transcript.

Brumm: What do you see as being the function of the artist?

Brodsky: The role of the artist—and his duty—well, if this can be said for poetry, for literature—is to write well, that's all.

Brumm: What then would you say are the main concerns of your poetry?

Brodsky: Once I made this statement and maybe it's correct. I think that the role of writer and of artist is to show to the people the real vision of the scale of things. For instance, I think that a good writer shows you life as some long chain and a good writer can indicate very correctly the number of your link in this chain. Or at least he has to move you to create such a possibility for yourself, for recognizing your own link in this chain. That is what I mean.

Brumm: How old were you when you first started writing poetry?

Brodsky: I don't remember. I was 17–18, I guess. But it wasn't serious. I started to write seriously, well, at least I think seriously, when I was 23, 22–23.

Brumm: Could you tell me how your poetry has developed or changed from the time when you first started writing until now?

Brodsky: The only thing which I can tell about it is that (pause) in the beginning I was well, as all the people in the beginning, I was very emotional and so on. But right now, (pause) I have more taboos, more vetoes than permissions. I make more vetoes for myself writing something than I permit myself. I think if I can talk about any development, my writing becomes a bit more hard, a bit more sober, maybe not a bit more—more sober, more dry—less emotional, just more deaf in some sense.

Brumm: Could you explain that more fully?

Brodsky: I can, I guess. When I was young, younger I mean. When I started, my poetry was—well, my poetry—my verses were very "sounding." I used a great amount of instrumentation. There were a number of sounds. It was just phonetically very beautiful, well, I think it was. (laugh) But right now, the sound is a bit more impersonal. It sounds like (pause) less exciting, I guess.

Brumm: Would you say that your poems tend to be rather sad and ultimately pessimistic, as for example, "Christmas Romance"?

Brodsky: No, that's wrong. It's not pessimistic and I don't think this is a good definition for poetry, pessimistic or optimistic.

Brumm: OK. It must be painful for you to write about your past experiences.

Brodsky: No, no, and as a matter of fact, I think my verses are rather retrospective than introspective. I mean I'd rather remember when I write. The hero of the poems I write rather remembers things than predicts them.

Brumm: Like the Greek poet, Cavafy, whom we discussed in class, you frequently use historical and mythical themes to make a broader statement. Is this what you attempted to do, for example, in your poem, "Aeneas and Dido"?

Brodsky: No, I wouldn't say so. You know, Cavafy is usually talking about very concrete situations. All the people whom he mentions are people who really existed and generally speaking, I would call his poetry some kind of development in the tradition of epitaph. And when you write the epitaph, you write this for some concrete people you know, for real citizens—those citizens of Asia Minor—yes?

Brumm: Who then are your Dido and Aeneas?

Brodsky: They are mythical personages. This is the first difference. If it's close to Cavafy, that's fine but I don't think I wrote this poem because of him. I remember very well what influenced me. There were two things. The first was Anna Akhmatova's cycle about Dido and Aeneas. That was a sequence of love poems about her separation from her beloved. She embodied herself in Dido and the man was some kind of Aeneas. By the way this man is still alive. The second thing which more or less moved me to write about that was Henry Purcell's opera, *Dido and Aeneas.* There was a certain aria which Dido sings that was so penetrating, so moving, so despairing. I remember this when Elizabeth Schwarzkopf sings, "Remember Me." It sounds absolutely incredible.

There were a couple of reasons why I wrote this poem. Moreover, this is not a love poem. "Aeneas and Dido" is a poem about destruction—the destruction of Carthage which happened before it happened in the flesh. It's rather a historical poem in some sense. Aeneas left Dido. She didn't want him to leave her but he did. And, accordingly to the myth, he created Rome whose army in some centuries afterward came to destroy Carthage. So you see what love is and what betrayal in love is. The consequences are usually invisible but I was trying to make them more or less visible. Well, on this point, that's all.

Brumm: You mentioned Purcell's opera. Has music generally been an important part of your life and development?

Brodsky: I would say, yes. Yes, it has.

Brumm: Are there some composers you prefer to others?

Brodsky: First of all, I guess, Bach and Mozart. Once some friend of mine, a long time ago in Russia in saying something good about my poems, said, "But, nevertheless, Joseph, you haven't this lightness or easiness—this light quality with which Mozart makes his stuff. Your poetry is a bit more heavy." So I was trying not consciously but sometimes even consciously to make some very serious statement in the poem and to make them light as if they had no weight. It's rather dangerous business because the means of poetry are rather limited. Sometimes, it starts to sound like a nursery poem and yet is far from it. You have a lot of examples like that in your English poetry, for instance, W. H. Auden's poem "In Memory of W. B. Yeats" was a model for my poem, "On the Death of T. S. Eliot." I was trying to repeat Auden's structure in the third part—this short meter. Some people accused me saying that this looks like nursery rhymes. But it isn't, it isn't, I think. In some sense, music is the best teacher of construction, of counterpoints, of some logic.

Brumm: Has art played an influential role in your writing? Again, are there any specific painters or sculptors which you find especially worthwhile?

Brodsky: Yes, yes, painting, yes, a lot. Well I would say so, yes. Painters—I like a couple of people very much. I like Georges Braque most of all and I like Raoul Dufy—both of them Frenchmen as a matter of fact. I'm talking about this century but most of all, I like early Italian art.

Brumm: The Renaissance?

Brodsky: Oh no, before the Renaissance—people like Sassetta, for instance. By the way, he has something in common with Dufy. It's a kind of light art, but at the same time it's very deep; it's very profound. The same similarity exists with Mozart. Not many people know about Dufy but I like him for a number of reasons. I remember I liked Umberto Boccioni when I was something like 19 or 20. I even wrote a poem which was trying to describe the same feeling of movement which he tried to. Well, it doesn't matter. I can talk endlessly about all that.

Brumm: Since your stay in the United States, do you find yourself writing more about Russia or the United States? Has the transition to the United States changed your poetry in any way?

Brodsky: I don't think so. It can't change the basic thing, although I think that I flew to the United States without my Muse. Maybe she didn't take the same plane.

Brumm: What do you discover yourself writing about most now? Are there any specific concerns that you have?

Brodsky: Right now, just these last few weeks, I wrote a couple of poems about the United States—about my life in the United States. That's correct! (laugh) But four weeks ago, I wrote about Russia. And I think that the day after tomorrow—(laugh). No, I think geography doesn't influence the content of a poem.

Brumm: Do you now or do you intend to write any poems in English?

Brodsky: No, well I did some but just for fun. Some limericks or a couple of serious poems, but I don't think they are good.

Brumm: So you plan to continue writing in your native language?

Brodsky: Yes, of course.

Brumm: What were your feelings when you wrote the poem, "A Jewish Cemetery by Leningrad"?

Brodsky: I don't remember; I was 18. This was one of the first poems which I wrote. Well, just sadness, I suppose. Sadness and compassion to those people. But now, I think it is a bad poem.

Brumm: Over and over again in your poetry, you seem to be saying be steadfast, persevere, stand alone. Is this your basic philosophy?

Brodsky: Yes, I think so. Well, I have nothing instead, so far. (laugh)

Brumm: Could you describe your philosophy of life?

Brodsky: It's not a philosophy of life. This is just a number of devices. If to call it a philosophy, I would call it a philosophy of endurance—of the possibility of endurance. It's very simple. When you have some bad situation, there are two ways to deal with it—just to give up or to try to stand it. Well, in some sense, I prefer to stand it as far as I can. So this is my philosophy—that's all, nothing special.

Brumm: You once said in class that the use of irony is the coward's way out. One should look at things directly. Could you comment on that?

Brodsky: This is true. Irony is really a deceiving business. When you say something funny or ironical about the situation in which you are, you have a feeling that you overcame it but you didn't. Irony doesn't lead you out of the problem or beyond the problem. It just keeps you in the same frame. When you make jokes about something awful, you continue to be the captive of this terrible thing. This is just one of the possible bad reflections. That's not overcoming. You can't overcome anything with irony. If you really want to overcome something, it's necessary to invent something else. If you see a problem, you must fight. No one ever won with irony alone.

Irony comes from the psychological layer of the mind. There are different layers: biological, political, philosophical, religious, transcendent. Life is tragic, so irony is not enough.

Brumm: So you believe in looking at things directly. Is this also the reason why you like narrative poetry?

Brodsky: Yes, that's right. Of course, you can use irony as a device. But it's impossible to use it as a general approach, as a general agiteur. In narrative poetry, you can see the scale of things. It is much closer to life than the short lyric poem. Good poetry imitates life. One should get used to reading narrative poetry even though it is not just a beautiful short masterpiece that one can read quickly and easily. Reading poetry is a struggle like everything in life.

Brumm: Do you think that narrative poetry will increase in importance in this country?

Brodsky: I don't know. I couldn't predict. I wish it would but I don't know what will happen.

Brumm: Are there any narrative writers with whom you are especially impressed?

Brodsky: There are a lot of them. I like two people whom they call old-fashioned. First of all, I like Robert Frost and I also like Edwin Arlington Robinson. Also some Australian poets, a lot of them—Judith Wright, for instance, although she doesn't write narratively—and that poem which I gave you in class, "Five Visions of Captain Cook" by Kenneth Slessor. This is also a narrative poem.

Brumm: What is your opinion of our confessional poetry?

Brodsky: Well, as a definition, this is not confessional poetry, by the way. (laugh) I don't think it's confessional.

Brumm: Poets such as Robert Lowell, Sylvia Plath, John Berryman?

Brodsky: I prefer Plath and Berryman. I like Lowell very much but I prefer these two people because in some sense they are stronger than he is. Stronger and more direct. They don't hide themselves. Lowell hides. But this hiding, of course, is the big new art. And maybe the future belongs to the new art and vice versa. In some sense, I think Lowell is a new human being—some kind of Homo-tragic or Homo-hidden. But I feel closer to Berryman and Plath.

Brumm: Although both Sylvia Plath and John Berryman committed suicide, do you still feel that they endured or looked at life directly?

Brodsky: I think so. And I don't think their suicides mean something because both of them were rather occasional things. I know something more or less about the details of Sylvia Plath's suicide and I know about John Berryman as well. I don't think that their suicides were some acts of the consequences of their philosophies as artists. It just happened so. If the milkman had come sooner, Sylvia Plath would be alive. And if Berryman wasn't well—I don't know what they say. He was a drunk or on some drugs—he would be alive as well.

I think that the note which the poet takes, the note which the poet sings, the note in the musical sense—this high note which his voice permits him to produce is a general justification. And such a high note in which Sylvia Plath sang "Lady Lazarus" or "Daddy" is not only her justification. This is an equal response to life. I think so. She was on the same level as life was. It was very tragic but the possibility to take this note and to sing in this high voice means she overcame it. And Berryman, because he was a man—in that short poem which I gave you, "He Resigns," I think it was not a resignation. It was a victory over the nightmare of his life. These suicides do not mean they have been defeated. It means they have been equal to life. You think another way. I guess?

Brumm: No, not really. Their suicides do not surprise me as I become more and more aware of their unbelievably profound, lucid, almost hallucinatory insight into life. I also agree with your comment that Berryman's suicide was a victory over the nightmare of his life.

Brodsky: Sylvia Plath attempted suicide having a pretty good chance for survival. All the other times it had worked that she would be saved. Of course, she also had a self-destructive instinct. She tried to make it a number of times. But when she had been saved, she continued to write poetry and if she had been saved this time, the last time, it would still be the same prolongation of this business, yes? It's silly to talk about death as a conclusion, generally speaking, that's all.

Brumm: She seemed almost to be playing a game with death.

Brodsky: Yes, she did, Well, it's not a game, of course, but . . .

Brumm: In the course on Russian and American poetry which you taught at the University of Michigan, you spent a considerable amount of time discussing the Greek poet, Constantine Cavafy. To what extent has Cavafy influenced your writing or your outlook on life?

Brodsky: The first time I read Cavafy was about two years ago. If one can find his influence in my work, this is the best compliment for me, I think. However, I don't think he influenced me very much. Probably what happened is that I recognized many things which are very dear for me in his work. It's impossible to be influenced by Cavafy. It's possible to like his work and so on but it's impossible to use him as some kind of example because he is unrepeatable. Because of the quality of his thought and of his logic, one cannot repeat it.

Brumm: Are there any specific poems by Cavafy that you like best?

Brodsky: Yes, I gave a lecture on Cavafy one day in this university. I chose for this lecture four poems. I chose "Thermopylae," "The Bandaged Shoulder," what else—of course, "Waiting for Barbarians" (that is his great hit you know; they include it in all the anthologies), "Darius" and a couple of other poems. From my point of view, the best which he wrote is "Myres: Alexandria, A.D. 340" and the last one, "Ionic." I like all his poetry, well almost everything, even his early stuff which has been included in some books. It appears also in the appendix in this Rae Dalven translation.

It's impossible to tell something about any one concrete poem. This is a whole system. And one can say that system works only by reading the whole body of his work.

Brumm: What is included in this "system"?

Brodsky: A lot of things. First of all that which I would call something like—this is my definition—a so-called political symbolism. He uses politics as other poets use, for instance, all this poetical . . . as other poets use moon, lakes, solitude and so on. Politics is everywhere for this is closest to everybody's mind. When you are talking about politics, almost everybody understands you. It is something like matter language. It is a kind of uniform of your mind—a kind of meaningless jargon. So when people are talking about politics, whatever country they belong to, they think they understand each other. For instance, when you are talking about World War II, if you are Frenchman, American or Russian, people know what it's all about. So Cavafy uses politics. But for him, this is just a part; he understands that politics is the lowest level step of the big ladder.

Brumm: Could you describe this ladder? For what level do you aim?

Brodsky: Politics is the lowest level of spiritual life. Cavafy leads you on this step only to indicate something more, to indicate the size of the whole ladder. But many poets just talk about the first step because they don't see the prospect of this ladder. For instance, the first impression people have, my students, for example, of the poem "Waiting for Barbarians" is that this is a satire on some kind of despotism or dictatorship using contemporary vocabulary. This is a satire on the totalitarian state, that's correct, but at the same time, it is so much more. In the poem, "Waiting for Barbarians," Cavafy is talking about some rather decadent state that is waiting for barbarians who will pour fresh barbarian blood into the old veins. Or something like a democracy which is looking for barbarians as a solution. Yet we never experienced such a decadent democracy so this is probably about something else. This is maybe about culture, about one culture which dried itself up and is probably looking for some wild powers, wild invasions of some wild people who will refresh it. This is of course not the best example, but the first which comes to my mind. It may be something like black poetry which, so to speak, will refresh the academical poetry in this country. Something like that, or something like the beatniks.

But I think this is not even just about the decadent culture. It is also about a decadent state of mind. It is about human beings when they are too sophisticated to take some steps and hope that somebody will come and help them to do it. But you remember the end of the poem. The barbarians didn't come. This political symbolism is one of Cavafy's devices.

Brumm: What other devices does Cavafy use that make him so unique as a poet?

Brodsky: Of course, there are many things. I like some other characteristics of Cavafy's work. For instance, the rejection of so-called *a priori* devices. He almost never uses metaphors. It's very hard to find any exclamation points in his poems. There are many more question marks. In fact, he poses more questions than answers, and his answers are very questionable. There is nothing in his work such as beautiful comparisons and so on. He uses only pure logic in the development of the poem. The poem develops not because of some image which follows another image but because of logic.

I also like in his work a kind of lack of exaltation. His is a very calm, very restricted, very sober and dry voice. In this hysterical epoch, I think that is very important. Cavafy has some really Greek feeling of measure. I like all these things and I would like to follow them if I could but it is very difficult. Besides, the contemporary tendency of poetry implies the use of some rather extreme devices. He doesn't and he succeeds more than all the people who are crying, shouting and what else.

It's very interesting that only forty percent of his work has been rhymed or organized metrically in old fashioned ways. This is what they say; I don't know. I am not a connoisseur of demotic Greek. The sixty percent is written in free verse. But his free verse radically differs from contemporary free verse. His free verse is very functional, I would say, because he has the line follow after the line not because of some metrical stuff, not because of some idea of harmony of speech or disharmony of speech or freedom of speech but because of some development of logic. I say logic, maybe it's wrong, but let's use it as a tentative description. It is logic which compels him to write down the next line because he tries to organize those things which are not supposed to be organized. And in this case, maybe the use of free verse is the best device.

Brumm: Let's turn to your poem. "A Halt in the Wilderness," in which you once wrote:

> What lies ahead? Does a new epoch wait
> for us? And, if it does, what duty do we owe?—
> What sacrifices must we make for it?

That was 1966. Have your expectations changed since then?

Brodsky: No, no, I think more or less that this new era is coming and is approaching us. I used to say in conversation that this is the post-Christian era. But I don't think that we have to make any sacrifices because of this coming.

Brumm: How do you envision the coming of this new epoch?

Brodsky: I wouldn't like to add to everybody's prophecies about the future. I don't like to increase the amount of senseless information. But I do think that the coming world, the coming epoch will be less moral, more relative, more impersonal, less, I would say, human. This picture is a bit obvious for me. But I don't think it's necessary to make any sacrifices to work right now for this epoch.

Brumm: What other significance did you attach to the "wilderness"?

Brodsky: It's a very old poem. I made some two or three remarks in this poem. I don't remember them very well but one of them was that it is one thing to baptize people, to lead them to the cross, in a metaphoric way, but to bear this cross is another thing, absolutely another. So what I meant in this poem is that we used to understand Christianity in very tentative terms and in a very formal way. Because if you really have been led to the cross, it does not mean that because of that, you will have a happy life or an absolutely secure life. It also means that you will carry this cross some day—carry, you know, on your own back. People try to take these things apart. I don't think that's a very serious approach or a very serious attitude. Well, a number of other things, I don't remember.

Brumm: Do you no longer like the poem?

Brodsky: Relatively speaking, I like it but it's something like six years ago.

Brumm: I find many of your recent poems very complex and intriguing. One which I thought especially challenging is called "Nature Morte." Could you perhaps comment on it?

Brodsky: I like some recent poems which have not yet been translated into English. I too like this poem, "Nature Morte." I like it because . . . (pause). It's a bit difficult for me to talk about my own stuff.

Brumm: (reading from Russian text; translated here by author):

It's time. I shall now begin.
It makes no difference with what.
Open mouth. It is better to speak,
although I can also be mute.*

Brodsky: All right—"Nature Morte" means "still life" but the title is "Nature Morte." Generally speaking, it is about the fact that Christ is in some sense, a still life.

Brumm: Did you mean to say that Christianity is static?

Brodsky: No, I mean, it's not. I mean, in this poem, "Nature Morte," I

---

*This translation was virtually identical to George L. Kline's in *Selected Poems* and has been altered to match it.—*ED*

was dealing with people and things. And I found that I am fed up with people—I'm sorry for this—and that I prefer things. For instance—it's better to look at the poem—but I thought that Christ is a thing and a man at the same time. That's what I meant. Well, it's even something more. It's silly to talk about it. I can't do it.

Brumm: The style conveys also a sense of balance. I notice that there are ten equal sections of three stanzas each.

Brodsky: I like one passage; I remember it.

Dust is the flesh of time.
Time's very flesh and blood.

This is correct, I think. (laugh) I can't talk about myself and about my poetry, I like it and I wrote it. But how can I do it? Do you think it's possible to talk about your own stuff?

Brumm: I guess that depends on the writer. It seems as though many are able to do so.

Brodsky: You think so. Some poets can, I guess. But this is some kind of self-apology—self . . . It's not modest. It's not about my modesty but maybe rather because of my impossibility to do it.

This is one of the best poems which I wrote, I think. Not recently—it's two years ago. I also wrote quite a good poem about Candlemas.* You know this celebration? This is about the transition between the Old Testament and the New Testament. It is the first appearance of Christ in the Bible when Mary brings him into the temple. It is also about the first Christian death—that holy man Simeon. This is rather good, I think.

Brumm: Yes, it certainly is. One of my favorites is your poem, "Adieu Mademoiselle Véronique." Is Veronica a symbol?

Brodsky: No, she's not a symbol. Just a French girl, just a person to talk to. It's not a love poem.

Brumm: What did you mean by the line in Stanza VIII, "In our past there is greatness—but prose in our future" and why do you draw on the symbol of Holy Week?

Brodsky: This is a poem about separation: In the future, there will be nothing like there was before. The Holy Week is a kind of model; it is also

*"Nunc Dimittis."

separation. There are similarities going on. It is a miniaturization of Christ's story.

Brumm: Could you comment on the "mode of masking, which came from the Greeks, is again in fashion" in Stanza VI?

Brodsky: It is! That's life. You can't express your own feelings. This is true anywhere. In the most important cases, you can't. You can't laugh or cry when you want to or need to most.

Brumm: Why do you feel that "it's the strong who perish"?

Brodsky: It's true! I saw many perish who were very strong—the good, the best, important people. I wrote the poem mostly because of Kennedy but it's true in general.

Brumm: Many of your poems seem to intertwine various aspects of Christianity. Is there any specific reason why you either use this as a base or weave it into the background?

Brodsky: I don't know. The only reason that I think . . . Maybe I'm Christian, not in the sense that I am Catholic or Orthodox. I say that I'm Christian because I'm not a barbarian, I guess. I like some things in Christianity. A lot of them, as a matter of fact.

Brumm: Could you mention some of these?

Brodsky: Well, I like the Old Testament; I prefer the Old Testament because the spirit of that book is very high and very . . . less forgiving. I like the Old Testament, generally speaking, because of the idea of justice—not concrete justice but divine justice—and because it insists on personal responsibility. It almost rejects those excuses which the New Testament gives to people.

Brumm: Would you then like to see a combination of the two—justice from the Old and compassion and forgiveness from the New?

Brodsky: What I like in the New Testament are those things which develop the Old Testament's ideology. That's why I wrote this poem about transition between those books. What I like, for instance, in the New Testament is this remark by Christ made during the agony in the garden. When he said, what I'm doing right now, I'm doing because it has been written in the books. And right now, that thing is supposed to happen which has been written and predicted by the books. I had a feeling there was nothing in the Old Testament more about him. So in some sense, he died. He has been crucified because there was nothing more in all those books which he read. It was as if the Old Testament were his script and he played his role which had been prescribed by it. And right now, there was nothing more. That was the last page of the script. (I'm trying to use this image of the "script" in order to explain because of my English).

Brumm: Could you talk about your poem, "Verses in April"?
Brodsky: This is a very average poem.

Brumm: Does this poem deal with your experiences in Siberia?
Brodsky: No, you mean because of the first line? Why Siberia?

Brumm: Because of the nostalgia for spring and the references to "losing my mind," "I am broken into pieces" and "ice cracks loudly."
Brodsky: No, it's rather a love poem. I think maybe it has been translated in the wrong way but this is a love poem. When I say I didn't become mad this winter and I see the coming of spring, it means I didn't become mad because of some of my personal troubles—nothing political, I guess.

Brumm: You once said that there is nothing more fearful in this life than a human being. Could you elaborate further on this?
Brodsky: That's right. Well, just one example. I remember very well when I was working in geology. I spent a number of times in the very remote areas of the woods—in the so-called taiga in Eastern Siberia. There are wolves and bears and so on but once I met a man in this wood and I was frightened more than if I had met some animal. (laugh) That's all.

Brumm: You also said that Robert Frost puts human beings on the stage and . . .
Brodsky: T. S. Eliot puts on a skeleton, yes. Yes, I think so because a skeleton can't produce anything bad.

Brumm: And a human being is likely to?
Brodsky: Yes, yes, very capable.

Brumm: Do you see human nature then as being essentially very negative?
Brodsky: No, basically, I wouldn't say that all the people are bad. But I would say that people are very capable for bad—for evil—incredibly capable.

Brumm: More so than for good?
Brodsky: It looks that way. It looks like that, yes. (laugh) I would say that

people are equally capable for good and for bad. But people as far as I know prefer easy solutions and to commit evil is much easier than to make something good, that's all.

Brumm: Ideally, it should be just as easy to do good.

Brodsky: Well, yes, but most people like to simplify their tasks.

Brumm: I guess that is why we also have so many stereotypes.

Brodsky: Yes, of course. And also gadgets, for instance (pointing to tape recorder).

Brumm: When the students in your class submitted their own poems, the one thing that seemed to surprise you was the fact that so many of them wrote with little or no attention to form. Do you yourself feel more comfortable writing in a strict form?

Brodsky: By strict form, you mean some so-called classical forms, some metrical organization? Yes, I think so, precisely for this reason. The strict form is a device to organize those things which are not supposed to be organized. And it's a very noble task, I think, to do it. I think when you try to . . . It's very simple. If you use strict form for your modern contemporary content, you can see when you put it in this form, that it works stronger because there appears something like tension between what you are saying and the form in which you are saying it. Between the content and the form—and this tension indicates the real scale of the new thing which you are saying.

If you will use free form or free verse for your new contemporary content, there will be no problem. Poems can go nude but sometimes we like to see them dressed. It would be just how you say . . . There are no limitations. It will not produce any scale. It will look natural, absolutely natural. But when you put it into some form, for example, into sonnet form, it will strike people. They are used to sonnet form. But they read in this sonnet form something awful. The same thing is true in life. You are walking on the street and you see something terrible on the street. This is terrible not because it is terrible in itself but because this is on the street where there is supposed to be calm and order. This modern contemporary content in strict form is like a car which is going in the wrong lane on a highway. That's what I mean.

Brumm: William Carlos Williams once wrote that the only way one can write adequately about modern life is in free verse. Modern life is so varied, relative and non-hierarchical, that it requires a variable, relative and flexible form with which to express its concerns. What is your reaction to this argument for free verse?

Brodsky: First of all, I don't like generalizations. What I am saying about strict form is my preference. I don't insist on that. To make such a statement like William Carlos Williams, well, I can't permit myself to do it, that's all.

Brumm: Did you ever write in free form?

Brodsky: I did, a lot, especially when I was younger.

Brumm: That seems to be characteristic of younger poets, doesn't it? That is probably why the students are still writing that way.

Brodsky: Because it's easier to express yourself in free verse. But poetry is not a question of self-expression. It's something else. It's also some kind of craft, you know.

Brumm: Which takes time—

Brodsky: Which takes time. You know, as Robert Frost said, to write free verse is the same as to play tennis with the net down. And with free verse, the first question should be, free from what, free from what? It's OK if you write free verse because you're tired and you can't write anymore. It's all right if you at least experience a strict form and if the free verse is a consequence of it. Because why did free verse appear?—as a consequence of strict form. So each poet has to repeat in miniature the same process. Free verse, freedom—this is a question of liberation. But he who has liberated himself has liberated himself from what—from some kind of, let's say, slavery. But if he didn't experience slavery, he can't experience freedom because freedom does not have an autonomous meaning. What kind of freedom can we talk about if physical freedom has been determined by states, political freedom by slavery and even religious freedom, if you talk within the framework of Christianity, is determined by the last judgment?

Brumm: Yes, that is a vital question to be considered. In returning, however, to your notion of poetry as craft, I wish to ask if you do much revision of your poems?

Brodsky: Sometimes I do, sometimes not.

Brumm: How do you feel when you know that a poem is "coming on"—when you feel like writing?

Brodsky: Oh, I like it. I like it.

Brumm: Could you describe it?

Brodsky: I don't know how to describe it. There are no rules. There is no set custom for this business of the coming of a poem. Sometimes I have two or three lines and a couple of other ideas and I'm trying to write them down. But during the process itself, something happens, something happens and very often the poem—the result of the poem is not that thing which I predicted in the beginning. But usually it contains those elements with which I started. Writing—coming of poem—it's unpredictable. Where will it lead you? The only one thing which is predictable is that you will not say something idiotic, maybe. (laugh)

Brumm: Do you often find it difficult to get words down on paper once you've got the initial inspiration?

Brodsky: Well, of course, it's usually difficult, yes, because of some element of craftsmanship. Sometimes, it's easy to write certain things because of experience but with others, it can be very difficult. But I don't trust myself when something happens very easily. Sometimes it's good but I'm used to experiencing some struggle with material.

Brumm: Are there any specific metrical patterns that you prefer to use?

Brodsky: (after a pause) I like iambic pentameter, usually because of the variety of possibilities of intonations. It is very rich. But I also wrote 1,600 lines of what I call "decima" with an ABABABABAB alternating rhyme. Each line has ten syllables, each stanza has ten lines, each section has ten stanzas. I used this in "Gorbunov and Gorchakov" to describe the state of the characters' minds.

Brumm: How do you feel about reading your poetry in public?

Brodsky: Right now, I have no feelings toward it. In the beginning I liked to do it. Afterwards, it began to seem absolutely dull and empty. When you repeat one statement twice or three times, it loses its meaning for you. It may have meaning for the audience but not for you. But if you do it something like ten times, it's dangerous for your mentality, for your mind. In the beginning, I felt some anxiety, some fear. Right now, I would say, I feel almost nothing. I just remember only one thing. Do your best. Try to do your best for the best people who are sitting in the audience. That's all. And I'm trying to keep myself on this level.

Brumm: I remember when I first heard you at the Donnell Library in New York in Fall 1972. It was on two different nights; I was there the second night. I really enjoyed it.

Brodsky: That was one of the first readings. The first night I was rather nervous.

Brumm: The audience really liked it. They seemed to be very impressed and they responded to you all the way.

Brodsky: Maybe they did. I don't know. (pause)

Brumm: You were born in Leningrad which is a large metropolis. What has been your impression of American cities?

Brodsky: Oh, I saw a lot of them. The bulk of them I like. I like some places. I like New York. Well, for very well balanced people, it's probably a bad place but for masochists like me, it's OK. Relatively speaking, I like San Francisco but less than Vancouver in Canada. I like American countryside much more.

Brumm: You recently spent six months living and teaching in New York City. How would you describe your experience?

Brodsky: Oh, it was great, just great. I really like New York. There was always something to do.

Brumm: Then you don't view the city as something fearful.

Brodsky: No, they are not fearful and not dull. But what I am really missing in this country is some normal European street, you know, a normal European street.

Brumm: How would you sketch this European street?

Brodsky: A normal European street is houses with old fashioned façades in different styles, with a busy streetcar on the street, with some kind of dirtiness, you know, European dirt, as well, with a possibility to stay on the street to talk with somebody and so on. It's impossible to do that in America, really. It's impossible to stay twenty or thirty minutes on the street and talk. I almost didn't see any people who were talking and standing on the street for a long time. You haven't got this culture of life on the street in America.

Brumm: I suppose it is true. We haven't.

Brodsky: No, you haven't. For you, the street is just some other form of highway. It is a place to move in some direction, not to live on. In Europe, they have it.

Brumm: In your city, for example?

Brodsky: Yes, yes, yes.

Brumm: Do you feel then from what you have seen that the pace of life is too quick in the United States?

Brodsky: Yes, more or less, yes. Of course, how you participate in this life depends on you yourself. You can participate; you can reject it. And in this sense, America is the best place in the world, because you can choose your own way. Well, maybe there are some bad consequences, but this is your own business—what is most important to you, the way of life or something else.

Brumm: How do you feel about apartment living? You once said in class that it was frightening and terrifying. The idea of people each living in their own boxes next door to one another . . .

Brodsky: Oh, yes, this is something strange in America. The Americans often say that their general fear is the fear of isolation. Yet the way in which they organize their lives leads only to isolation.

Brumm: What has struck you most about American life? What surprises you?

Brodsky: I hadn't any big surprises. I hadn't—just lack of (pause) I don't know how to say it. Lack of . . . if it's possible to say . . . cordiality. Lack of cordial relationships, you know, lack of involvement, of cordial element in the relationships.

Brumm: Caring for one another?

Brodsky: Yes, you know. This is some sense, the general idea of American life, the general approach to other people. This is your problem, partly. That's correct. It's true because we have our own problems and nobody will solve them but us nor support or disapprove them. But because of this situation, because of this condition, it would be better to be more cordial, more close to each other. Of course, it could produce false expectations which happened in Europe. They have the same thing but the lack of compassion, you know. Not compassion, precisely, people, of course. I don't know how to say it.

Brumm: What do you think might be the reason for this?

Brodsky: First of all, the real understanding that you can't help your partner. This is his problem, really. This is some kind of . . . I really don't know. I don't like to make generalizations. I can talk only about those people whom I knew and each case has its own reason for the lack of participation in the other's life. Yet this is probably a very social way of social organization.

For instance, in Russia, it wasn't always very pleasant but some people could come to my house without any call beforehand, before any warning, before any information. They bumped at my door. I opened and I saw a man about whom I hadn't been thinking and he said, "Can I come in?" "May I come in?" "What are you doing?" They interrupted my life, my work and so on. But in some sense it was life. It was natural; it was unpredictable. The bulk of American life, the bulk of time is predictable. You know what will happen in two hours. This is like an established schedule of life. And it makes life not very exciting, less exciting. You know, your idea of "happening" has been produced and appeared because of a lack of happening in the life itself.

Brumm: That is a very good observation.

Brodsky: I think so, yes.

Brumm: Have you had a favorable impression of American women?

Brodsky: Some of them.

Brumm: Do you sympathize with the women's liberation movement?

Brodsky: No, not at all. For instance, we have in Russia all this stuff. We have some kind of organized matriocrat which tends to be a factory. We have women judges, engineers, doctors and whatever else. All the male opportunities—they've got them.

Brumm: Automatically?

Brodsky: Yes, automatically, because of our constitutions. It doesn't work. You see, this is a dirty bit, because of one reason, because it is a generalization. Some women are really talented. They really want to do it and so on. But to make it the general law, the general rule—that a woman has the same rights as a man and has the same right to his job. OK, what will happen? She will have the same rights but she will not have the same qualities, the same sense of responsibility, for instance, the same energy, let's say, the same dedication, whatever else. What will happen? We have in our life, enough wrong people in wrong places, so we can only increase this. Some women will be all right but it's senseless to insist that all will be. It's senseless. What is sad about women's liberation is that they are running for male opportunities. But these opportunities are not a very charming thing as a matter of fact. They will be very much surprised when they achieve their goal.

Brumm: Do you think women should be in the university?

Brodsky: Why not, if they're bright. Well, generally speaking, for American universities, it's not the question. There are such a big number of dull people that it doesn't matter, woman or man.

Brumm: Have you really gotten that impression?

Brodsky: Yes, I've been surprised. Maybe I have no right to talk about it, but I've been surprised with the level of academical life. Well, you have absolutely great people in academics but at the same time, you have an incredibly high percentage of "sensible emptiness." I think so.

Brumm: Did you find that here at the University of Michigan also?

Brodsky: In Ann Arbor? You know, it's strange. It's not because I'm patriot. In some sense, I am a patriot of Ann Arbor but this is the best school which I experienced so far. Oh, you know. Well, it's a special problem, academia. This is not my problem. I'm rather an occasional person in academia, so, well, I don't like to talk about it.

Brumm: Which of the contemporary American poets do you find especially promising?

Brodsky: Well, I like . . . I just like Mark Strand. I'm talking about this recent generation, about people between thirty and forty. That's all, I think.

Brumm: Do you still like Peter Viereck, whom you gave us in class?

Brodsky: Oh, Viereck, yes, but he's older. He belongs to the post-war generation like Richard Wilbur and Randall Jarrell. He belongs to that generation, the bulk of members of which are dead already. That was a great generation. One of the greatest living poets is Czeslaw Milosz. I think he is one of the best among the contemporaries.

Brumm: Which of the Russian poets has influenced your work or which do you particularly admire?

Brodsky: Two or three. The first one is an eighteenth century poet, Derzhavin; another is from the nineteenth century, Baratynsky and the third from this century, Tsvetaeva.

Brumm: What do you find especially interesting in Derzhavin?

Brodsky: Oh, he's a great poet. He reminds me very often of John Donne. He's a bit more lapidarian, something more primitive. His thoughts and psychology are equal to John Donne but because of a young language, young nation and young culture, he expresses it in a rather more primitive way, for example, with primitive metaphors. But the drive which he has in his voice, the expression!

Brumm: What is your opinion of Anna Akhmatova?

Brodsky: Oh, she's a great poet and a very dear friend. But I don't think there was any influence from her. I would say, she's a great human being.

Brumm: She came to your aid, didn't she?
Brodsky: Yes, she helped me a lot.

Brumm: When you were in prison?
Brodsky: I would say I've been released because of her. She initiated all the activity and moved all the people.

Brumm: Do you want to say anything about your experiences in Arkhangelsk?
Brodsky: No. No, first of all, it was a long time ago.

Brumm: Do you still think about it?
Brodsky: Sometimes, sometimes.

Brumm: Do you think you'll ever put it into your poetry?
Brodsky: Yes, I did—and maybe I will. Yes, it was a part of my life but if I put it into my poetry, it was in a rather indirect way.

Brumm: Have you found anything surprising about your students? Do you consider them aggressive, dull, interesting? What has been your impression?
Brodsky: All the qualities. I found all the qualities. (laugh) I think I had a number of absolutely great people, absolutely great, absolutely bright. Of course, the proportion was very small and this is the normal proportion of bright people in any community. (laugh) I think so.

Brumm: When you first came to an American campus, did you expect the students to be more submissive, more docile?
Brodsky: I didn't expect anything. I couldn't expect anything when I first came. I had no idea in which way it would go.

Brumm: The reason I ask is that sometimes when people come from European countries and teach in this country, they are often rather surprised at how much freedom the students have in this country and how much they participate in the class discussions.
Brodsky: Yes, of course, they have much more freedom than anywhere, I guess and not only in Russia but more than anywhere. But the matter of freedom or lack of freedom is a general matter for me. For me, their intelligence, their knowledge, the level of their perception and the quality of their response was important. And I didn't have a big disillusion. I've been surprised at a number of them. For me, it was a big surprise, first of all, because of my English. When I started, especially the first semester, it was a constant

challenge, a constant adventure. Each class was an adventure for me. Right now, it's a bit easier because I have become more self-confident. Not self-confident, I just tire to worry about it. (laugh)

Brumm: What is your attitude toward the use of drugs and marijuana by some young people?

Brodsky: I don't know. This is their business. I wouldn't advise them to do it. As for myself, well, as W. H. Auden said once, I belong to the cigarette and alcohol culture, not to the culture of drugs.

Brumm: The last day of class, you left your students with some very meaningful lines by W. H. Auden. Have they always been important to you?

Brodsky: Yes, they are very good lines.

Come to our jolly desert
Where even dolls go whoring
   Where cigarette-ends
   Become intimate friends
And where it's always three-in-the-morning.

A Poet's Map of His Poem: An Interview by George L. Kline

George L. Kline / 1973

From *Vogue,* 162 (September 1973), 228, 230. Reprinted by permission of George L. Kline.

The poet Joseph Brodsky was born in 1940 in Leningrad and forced to leave the Soviet Union in June 1972. During the academic year 1972–1973, he was poet in residence and special lecturer at the University of Michigan; this fall, he will hold similar posts at Queens College in New York. Mr. Kline, who has known Mr. Brodsky since 1967, is professor of philosophy at Bryn Mawr College; he talked with Mr. Brodsky about the poem in Russian and translated their conversation.

Kline: Joseph, when did Biblical themes first appear in your work? Was it, as I seem to recall, in the long poem "Isaac and Abraham" of 1963?

Brodsky: In a serious and central way, yes, although I had touched on Biblical themes in certain earlier poems.

K: Why was it precisely in 1963 that you turned to such themes "in a serious way"?

B: For a very simple reason: it was in that first year that I first read the Bible. I wrote "Isaac and Abraham" literally within a few days of first reading Genesis.

K: It would seem that "Nunc Dimittis" is your only poem devoted entirely to a Biblical theme?

B: Yes, it is.

K: Am I right in interpreting this poem, and in particular the central figure of St. Simeon, as representing a "point of transition" between the Old Testament and the New?

B: You are.

K: And when you say of Simeon: "He moved and grew smaller, in size and in meaning," do you mean that as an Old Testament figure he diminished in importance because the world of the Old Testament faded as the world of the New Testament was born?

B: Yes, but there is a second, literal sense: from the standpoint of Mary and Anna, who are looking on, Simeon appears to shrink physically as he leaves the temple.

K: What about the "strangeness" that the two women experience? Do they find the emerging world of the New Testament incomprehensible and alien?

B: In a sense, yes. But there is also another factor. Technically speaking, this poem is written in a very traditional style, but with absurdist elements, for example, a number of grammatical repetitions. Stylistically, the New Testament is distinguished from the Old by its repetitions, which often have a faintly "absurdist" air.

K: Absurdity, then, is suggested mainly through repetition?

B: Yes, but also by using words in such a way that they suddenly take on quite different meanings, become semantically greater than they are. For example, when Robert Frost in "West-Running Brook" speaks about the *source* of the brook, you suddenly realized that the word 'source' means much more than the word 'source.' It means even more than the word 'God'; it is an absolutely transcendental word.

K: Returning to "Nunc Dimittis"—how would you characterize the role of the Christ Child in the episode which culminates in Simeon's death?

B: That seems to be quite clear. The image of Christ lights up what had hitherto been hidden in darkness, in non-being.

K: Yes, but at this point Christ is only a sleeping baby, "who stirred but as yet/was conscious of nothing. He blew drowsy bubbles."

B: Precisely, but even as a baby he functions as a source of light. What is central in the poem is the relation between the old man and the baby, between the end and the beginning of life.

K: Is Simeon's death, then, the "first Christian death" in human history?

B: Yes, exactly so. Simeon is the first human being to bear the image of Christ into the world beyond.

K: And he dies, not perhaps joyously, but with a clear and calm awareness of what is happening to him and in humble reconciliation to the event. It seems clear, that, although he is very old, Simeon is still vigorous; he does not die from weakness.

B: No, but he is tired of living. Having to live so long—until the birth of the Christ Child—has been a kind of punishment for him.

K: Your images of his dying strike me as particularly original and effective: "He strode through a space that was no longer solid," and "The roaring of time ebbed away in his ears." This last seems to anticipate a passage in your most recent major poem, "1972" (written in Ann Arbor in December), about "growing old" as involving a dulling of the "organ of hearing," which prepares it for silence.

B: Yes, there is a definite connection.

K: Do you mean "silence" in the sense of "eternity"—without the "roaring of time"?

B: Yes, but also in the sense that as the body grows older it fills up with silence—with organs and functions which are no longer relevant to its life.

K: So you are again emphasizing what is central in your very long poem "Gorbunov and Gorchakov" (1965–68)—the connection between life and speech, and between death and silence or non-speech, as when you write: "Life is but talk hurled in the face of silence."

B: I am very pleased, George, that you have noticed this connection, because it does indeed exist, and I consider it important.

K: There is also the relation between "word" and "bird," as when Simeon's words soar upward like a bird "high over their heads in the tall temple's vaults."

B: Yes, Simeon's words fly upward . . .

K: . . . to all men, up the ladder of history?

B: Yes, up the ladder of history, but also upward to God. The uniqueness of Simeon's "Nunc Dimittis" speech lies in the fact that what one man says at a shattering moment in his life becomes universal, becomes a prayer on the lips of all men.

K: What about the two women? Do they understand what is happening?

B: No, they don't really.

K: They seem to be more particular, more private, as persons than Simeon.

B: Yes, they are, and this is true of most of the women in the New Testament; they are less universal than those in the Old Testament.

K: But Anna, at least, is an Old Testament figure, too; she is very old and she remains in the temple day and night, "departing not from it."

B: Yes, she is a kind of Eleanor Rigby. You remember the Beatles' song:

"Eleanor Rigby picks up the rice/in a church where a wedding has been . . . / Waits at the window . . ."

K: I've saved this question for last and perhaps it's unfair. But why is the figure of Joseph missing from your temple scene?

B: That's quite simple. I couldn't have as a major figure someone with the same name as mine.

K: Of course, Joseph has no special role to play in this drama. Yet he infallibly appears on the icons.

B: Yes, and this troubles me, because I have been planning to bring out an anthology of Russian poetry devoted to Biblical subjects—some of Pasternak's Zhivago poems, for example—and to illustrate it with Russian icons. And I realize that I won't be able to include my own "Nunc Dimittis."

K: Unless you can find a special Brodsky icon, one that doesn't show Joseph.

B: Yes, a special Brodsky icon!

Poet in Exile—Joseph Brodsky

Jane Ellen Glasser / 1975

From *The Ghent Quarterly,* 1 (Summer 1975), 58–65. Reprinted by permission of Jane Ellen Glasser and Sam Martinette.

Joseph Brodsky was born in the Soviet Union in 1940. After leaving school at the age of fifteen, he educated himself through his own efforts. Brodsky began to write poetry in his late teens, and by his mid-twenties found himself in trouble with the Soviet authorities. After being found guilty of "social parasitism," Brodsky served almost two years of a five-year term at hard labor. In June of 1972, the Soviet government exiled Brodsky from his native land.

The poetry of Joseph Brodsky has been translated into a dozen different languages. He has been called by many "Russia's greatest living poet," a title which he disdains. His work may be sampled in *Joseph Brodsky: Selected Poems,* translated by George L. Kline.

Brodsky visited Norfolk on April 5, 1975, for a public reading of his poetry, at the invitation of Dr. Leonid Mihilap of Old Dominion University. On the following morning, an informal interview was conducted at 1009 Brandon Avenue, with Poetry Editor Jane Ellen Glasser questioning Brodsky on his work, his ideas, and on himself. As editor, I sat in on the interview, accompanied by photographer Richard Glasser.

S.M., Jr.

TGQ: Do you want to be called Mr. Brodsky?

JB: Joseph.

TGQ: Joseph, you were sentenced to exile to Northern Russia in 1964, having been found guilty of "social parasitism," and then in 1972 forced to become an involuntary exile of the Soviet Union, yet your poems do not reflect an alienation or bitterness towards your country. Why were you asked to leave Russia, and how do you feel about a country which cannot accept, no less revere, its great writers?

JB: The question sounds wrong, because it is not the country which doesn't accept. This is the regime. This is the state. It's important to distinguish, otherwise you're getting mad at the wrong people. As for the state, that's nice, but for the regime, I think they are a bunch of criminals. And the country, well, it's a great country. Its vices and advantages are linked in proportion to its size. What's more, I can't develop any attitude towards Russia. It's my country, my homeland. Whatever treatment you get at your homeland, it doesn't matter, it's still your homeland.

TGQ: What drove you to dedicate your life to becoming a writer in a country where the regime regards poets as nearly synonymous with criminals or enemies?

JB: Well, it's very simple. Nothing drove me. I started to do it because I liked it. I didn't take what was going on very much into consideration. I just liked to do it—writing—and when you're doing that for two, three, four years, you're carrying on partly because of your desire to do it, partly because of your inertia.

TGQ: Are you bitter that your works are now being translated and read all over the globe except in Russia, that, in fact, only a handful of your poems have been published there?

JB: I would prefer them to be published there. Still, there's a great deal of underground circulation, and in Russia it's sort of equivalent to the number of copies they print in this country.

TGQ: What is the literary underground in the Soviet Union?

JB: It's not an underground, literally. There are some people who are interested in poetry and are trying to satisfy, let's say, their needs or interests by the means which are not provided by the State. There's an entire civilization of friendship in Russia. You know the people whom you can trust. You know the people who possess some kind of interesting materials, etc., etc., so you are going to those people sooner or later.

TGQ: Are you still in communication with these people?

JB: I wouldn't say so. Still, I am sending my stuff through rarest channels.

TGQ: Why did you decide to settle in the United States?

JB: Oh, because I'm used to living in a big country.

TGQ: You have been poet-in-residence at numerous American colleges over the last two and a half years. How do you evaluate the creative efforts of our young writers?

JB: You see, I'm not teaching creative writing, so consequently, if I have any evaluation, it is not on the grounds of being introduced to it by these schools, but something outside. Well, it's pretty good. This is my basic attitude: they have the best poetry in the world in this country. I am serious.

This is the best poetry which is written in this country, which is written in English, with some two, three, or four Russian exceptions.

TGQ: Is English a particularly fluent language for poetry?

JB: Yes. Yes, it's a great language for poetry. It's really great precisely for poetry because, for one thing, the average length of an English word is one or two syllables. So, consequently, you can say more in a very short space, in the space of a very short line, than in any other language, for instance, than in Russian because the average length of a Russian word is three or four syllables, minimum. Well, Solzhenitsyn is minimum at six syllable words, which turns me off.

TGQ: Then you are writing in English?

JB: I have done something, about three months ago, a W. H. Auden memorial issue.

TGQ: Do you always write in strict rhyme schemes?

JB: Sometimes yes, sometimes no.

TGQ: Why do you write predominantly in traditional forms?

JB: There are plenty of reasons. For one reason, I love the song, the organization. Should I say, because it is much more difficult to do than anything else, than free verse, for instance, even than blank verse. It really gives you a very tight frame of structure, and, then, there's no question of your own freedom. It's a question of freedom of language, whether the language can make it within this tight structure. It's merely a sense of discipline.

TGQ: Do you ever find it contrived?

JB: When I do, it means that I have nothing. Well, it means that the issue I am trying to ponder over, the statement I am trying to make, is wrong.

TGQ: Do you ever write in free verse?

JB: When I was eighteen, nineteen, twenty or twenty-one. Then I dropped it because it was very easy. Not very easy, fairly easy.

TGQ: Many of our young writers are continually trying to be inventive. They think that poetry should go beyond what it has been and they are searching for new forms, new means of expression.

JB: Still, you don't have many forms. You have merely one form, and you are doing it with words and words have their logic. What's more, all these magical patterns, they are not merely technical devices. Our bodies are iambic pentameter. All these metrical patterns are spiritual units, if you wish, spiritual magnets.

TGQ: There is a growing movement in this country to reject the traditional approach to poetry for an experimentation with, an openness of structure, content, and language.

JB: All these movements, they are behaving in a pendulum type thing, let's say from baroque to classicism, from classicism to romanticism, from romanticism to realism, back to realism, from realism to surrealism, expressionism, etc., etc. Basically, it's from the vague to the precise, and back. So, consequently, people who are exercising right now all this free verse, self-expression enterprise, they are sitting on the safest side of the pendulum.

TGQ: What is your opinion of our growing ranks of so-called "confessional" poets?

JB: Well, it's a sick thing that is growing. For one thing, to be literal about it, speaking about the confession as such, you reveal all your life to the priest, let's say, in order to be really honest, you should make a step back. To cover with the light your life, you should make one step back in the shadow. So, consequently, each confession has a little reservation. First, I don't believe that our egos are the best material for the poetry, even wounded egos. There are some things which are linked outside.

TGQ: How critical are you of your own writing?

JB: Well, I think I'm pretty critical.

TGQ: Do you have a tendency to redraft?

JB: Well, yes I do. To destroy or just to suppress it for good.

TGQ: What are your primary thematic concerns?

JB: It's always hard to define. Well, should I say, things in their transition. I would quote Frost about "Neither Out Far Nor In Deep" when he says:

As long as it takes to pass
A ship keeps raising its hull;
The wetter ground like glass
Reflects a standing gull.

Well, this is the primary concern.

TGQ: There is a darkness, an anguish, a pain suffered in silence in your poems. Is this the pain of the poet in exile or the existential pain of the human condition?

JB: The latter.

TGQ: Why don't you participate in or conduct writing workshops?
JB: Well, because I don't believe in that kind of thing.

TGQ: You don't believe you can teach people to see more clearly?
JB: That's a good definition. You can't teach people to write a poem. You can teach them technical tricks. What's more, you can teach them to see more clearly. Still, the formula of any exploit is not just muscles doing all the act. It's not even the courage you have. It's not even the craftsmanship, that is, your ability to handle your weaponry. There's one extra thing in any exploit. Some divine intervention. You can't possibly teach this kind of thing. It's up to a person, or down to a person.

TGQ: I think workshops can be effective in the sense that the writer is writing both for himself and for an audience, and a workshop can point out failures in communication.
JB: It depends on who you are trying to communicate to. If you are trying to communicate to your colleagues, or even the critics, or whoever will pronounce judgment, it sounds wrong. You should communicate to somebody, either somebody in particular—he, she—but not so much he, she, as the subject of your love or hatred. And, the best thing, when you get to a certain angel or devil, to try to convince him, on his high level, that he's wrong and you are right. You are talking to someone else who knows all your arguments, who knows all your models. Still, you are trying to make a statement beyond his grasp. That's the trick. It's very easy to find yourself speaking to nobody, literally. But there is still someone who is better than you are, to say the least.

TGQ: But, for example, when you give a reading, you want people to respond.
JB: It's not that. The main thing I try to convey is a fair idea for Russian.

TGQ: But, assuming that you had a Russian audience.
JB: I would do the same. I don't care that much for the response. I'm just making my statement on a certain level and it's up to them to accept it or not, to be smashed by that or excited by that. But whatever the response will be, it is not an adequate response. I would address to them as if I was addressing to myself or some certain being, whether human or inhuman, which is superior to me. That is a kind of defense. That is a kind of trial, and you, to some extent, defend yourself, listen to your arguments about your existence.

TGQ: When you talk about this other being, are you talking about another part of yourself, or something spiritual?

JB: Well, it's not a spirit. There is somebody, there is something beyond my grasp. I am trying to convince him that I am alright.

TGQ: Which poets, living or dead, have had the greatest influence on your work?

JB: Oh, many of them. Really many. If you talk about Americans, let's say, Edward Arlington Robinson, Frost, Marianne Moore, although in some strange ways, and I hope all these people, Richard Wilbur, Lowell, I hope I oblige them to a certain extent. But I am talking only about the American ones.

TGQ: Admiring such poets as Robert Frost and Robert Lowell who speak for their country, your poems have been characterized as apolitical and personal. What voice addresses what audience in your poems?

JB: Well, I don't know. The best answer is given to such a question by the late Russian composer Stravinsky. Being asked for whom he writes, he said, "for myself, and for the probable alter-ego."

TGQ: Are there any American novelists who have influenced you?

JB: I don't know which way, but I think he did. William Faulkner.

TGQ: Are you familiar with the strain of American literature that deals with social criticism, such as in Sinclair Lewis's writings? I am not familiar with any Russian who has left his country and has written in this manner. The Russian authors I have come across seem to retain an uncritical love for their homeland once they have left, with the exception, perhaps, of Solzhenitsyn. Is there a Russian who writes in the manner of Lewis or Sherwood Anderson?

JB: Well, certainly each work of art, especially if it's prose or poetry, contains a certain element of social comment, but not entirely. I don't know anybody whom I would compare—at least not as much out of the content of the word, but the quality, the level—among the living writers with Lewis or Anderson. There are some people who create their own universes. There's a pretty good writer, Voinovich (you don't know this name), pretty soon his book is going to come out by Farrar & Straus. It's a kind of mortuary, a kind of novel-anecdote. There was a man . . . in comparison, all these people—Solzhenitsyn, Bulgakov—look like kids. His work is not very widely known in this country at all. Andrei Platonov is the greatest Russian writer of this century, and he was much beyond the level of those you mentioned, and his social comment was much more great.

TGQ: How do you feel your poems have been received in this country?
JB: Oh, well, I think it has been received okay. No complaints.

TGQ: Joseph, how do you account for the way the world has embraced not only you, but Solzhenitsyn?
JB: Does it embrace me?

TGQ: I think it has. Your name is known.
JB: But I am not my name.

TGQ: It might be easier for you to relate your reaction to the world's response to Solzhenitsyn.
JB: In his case, it provides him with somewhat the wrong behavior on two levels: A. He's starting as a kind of teacher of humanity. Whether you have a real capability, or possibility, or even guts for that is a very dangerous position. Well, because it reduces the self-checking process as a human being. B. On merely stylistical grounds, being abroad, having no censorship, no editing, he finds himself in the position of Caesar's wife, that is, beyond any suspicion. Nobody would come to the man to say, "cut down this passage, you told that five pages before."

TGQ: How do you evaluate yourself in terms of the great Russian writers and your place in the posterity of your native literature?
JB: I don't know.

TGQ: You have been described as the greatest living Russian poet.
JB: Well, this is the responsibility of the people who did it, not mine.

TGQ: What is your response to the description?
JB: It's merely a fun and tasteless statement. It's impossible to say anything like that during the time the person you are talking about is living. I don't care that much about posterity.

TGQ: Does it put any pressure on you, or do you ignore it completely?
JB: Well, I don't know how to say it. Well, I hope it will survive something; I hope it will survive myself. But for how long, I don't care.

TGQ: Don't all great writers dream of having an enduring influence?
JB: Not necessarily great. All poets do have this kind of thing. Let's hope I will, but if not, so what! I have enjoyed this interview, at least.

TGQ: Do you think you will ever be able to return to Russia, and if so, would you choose to?

JB: Certainly I would choose to, certainly.

TGQ: Do you foresee that you will be able to?

JB: That's quite vague now, but I don't live in the human "never." I just don't believe in that. I just can't believe when they tell you that you'll never be back, whoever they are, however strong they are. In the future not that much foreseeable, but still, if a future does exist, I will find my way back, either through deceiving them or, perhaps, there will be some changes, but I do not hope. I do not have any hope for beautiful changes over there. Still, I think I will be back to those streets and people.

TGQ: Do you know where you will be in ten years? Do you have any goals?

JB: No.

TGQ: Is there anything you want to do with your sensitivity, your message?

JB: No, how could I?

TGQ: What has motivated you to produce what you have written to this date? I don't know that I can take your statement seriously that you have no goals.

JB: You may take it seriously. Masochism.

Questions and Answers after Brodsky's Reading, 21 February 1978

The Iowa Review / 1978

From *The Iowa Review,* 9 (Winter 1979), 4–9. Reprinted by permission of *The Iowa Review.**

Q: Do you like reading the poems in English?

A: No, no, I don't think so, no. Well, I'm just doing that from time to time. Mostly for fun. In this case, for something other than fun. But mostly for fun.

Q: Can I ask you to reminisce a little about Akhmatova? What was she like?

A: This is a cruel thing to do. This is a big topic. She was well-known . . . what can I say? Well, in short, let's say in two minutes . . . I don't know . . . well, she was awfully tall . . . (Laughter) . . . I guess I'm 5′10″ or something like that, and, by Russian standards, it's quite a bit. Well, anyway, I never had any pangs, any feelings, about my height except when I was walking with her because she was awfully tall. When you were looking at her you could kind of grasp the reason why, occasionally, Russia has been ruled by the empresses. She had, if you wish, an imperial look.

Mind that she was old—at that time she was seventy. She was extremely witty. One thing, I guess, everybody could learn from her is how to bear everything that befalls one. If not for some kind of Christian teaching, if not for all that Christian propaganda, the knowledge of her only will give you quite a bit of Christianity.

What else about her? We didn't talk much about poetry; well, we did, certainly . . . but we were mostly talking about something completely removed from that. She used to say that metaphysics and gossip are the only interesting things. (Laughter) In that she was quite in line with that French philosopher Cioran.** What else about her? Well, it's impossible to do it in two minutes.

**We thank Gail Hanlon for preparing this manuscript, from tape, and Mr. Brodsky for helping correct it.*

**E. M. Cioran was Romanian, although he lived much of his life in France.—*ED*

Q: Did she ever speak to you in a gossipy way, or even metaphysically to you, about Mandelstam?

A: Certainly.

Q: Which way? (Laughter)

A: Well, she used to say that Nadezhda, his wife, is the happiest of all Russian literary widows. (Laughter) Because lots of the awfully good people, writers and poets, got killed and the recognition came to many of them. In the case of Mandelstam it did, and it was a universal one. . . . We were discussing lots of things . . . we were discussing the origins of his . . . development, so to speak, because there was a great deal of discussion about where it's from. Akhmatova held that this was mostly from Pushkin. What else? She was never trying to compare herself to him. She knew the size of the man, the size of the poet. She was awfully humble. She used to say that "in comparison with him and Tsvetaeva I am just a little cow. I am a cow," that's what she used to say.

Q: Who do you read in Russian? I don't know much Russian and was wondering where to start.

A: Well, if you are talking about the twentieth century, I'll give you a list of poets. Akhmatova, Mandelstam, Tsvetaeva (and she is the greatest one, in my view. The greatest poet in the twentieth century was a woman.) I said Pasternak, no? Well, this is kind of obvious; also Klyuev, Khodasevich, Zabolotsky. That should occupy you for quite a while. In terms of prose it's a little bit harder because out of the nineteenth century an idea emerged that Russian literature is still just as great as it was in the nineteenth century, some kind of inertia. . . . And, very often, the things called the desirable were taken for the real . . . as when you try to impose all the lingo you usually apply to the great dead on to the living writers.

Andrey Platonov is the greatest of them. He is an awfully interesting man. It is kind of hard to translate him in English; on the other hand, he has been translated into English. When you are reading that, his work in English, you should sort of make an imaginary correlative. It's not what you're reading, really, it's kind of one-tenth of what's there. Because he was using syntax in a rather peculiar way. He will lead the sentence into some kind of logical dead-end. Always. Consequently, in order to comprehend what he is saying, you have to sort of "back" from the dead-end and then to realize what brought you to that dead-end. And you realize that this is the grammar, the very grammar, of the Russian language itself. And if you sort of estrange yourself and look at the page of what he has written it looks like kind of a big supermarket with all the items turned inside-out. Not only that, because he was never doing that for the game's sake. This kind of variety was the result of philosophical madness, not of aesthetic madness, and that's a big distinction.

Well, and who else? Well, I wouldn't say that there were people parallel to Platonov. There is a big interval after him, in my view. Well, this is my hierarchy, after all. . . . There are awfully nice writers . . . but in my opinion, the best Russian prose in the twentieth century has been written precisely by the poets, Mandelstam and by Tsvetaeva, and a little journal entitled in English, *The Safe Conduct,* by Pasternak. *Dr. Zhivago* is something else . . . it's a kind of book, yah? (Laughter) Well, he was one of the greatest poets, but it's awfully hard to talk about it because the level of the adoration of those people is such that you can't really talk in this fashion. On those heights there is no hierarchy.

Q: Do the Russian people listen to and respect their poets more than other countries.

A: I wouldn't say so.

Q: What about the government? Why are they afraid? Or are they?

A: Because when you have a centralized government it tries to oversee all walks of life, and, most of all, well, whatever has to do with the printed matter. Government itself has a language, or a lingo or jargon, in which it operates. A writer has to, in order to sell himself (if not really "sell" himself, but at least to the public, to make himself noticeable, etcetera), he should try to utter it in some different, differing idiom from that of the State, which immediately puts him into the category of suspect, yes?

And it's more interesting than that. There is a great deal of humbug about censorship. There is a terrific, well, choking censorship, that's quite right. And yet it's "life-size," if you wish. Or, at least for the writer, it's often a profitable thing in a way. Because the censorship turns the entire nation into the readership; it creates a certain stylistic plateau, yah? (Laughter) On which, when you are trying to do something on your own, you immediately get very noticeable. Besides, censorship accelerates the metaphoric speech. The metaphorical structure, yes? Because, while we are not allowed to say "the tyrants," well, sometimes, when you are saying "that man" (Laughter) it gives some kind of boost, a metaphorical boost, if you wish.

Why are they afraid? Well, they are not afraid, they're just stupid. (Laughter) No, no. I can understand how laughable it is, but it's not a laughable matter because, well, the stupid people are awfully mean.

Q: What sort of proof was offered in the trial where they proved that you weren't a poet?

A: It's the other way around, because in our courts you ought to prove that you are something or are not something. There is no presumption of innocence in Russian courts. Whatever they charge you with, it is you who should prove that you are not guilty. It is not they who should prove that you are guilty, that's the point, whatever it is, poet or not poet. And actually I couldn't prove that. Nor could they prove that I am not. (Laughter) And besides it was years ago. It was . . . fifteen years ago.

Q: Would you like to go back and live in Russia again?

A: I would love to. I would really love to. Now it's getting a little bit complicated because I am for five years already here. And I'm just a little bit scared that I've changed quite a bit . . . well, not scared . . . got, well, if you wish, corrupted or whatever. (Laughter)

I would go there on one condition. And I think I am in a position to make conditions, to make demands. The condition would be that all my work would have to be published. Then I would like to return there and live the same life as I did. If something like that happens . . . if I am going back . . . I would like to bring some kind of change within this business of poetry.

Q: Do you think that's possible?

A: I don't think so. At least I don't see it.

Q: How do you think being involved in an institution like the University of Michigan has changed you . . . while in Russia you weren't affiliated with any academy?

A: No, I wasn't. No, when I said that I had changed I didn't mean exactly the University of Michigan. Nor did I have in mind America in particular. What I've been thinking about is about getting older, more demanding, so to speak. Less willing to compromise, perhaps, because, well, there is not that much left to compromise. No, the University didn't change me. For myself, I like to teach. And there are a couple of people in this audience who can testify that I'm not lying. (Laughter)

Q: I've noticed, and found it very interesting, that you do not write only about Russia. You write about subjects that are around you now. Do you ever find yourself at a real loss for words in Russian to describe, say, particular plants or trees or particularly lovely things?

A: Good question. Never. (Laughter)

I was scared a great deal that such a thing might happen. And this is the kind of scare which sits pretty tightly nearby. So far, such a thing has never occurred. It's kind of a mind-boggling thing when, for instance, you're looking for something that needs a rhyme, and then there is no rhyme, and then you think, "Am I forgetting the language, or is there no such rhyme for this word?" Then you think there is no point to get paranoid because you ought to stay sane. But then you ask yourself "What for?" if you are really forgetting the language . . . "What for?" . . . just to stay sane?

Well, it's good to think about that. Are you doing that in order to prove to yourself that you can still write, or are you really writing out of necessity? In other words, all those questions which a writer usually encounters in his practice are kind of a little bit blown up . . . getting sort of more ominous in size than before. There is something in this quarrel between madness and sanity, perhaps. Though one could do without it . . .

Q: What's your opinion of Solzhenitsyn and the legend which has been built around him?

A: (Long pause) Well, let's put it this way. I'm awfully proud that I'm writing in the same language as he does. I think he's one of the greatest men ever . . . one of the greatest and most courageous men who has ever lived in this century. I think he is an absolutely remarkable writer. As for legend . . . you shouldn't worry or care about legend, you should read the work. And what kind of legend? He has his biography . . . and he has his words.

Is that enough or should I say something else?

Q: Please go on.

A: He has been reproached quite a bit by various critics, by various men of letters, for being a second-rate writer, or a bad writer. I don't think it's just . . . because the people who are judging the work of literature are sort of building their judgment on the basis of systems of aesthetics which we inherited from the nineteenth century. What Solzhenitsyn is doing in literature cannot be judged by this aesthetic standard just as his subject-matter cannot be judged by our ethical standards. Because when the man is talking about the annihilation or liquidation of sixty million men, there is no room, in my opinion, left to talk about literature and whether it's a good type of literature or not. In his case, literature is absorbed in the story.

What I'm trying to say is this. Curiously enough, he is the writer, but he *uses* literature, and not in order to create a new aesthetics but for its ancient, original purpose: to tell the story. And, in doing that, he's unwittingly, in my opinion, expanding the framework of literature. From the beginning of his career, as far as we can trace it on the basis of his successive publications, you see quite an obvious erosion of the genres.

What we start with, historically, is a normal novella, *One Day,* yes? Then he goes to something bigger, *Cancer Ward,* yes? And then he went to something which is really neither a novel nor a chronicle but somewhere in between, *The First Circle.* And then we've got this *Gulag* which is, I think, a new kind of epic. It's a very dark epic, if you wish, but it's an epic.

I think that the Soviet rule has its Homer in the case of Solzhenitsyn. I don't know what else to say. And forget about legends, that is real crap . . . about every writer.

Q: Are your comfortable with the English translations of your work?

A: Sometimes, yes. Sometimes, no. An acquaintance of mine, a Swedish poet, Tomas Tranströmer, who has been, in my view, real botched up by Robert Bly (Laughter), once said that your attitude toward a translator sort of goes through three stages. First you trust him, and he kills you. The second time you don't trust him and he kills you just the same. The third kind of attitude involves certain masochistic traits in you. (Laughter) You say "kill me, kill me, kill me. . . ." And he kills you. (Laughter) It's not my joke . . . it's a quiet Swedish joke. (Laughter)

Q: I've understood that the way contemporary Russian poets deliver their own work, the sort of declamatory style, comes from Mayakovsky's delivery. Is there any truth to that? That there is a school of declamation?

A: No. Not much. Not much. Well, actually, I never heard any recordings of Mayakovsky, but if it's so, if his style is declamatory, it comes from something much further back in our history. The first literature which appeared in Russian was liturgical literature: the chants, the recitals . . . *qu'est-ce que c'est? psaltines?* [sic]

Q: Psalms?

A: Yes, psalms. So, they've been rendered in Russian in kind of rhythmical form. And, in the Russian equivalent of high school, although there is no real equivalent, the children are made to memorize lines and lines of poetry. Pages and pages. And, after that, they are compelled to deliver that with so-called expression. That is, if they deliver it they should underline by their intonation, by stress, whatever it is, their understanding of the text. OK? So, this comes in the schooling, the normal schooling.

I remember as a child knowing by heart lots of things, lots of Pushkin, lots of *Eugene Onegin*, lots of Griboedov, and other people. And this is what sets forth or releases this mechanism of mnemonic devices. And, in a way, this fashion or manner of recital, whatever it is, is in its own way a direct consequence of that liturgical tradition. All the more so because, as Theodore Roethke once said, the writing of a poem starts, if I remember the quote correctly, a "psychological mechanism of prayer." So, here you are.

Q: One of my Russian friends insists that no American, or even any non-Russian, can ever understand Russian poetry. What do you say to that?

A: Nonsense. Nonsense. Although, one thing should be said, and this is a really nice way to end the talk. In the fourth book of his *Histories* Herodotus tells a story. It deals with Scythia, with Scythians, the tribe that lives up north of Thanais, which I believe is the present day Donez. And the name of the tribe is already suspicious for a Russian ear. It's called Budini, well anyway, it has to do with the verb "to be," "byt," "bydi," of which the future tense could have sounded "budini," anyway . . . forget all that. He describes them in very general terms. And they are living in that area for timber; they make boats and build their houses and temples out of wood. And he says, and I checked that line even in Greek because I was astonished, "And they are in total amazement towards their own language." "They are amazed by their own language, astonished by their own language." There you are. Alright?

Interview with Joseph Brodsky

Eva Burch and David Chin / 1979

From *Columbia: A Magazine of Poetry and Prose* (Spring/Summer 1980), 50–68. Reprinted by permission of Eva Burch and David Chin.

Do you think that your new book A Part of Speech *(Farrar, Straus & Giroux) marks any particular crossroads in your poetic career?*

What I really can detect if I look, if I am capable of assessing myself, are simply prosodic shifts, like one from tetrameters into pentameters, acquiring a bigger swing, or another one, away from predominantly pentametric structures. Somewhere about three or four years ago, I began to drift to something like an accentuated verse, stressing the syllabic element, not the syllabatonic—returning almost to the slug, a slow speech. Not exactly slow, but the kind of poem that proceeds without any *a priori* music.

Do you attribute the prosodic shifts to anything in particular?

It had to do with a very simple thing, a sense that the existing meters began to satisfy me less and less and that some different music entered. Not that I had exhausted the possibilities of the strict meters—since one has, at any time, all these temptations. But there is a certain domineering note, or tune, that is going through one's mind. It's a very strange thing. I say tune; I can just as well say noise. In either case, whatever it is, it's not just exactly a tune, a musical hum. For this hum has a certain psychological overlay. It's an extremely grey area—not grey, it's a certain frequency, so to speak in which you operate and which, at times, you change. However, at any point, you just opt for several things. Once you have the experience of the strict meters, you always long to return to them, as well as deviate from them. At any given point, you are under the spell of several of them. So it is not as though you have really abandoned the previous prosodic idiom, but you have just departed from it.

Would you say there was any particular influence? For instance, Derek Walcott's work?

No, not really. At that time I hadn't read Derek's work. I think what really prompted it a bit, if we talk about the literature, is that I had read two or three poems by somebody in French. French poetry is technically speaking syllabic. And I realized that the beat was somewhat . . . well, when you read a poem, very often you get a certain prosodic taste in your mouth. This is what happened, I think, once again. I must say I was using these things before, but never in such an extensive fashion. I wouldn't call it a shift, really: neither thematically, nor, of course, mentally. It was simply a prosodic alteration, and a noticeable one at that.

When you start to work on a poem, do you have a form already in mind or do you work from the subject materials toward the form?

I always have, I think, some sense of form. In fact, what I have is a volume, an idea of quantity. It is not exactly a vessel. I have some sort of outline. I know how many chunks there are going to be. I think in some sense I have an image of its flesh and I know more or less how long it is going to last. Somehow, however, in the course of the writing, it starts to spin itself off, it extends, expands, or it shrinks.

So the chunks you've been working with are really dictated by some phonetic sense of rhythm or psychological sense of rhythm rather than blocks of images?

The former. Very often you don't have images, and really you don't have things to say. Images, et cetera, are suggested by the language, in the process of its deployment. Sometimes things are prompted by rhyme, by what is said before. You've got these two or three things and you think, well, I should take the next step. There's always a considerable temptation to make a next step. And very often submission to this temptation pays off.

Do you think these things are preserved in translation?

The succession of images and sometimes the succession of thought, the development, the psychology of the next step sometimes are preserved.

But not the prosody itself?

Sometimes there is an attempt to preserve it; if the translator is a conscientious person, he will try to imitate the structure. However, there is a large question that looms over those things. It certainly involves the biography of this or that structure within various cultures, various languages, various prosodic traditions. The same structure may mean, imply or allude to different things. I never know whether the nuance—and poetry is all about nuance, linguistic nuance—really survives. However, I think quite a lot of a poem survives translation. Besides, one is not able to say something so qualitatively different that in translation it could be so utterly lost. Man's capacity for utterances is somewhat limited: you cannot lose much, even though you only understand the man in half.

In your introduction to Platonov, I believe you said that the translation necessarily had to miss Platonov's very special grammatical constructions, which I believe you called a backing-in operation, a dead end.

A cuneiform, in a way.

Do you think the same kind of loss occurs in the translations of your poems?

No, because . . . well, it occurs, certainly, but in my case it occurs to a lesser degree than Platonov's because his main tool, so to speak, was his texture. That was his main device. A device that is really unreconstructable in English. Or you can reconstruct it, but only to a certain extent—beyond this it becomes tedious in English. In Russian it's all pleasure.

In addition to the prosodical feature you already mentioned, what do you see as your main device?

Well, actually, I would say precisely the readiness to submit to this temptation of making the next step. That is, when you think the subject, emotion, even an image and its implications, are exhausted, I try to make a next step—to plumb some impossibility of image or of sentiment. I tried it once, in that large dialogue thing ("Gorbunov and Gorchakov"), fourteen hundred lines, and I liked it. For one thing, it was written in decima, ababababab, which is bloody monotonous, mind-boggling in itself, every stanza. So any attempt to make a next stanza was nearly unthinkable to me at the time. Also, in terms of the argument, the points of the argument, any continuation of the conversation seemed to be unthinkable. Those characters couldn't have had anything to say to each other. And yet we know the nature of conversations; they always linger. They always resume—it's like crickets—in the same note they quit last night. This is one of the frightening powers of exchanges, of dialogues. So I was trying to ape those powers . . . I can talk at length about the poem, merely because it is one of the most serious things I've ever done in my life. I don't think I'll ever be able to repeat anything of a parallel scope because I don't have any more of that patience or whatever it is. That poem displays one of the main devices—making that next step, which seems a) impossible, b) even unnecessary. Perhaps it's not my main device, but this is what I respect myself for . . . Pity that the translation of that poem is really nowhere. I struck it out of the book.

The poem seems to investigate how inevitably a kind of betrayal or self-betrayal got perpetuated. Could you comment on that?

True, and this one of the essential, perennial themes of Russian literature. It's all about betrayal. In that respect I think I am in the tradition—well, more in that of prose than of poetry. This is the literature or mentality which is considerably poised by that expectation of betrayal. To a certain extent I think that it affects the language itself. I suppose I shouldn't venture into these dark areas. For instance, in Russian, however strong an accusation is, it always has this expectation of reversal merely because, I presume, the words are polysyllabic and are invested with a great deal of phonetics. Also, there is a somewhat self-effacing element, merely because there are too many syllables to take that accusation at face value. That idea of reversal, of ambivalence, of betrayal creeps into the language. We are talking now about the nuances. So, in Russian, in fact, it's easier to a certain extent to speak with a very poised voice regardless of the sentiment. The sentiment may be a straightforward "I approve of this" or "I disapprove of that." Yet merely because of the language, the expression of this sentiment is tinged with ambiguity. There is this slight poise, even poison, I would say. A reader senses it. You can play on that endlessly—because nearly every statement reeks with uncertainty.

Would you say that language is using its speakers or that its speakers are at the mercy of language?

Both, I presume; although my verdict doesn't count: I am in a peculiar position—that is, I am outside the language, and I became its observer to a certain extent. Well, a writer is always an observer. So, his assessment of the language is, to say the least, somewhat biased. However, I would say, we are the victims of our language. Victims, that is, as a nation, and as writers we are servants. Not that we perfect it—we rather proliferate it, unwittingly.

Do you think the same obtains for English?

To a certain extent the same thing goes for English, but in a different line of regard. English is an analytical language and does not really allow for much nuance. Or you get circumvential, Henry Jamesian, to say the least. There is English and English: Jane Austen and Orwell, on the one hand, and James Conrad and Nabokov on the other. I prefer the Austen/Orwell tradition. Jamesian English has a sense of texture similar to that of Russian. And once you're working with texture, your statements get . . . not exactly compromised, but less important—you are striving for the cumulative effect. So it depends on whose English we are talking about. English *per se*? Well, there is no such thing, I think.

In the title poem, "A Part of Speech," does the image of language as mice refer to some quality of the Russian language?

It refers in a way to the phonetics of the Russian word for "future," which phonetically resembles the word for "rodents." Therefore, I spin it off into the idea that the future, that is, the word itself, gnaws—or whatever it is, sinks its teeth—into the cheese of memory.

Time seems to be a constant, recurring theme throughout your poetry.

This is the only thing in the world. It's much more interesting than space, for instance. Because space is a thing, whereas time is an idea about things, about the Thing. And, if I were to describe the thing I'm interested in, it is what time does to a man. That's, in short, what it's all about.

Do you connect your interest in time with, say, Pasternak's or Mandelstam's?

I don't think that my notions of it are that different from theirs: they are just human notions of time. They simply involve that rather Christian notion of linear time, that is, not an African kind of thing, a circle or spiral that goes backward. In that respect we are not altogether different. It's awfully hard, again, to assess myself, but I would say I am more interested in the purely abstract notion of time. I think I may safely say that I am using the concrete notions of time as the point of departure into the abstract speculation. And what I'm trying to do is to make these abstract speculations palpable by means of imagery, concrete emblemata, and all those things. Sometimes it works.

In "Mexican Divertimento," does the concluding image of the lizard looking up at a space ship serve as a catapult from the various Mexican emblemata to some such speculation?

The only thing which I think is worthwhile to say about that poem, at least for me, is that the subject was Mexico—not exactly Mexico, but one's state of mind, I think, set against the least congenial background. Or I guess that was the subject. I was trying to employ the traditional Spanish meters. The first part about Maximillian starts as a madrigal. The second, "1867"—that business about Juarez—it's done to the tune of a choklo, that is, an Argentinian tango. "Merida," the third section, is done in the meter that was employed by the greatest Spanish poet, I think, ever, Jorge Manrique, in the Fifteenth Century. It's an imitation of his lament for his dead father. And "Romancero" is a traditional Spanish thing, those tetrameters. There is an approximation to a modern poem in that chapter, "To Evgeni." And a kind of classical iambic pentameter, a normal, regular thing, bringing this home in that final part for the encyclopedia, the "Encyclopedia Entry." After all, it's called a divertimento. It has to do with fashions, with the styles employed there. It's not exactly stylization. It's paying a tribute to the culture in question, so to speak.

I wonder if in that poem you have a more public, a broader voice?

Could be, but at the same time I resented that. And I was trying to subdue it. I was somewhat surprised that the *New York Review of Books* picked it up, because it is not exactly the most liberal stance that has been displayed there. I am afraid that it may have irked some people in Mexico, because it is somewhat Evelyn Waughish.

Of all the poems you've written, which are your favorites?

One was written about two or three years ago—"Letters from the Ming Dynasty"; Derek Walcott has translated it. Also, I like "The Butterfly." I was trying to combine two things, Beckett and Mozart. Many years ago, in Russia, I was after a girl. We left a concert, a Mozart concert, and she told me as we walked down the streets, "Joseph, everything is lovely about your poetry," et cetera. "Well, you know that," et cetera, "except you never execute in a poem that lightness and yet that gravity which Mozart has." And that kind of got me. I remembered that very well, and I decided to write that butterfly poem. Well, I hope I managed. Actually, George Kline did an excellent job translating the poem.

Would you comment on the relationship between Christianity and modern culture? Is your interest in Cavafy in any way connected with this?

The relationship between God—well, Christianity, or those religious things—and the modern culture is quite direct: it's the relation between cause and effect, if you like. If I have those things in my poems, it's merely an attempt of the effect to pay tribute to the cause. It's as simple as that. It's not that I am exactly religious, not at all. Fortunately or unfortunately, I don't really know. I don't think that I belong to any kind of creed. In fact, when they asked me in the hospital, well, that crucial question, because everything can happen, I felt quite a loss.

As for Cavafy, and why it's important for me to teach him, I don't have a one-line answer. One thing—because I love his work immensely. I think he is perhaps the only poet in this century (although this is not what I love him for) who has a kind of clear-cut system, or who at least is faithful to himself, to his idea of what it ought to be. The others, however great they may be, seem eclectic. But then, after him, everybody looks so. Therefore, one of the advantages of studying Cavafy is, you know what it is the man aims toward, what are the means he finds suitable, and what he rejects. This is very important knowledge for any student of literature.

If we reduce it to an extremely pedestrian level, what he tells you is a very simple tale about ambiguity being the ancient state of mind. This is something we fail to perceive, because we think that we are the most complicated creatures. And yet you can get this sensation from somebody as old as Plutarch or Herodotus, as much as you can get it from Cavafy. However, people don't read the classics that much these days. To say the least, I think that reading Cavafy for the sake of sheer historical content may humble a modern man considerably. Still, as I mention all these things, I am far, very far away, from saying why I like Cavafy. Well, I presume the main reason is that note of *ennui,* very sustained, which is the essential sentiment of a man about life and which hasn't been displayed until him or after him with such a constancy in poetry. Whereas everyone else who displayed it would do so in a romantic or expressionist key, which is a betrayal of the entire sentiment, Cavafy's poetic operation was, in my view, on the same plane of regard as the sentiment itself.

What about Auden? Why do you like him so much and like teaching him?

Because, for me, there is no better poet in either language. Well, actually, for me, there are two poets—Tsvetaeva, she's a Russian, and Auden. They are extremely disparate. She is all tragedy; but they have one thing in common. Both espouse, or their poetry espouses, the philosophy of discomfort. That is, almost to the extent of "the worse, the better" or, in the case of Auden, "the more interesting." I'm afraid I may sound almost like an Englishman. I guess what attracts me to both of them, and especially to Auden, is that kind of a drama which never manifests itself in the dramatic fashion. If anything, it manifests itself in the anti-climatic fashion. He was great with that technique, the anti-climatic technique, just astonishing. This to me seems to be an extremely noble posture in the art of letters. Also I am completely . . . it's a peculiar thing, I think, for a man from a different culture to be so taken by a foreign poet. I seldom derive such an amount of joy from reading as I do in the case of Auden. It's a real joy, and by saying joy I don't mean just a pleasure, because joy is a very dark thing in itself. For me he is a lot more profound or "sublime" than anybody else, more so than Yeats or than Eliot, merely because he does all those things that they aspire to and make a great deal of in a very oblique, parenthetical fashion. And this is what I respect a poet for. Well, I don't really know. Auden himself would certainly disagree with that and would boo me for what I'm saying. At one point I was bold enough to . . . well, it was really because my English wasn't very good at that point. I visited him at Christ's Church in Oxford. And suddenly there was that meaningless pause, because I didn't know how to fill it nor was he willing to fill it with anything. Then I interrupted it by saying, "Wystan, do you know what I think? I think that you and Tom Eliot make one great English poet." Well, that was the most idiotic thing. He just gave me a daunting look.

To teach him—although that could be done a lot better than I do—for me seems to be almost a natural thing to do. If only because to deal with him in person or in verse is the best occupation one may have on earth. Actually, I consider myself extremely lucky for that. It's not just luck; it's an astonishingly generous fate. Because there is nothing better in my view in the entire English language than the poetry of this man. For me to talk about him is . . . the most sensible and, say, just occupation. It grows on me the more I read him. It's not just a question of language. I can read and reread Eliot or Yeats, for that matter, and see the sparks of wisdom and profundity. Yet for me, for all their beauty, it's a little raw in either case, especially in the case of Yeats. I must say that I have a great deal of admiration for the raw stuff. Still, Auden, having most of what they had, possessed a unique intelligence. To say the least, he was really the first poet who was at home in his century, who didn't pretend he deserved or was destined for something better. Or worse. That's a very dignified stance.

Do you feel something toward him as Statius does toward Virgil in the Purgatorio?

Ah-huh . . . Exactly. And this is in part what helps me to operate, or justifies my operation, in the English language. Somehow I think that to work in the same language that he did is one of the most demanding—certainly demanding, no question about that—one of the most challenging, most rewarding things. Well, it's . . . I really love him very much. It's something haunting really, because the more I read, the more. . . . As the narrator in Anthony Hecht's poem ("Behold the Lilies of the Field") would remark, "I wish I were like them."

Are you writing poems in English at all?

I've written several. Some of them were published. Others weren't. I'm not aspiring to all that, but when I write prose, I wonder what would he say—whether he wound find it rubbish or a sensible thing. Auden was an astonishing critic, among all the other things; he had that peculiar mastery of common sense. And with the exception of Orwell, I consider him the greatest stylist of English prose.

Are you writing more and more prose?

No, not really, no. I wish I had more time, or I wish my time were better organized, or I wish I could organize it better. Unfortunately, I am a mess.

Do you have another book of poems in the works?

There are about two books of poems. It depends on what you consider a book, how many pages. If you use American standards, there are about two books ready. However, since translation by definition lags behind, poems amass, and you end up with a fatter book.

Are the poems in these untranslated books similar to those in A Part of Speech?

The shorter poems are quite similar. The longer ones—I don't know if I can say how different they are. Perhaps they are worse in some sense. Sometimes they are more monotonous. However, the monotony is always, at least to my eye, deliberate. I just hope that a reader may grasp it. But he may not, and then I am in trouble. But then again, so what. Basically, it's always done for your own . . . whatever it is—for yourself and the hypothetical alter ego. At any rate, it is for somebody invisible. Perhaps for an angel, for all I know.

Are the poems more didactic?

They are more angelic, I think. . . . So that He understands.

Do you like living in New York for half a year and in Michigan for the other half?

I do, although I'd rather stay somewhere on the East Coast for the second semester as well—not necessarily in New York, but on the East Coast. Because it's somewhat claustrophobic over there in Michigan. It's too deep inside of the continent, you see—like some comma in *War and Peace,* pages and pages to go either way. I used to live for all my life, or at least for thirty-two years, by the sea. It's something really biological, I think. Not that I have fits of claustrophobia literally, but the meaninglessness of space is really bothersome. But then again the telephone in Ann Arbor doesn't ring as though it were invented yesterday.

I've noticed that a number of your poems, for example, "In the Lake District," have comic undertones.

It's a humorous poem. I don't understand what's going on—not that I've read that much of what people say—but there is a great deal of comic undertone, I think, in what I'm doing. Yet people always ask about the religious significance.

I think of the metaphor of the ruins of the Parthenon as decaying teeth.

The whole point is that it is not a metaphor actually. It's very literal—especially since I came to Ann Arbor, with my Russian dental work, so to speak. It's not dental work, actually, it's something opposite to dental work. I was having some trouble, and friends took me to the doctor. He extracted about five at once, at one round. I don't really remember how I made it home. The moment I hit the bed, the postman rang the bell, and there was a bill. So I almost had the feeling that the doctor was dragging my teeth out with one hand and writing the bill with the other. But the thing is, the building I teach in is right next to a dental school, and there are all kinds of emblemata and even statues. Some modern sculpture that manifests the progress of this discipline. Hence the poem.

Comic undertones, then, play an important role in your poems . . .

Certainly. Basically, there are two or three things. Russian poetry as a whole is somewhat serious, and people very seldom allow themselves cracks. You see, when you write poetry, especially when you are young, you always know, you always anticipate that there is some sardonic mind that will laugh at both your delights and sorrows. So the idea is to beat that sardonic mind. To steal the chance from him. And the only chance to steal that from him is to laugh at yourself. Well, I've done that for a while. Yet irony is an extremely insulating thing. It's not liberating really, especially if irony is directed, if irony has a consumer, a designated consumer, that sardonic reader. The only way to beat the guy, in case he does exist—but you better suspect he does—is by the sublimity of the statement or the importance or gravity of it, so he won't be able to sneer. I proceeded to do those things, or I hope I did. The technique of laughing at yourself or making cracks stayed with me, and from time to time I resort to that.

Another thing about irony is that sometimes you resort to it just in order to avoid a cliché. Say, a rhyme kind of creeps in, and there is no better one in sight. Yet it has a tinge of cliché. So you had better reinforce it a bit. . . . You may use an assonant rhyme, and the essence of assonance in itself is quite ironic. . . . there are lots of tricks. It would be just to say that irony is a product of the language itself, as much as the rest. It's one of those things, so why not have it in the poem? It's a pleasure. But you shouldn't overdo it, and you should always juxtapose it with something. It should never be a goal in itself.

I think of the lines: "To ask/ the sense of ich bin, otherwise, is mad. . . . What, qua *poet, he gains;* qua *man,/ he loses." Those lines to me have a comic twinge, but there's something very profound attached.*

That was a nice poem. That was 1965 in the village of Norenskaya, a long time ago, fourteen years ago, years past, astonishing.

Do you think being in exile aided your interest in observing language with some detachment? And your themes dealing with estrangement?

To be absolutely honest, I think it did. However, I pretend, and with good reason, that it didn't, because basically every country is just a continuation of space. When I came here I told myself not to make a big deal out of this change—to act as though nothing had happened. And I acted that way. And I still, I think, to go on. However, for the first two or three years, I sensed that I was acting rather than living. Well, more acting as though nothing had happened. Presently I think the mask and the face have got glued together. I just don't feel it; I can't really distinguish.

In terms of my interest and the way this change influenced me, I wouldn't know what to say with conviction. Because certain things really happened. I became less nostalgic for certain cultural phenomena, for example, for the idea of the avant-garde in art. Presently I think it's ninety percent bullshit, if not more. If I had stayed in Russia, I would have continued to think that the theater of the absurd is a grand thing. However, I really don't know. I think that what makes one change his attitude or his perceptions is not so much actual experience, an actual taste of this or that thing, but aging itself. You get less excited. You don't exactly grow smart, but you get more earthly, so to speak. In a way it's a damaging thing because what's required by the popular version of poetry, what's required from the poet, is a certain elevated state. And I must say that while in Russia, I was in general a bit more, how to put it . . . ethereal. *I* never was ethereal, but I had somewhat more ethereal concerns. As I wrote a poem, I would more often lapse into that groping for the invisible. However, that would often lead me toward a kind of mystical incoherence, which even then I despised considerably. If anything of this kind takes place today, it's more precise and therefore less frequent. Again, I wouldn't ascribe that to the change of milieu so much. It's due to that noble name for aging—maturity; although very often I feel as uncertain as when I was nineteen, eighteen. Poetry is the best school for uncertainty. As for my attitude toward language, toward my language, so far I don't think anything really bad has happened. On the contrary. At home you use the language in haste. You kind of trust . . . well, you don't trust really, but it's a kind of automatic thing, writing. For instance, there are lots of passages in those poems—although I don't look at them often because I just can't bear it—in which I see the language has been used somewhat slovenly. These days I would be more careful, leaner.

I wonder if being away from one's own language and not hearing so many competing voices gives one a different perspective on one's own voice?

Language is an awfully private thing. By being displaced, you arrive at the ultimate privacy. It's a *tête à tête* between you and your *language.* There are no mediators. It certainly gives you something of a boost to hear your language on the street, some twist of phrase, some turn, and so forth. But then again I think that the poet should develop his own idiom. Since he has his own way of thinking, that is unlike other poets', he also develops his own way of speaking. However, the purpose is to be more concise within your own idiom. That's some sort of a purpose. I think being displaced doesn't obstruct that course of events. For all I know, it just encourages it. When you're writing in your own language in a foreign realm, a peculiar thing starts to happen. Suddenly there are lots of fears—you forget this, forget that. When you grope for the rhyme and you don't find it, you wonder, Jesus Christ, what's happening? Could it be that there is no rhyme, or did I forget something? Those things do happen. And, well, it's enough to make you nervous. As you are going to say something, you unleash all the sluices of your linguistic memory, and you try to imagine the alternative ways of saying something, which you would not really do while at home. All in all the volume of your linguistic operations stays the same. What sustains the language, I think, is not so much speaking as reading. In short, being out of your existential context helps to winnow a cleaner notion of yourself, of what you are both physically and linguistically.

Could you suggest some reading for young poets in addition to Cavafy and Auden?

Young poets? I used to be in that category for quite a while. Hardy, in the first place. Edwin Arlington Robinson, especially "Eros Turannos," "Isaac and Archibald," and "Rembrandt to Rembrandt"—those are quite interesting things apart from his shorter poems like "Richard Cory," and that Tilbury Town thing.

We are talking about Americans presently. Let's think about foreigners. I think reading foreign poetry loosens your imagination or your intuition. I would certainly suggest a Yugoslav, Vasko Popa. Or there are several great Poles: Czeslaw Milosz and Zbigniew Herbert, for instance; Herbert especially because he's so conceptual. It should be fairly easy for an American to grasp him. "Conceptual" is a bit of a put down for Herbert because he is much more interesting than that. Polish poetry is extremely rich, and I would add to a reading list poets like . . . well, there are not that many translations . . . Wislawa Szymborska, Stanislaw Grochowiak, Tadeusz Rozewicz—although what bothers me about him is what is known as the International Style. Auden said, in our era of global uniformity, it's only in poetry that an international style is impossible. However, Rozewicz is that kind of a poet, but all the same, quite profound. There was another Polish poet you should read, who was as great, I think, as Baudelaire. Norwid. Cyprian Kamil Norwid. There is a magnificent Czech poet, he's still alive, I hope, a tremendous man—Vladimir Holan. There's a Penguin collection of his. He's the best possible news on the horizon. Let me finish with the East Europeans. János Pilinszky—his book, translated by Ted Hughes, has been recently published; however, they are not the most successful translations. Also, there is a magnificent Hungarian poet, Miklós Radnóti, whose luck was real sour. He was killed by the Germans in a concentration camp in Yugoslavia. After he was buried, his wife came to the camp. When they dug the body out—it was a kind of common grave—she recognized him by finding in his breast pocket a bunch of elegies, written in classic alexandrine verse. That's something.

As for Germans, there is Ingeborg Bachmann, first and foremost, and then Peter Huchel. He is a magnificent poet. Well, I'm sorry for these "magnificent poets," but he really is. And his friend and contemporary, Günter Eich. Huchel is in the Michael Hamburger collection. Paul Célan is also a very good poet. He committed suicide in Paris in 1971 or 1970. We shouldn't buy this thing from Europeans—I mean both we Americans and we Russians; we shouldn't buy these kinds of self-dramatizations. It's a reversal of self-aggrandizement. They really had a rotten lot, all of them in this century, those who had the misfortune to be born in the twenties and thirties—the war, et cetera. All the same, I think some of them were making too much of their unhappiness or catastrophes. They thrived on it in a way; they built their identity around it, unlike Czeslaw Milosz. For a poet's identity should be built more on strophes than on catastrophes. . . . Still, Célan. Also, a man I had in mind is Georg Trakl.

For the French, I really don't have any kind words except for one man I just happened to come across in my own, well, silly and unsystematic reading. Actually, there are two men, who were minor poets: René de Cadoux and Jules Supervielle. I mention the minor French, because the guys like Reverdy, René Char, and Michaux—I don't like them. They are quite well known, and I don't think there is any point in my making propaganda for them.

I know nothing about poetry in Spanish. Except for Jorge Manrique, Gongora, St. John of the Cross, and Machado. In comparison to Machado, Lorca and others look pale. A very good Dutch poet is Nijhoff. His poem "Awater" is the poem to reckon with, one of the grandest works of poetry in this century. It's a completely different thing. This is the future of poetry, I think, or it at least paves the way for a very interesting future.

The Russians: Tsvetaeva, Mandelstam, Klyuev, Zabolotsky. There is a collection of Zabolotsky's, *Scrolls,* in English. For all the inevitable pitfalls of translation, you see how avant-garde he is—imagery alone saves it.

If we have a civilized poetry—not only civilized in terms of tone, but in terms of sustaining civilization—it's Italian poetry. For one thing, there is Umberto Saba, the man from Trieste, a traditionalist, but with all kinds of devils. Then, Guiseppe Ungaretti, except I'm afraid he took Mallarmé literally—that dictum that there shouldn't be too many words on the page. And there are not many. I think a poem is a poem, and it should have enough words on the page to make it dark. Otherwise it becomes tanka-like or haiku-like, which is a very nice thing, but it's done better by the Japanese themselves, by Basho. Then, there is, of course, Montale. Of lesser known poets, I would mention Cesare Pavese. There is one book by him which is extremely crucial for anyone who concerns himself with poetry—*Il Mestiere di Vivere* (in translation, *The Burning Brand: Diaries 1935–1950*). It's a diary or confession. As for the poems themselves, they have been rather decently translated into English. Also, there is Zanzotto and that peculiar character Sandro Penna, who is virtually nonexistent in English.

The reason I am suggesting Italians is because of their level of mental operation, the subtlety. They are quite cultivated because of their education, a solid kind of European education. But apart from their actual knowledge of Greek and Latin, apart from the Renaissance texture of their actual surroundings—apart from all this, there is that familiarity with an artifice, that familiarity with columns as omnipresent as trees. The result of such a situation is that artifice is regarded as natural, and vice versa. I think we are fairly removed from them, removed enough to appreciate this kind of sensibility. Perhaps their poetry is not as good as it seems to us because of the refinement of its texture. This is what we in America are somewhat lacking. But one always profits from nostalgia. If we are talking about poetries, then, while the texture of Italian poetry is mostly cultural or historical, the fabric of American poetry is rather anthropological. It's not that I'm deriding the latter, praising the former. The whole point is that they provide us with something to grope for. And there are examples of such groping motions in those magnificent Italian poems of Richard Wilbur, Anthony Hecht, and Stanley Kunitz. In fact, one can make an excellent anthology of American poetry on Italy. It's a poetry of a very hungry eye. This is the way civilization works: by induction.

If I were a younger poet, or whatever . . . a trooper . . . I would rather read the ancient stuff. I think no one has a right to touch paper before he's read *Gilgamesh.* No one has the right to write in the English language without reading the *Metamorphoses* by Ovid. The same goes for Homer and for Dante. Before we get to Dante, there are a lot of excellent Romans. I would single out Martial. The Loeb Series is awfully good. There is nothing more crucial. You should watch some translations, though, because sometimes Martial comes out sounding like a New York cabby. And it's really silly. Martial is so multifaceted. He was the worst possible ass-licker in the history of poetry. His praise of tyrants is just mind-blowing. Yet I have never read anything more vicious than his epigrams. For their sheer force you should respect them. Also he is an excellent lyric poet. He was a native of Iberia, of Spain, and returned there from Rome to settle. In one poem he looks back on his life in Rome. He talks about how half of his life has been covered, and there were good days and bad days. If we take white pebbles and black pebbles for good and bad days, he says, there are more black pebbles on the table. If you want to live happily, he says to his friend, don't befriend anybody very closely; thus perhaps there is less happiness, but there is less grief. When this kind of message comes from a millenium ego, it moves you considerably.

In general, one should have his left hand on Homer, the Bible, Dante, and the Loeb Series, before grabbing the pen with the right.

All these authors are a lot more important in my view than our contemporaries, if only because the contemporary literature is the effect of that ancient cause. If you want to learn a pattern of metaphoric thinking, reading Ovid is crucial, to see how this guy animates mythology. Well, in his myth about Narcissus and Echo, Narcissus appears in the water, and Echo appears. She is in love with him, but Narcissus sends her away. And he, well, he just pumps. But when Ovid tells about the grief of Echo . . . It's not that you begin to cry . . . You may cry: it depends on, well, your kind of nerves. This is such a beautiful description of her reactions, her hesitations. It makes Virginia Woolf's stuff sound like a kindergarten. Honestly. This is most puzzling: we think that because today we are present, we therefore are smarter than those who are absent. From reading the ancients, we learn that idea is not accurate. It may be true in terms of technology, but it humbles you a great deal in terms of poetry.

If I were younger, what I would do is write a book of imitations. It's an old dream of mine to do a collection of spinoffs, especially of the Alexandrian school, and especially of one guy whom I like best, Leonidas from Tarentum. He is one of the most imaginative guys. I thought about doing such a book, a kind of small pamphlet. It would have a watercolor of some ruins on the cover, and my name.

The Art of Poetry XXVIII: Joseph Brodsky

Sven Birkerts / 1979

From *The Paris Review,* 24 (Spring 1982), 82–126. Reprinted by permission of Russell & Volkening as agents for the author.

Joseph Brodsky was interviewed in his Greenwich Village apartment in December 1979. He was unshaven and looked harried. He was in the midst of correcting the galley proofs for his book—*A Part of Speech*—and he said that he had already missed every conceivable deadline. The floor of his living room was cluttered with papers. It was offered to do the interview at a more convenient time, but Brodsky would not hear of it.

The walls and free surfaces of his apartment were almost entirely obscured by books, post cards, and photographs. There were a number of pictures of a younger Brodsky, with Auden and Spender, with Octavio Paz, with various friends. Over the fireplace were two framed photographs, one of Akhmatova, another of Brodsky with his son, who remains in Russia.

Brodsky has been in the U.S. since 1972. He had been on trial in 1964 for "parasitism" and served 20 months of a 5-year hard labor sentence in the Arkhangelsk region. In 1972 the authorities "asked" him to leave. His *Selected Poems* was published in 1973, soon after his arrival in Ann Arbor. At the time of the interview he divided his teaching duties between Ann Arbor and New York. Since the time of the interview Mr. Brodsky has been vocal in his opposition to the military crackdown in Poland.

Brodsky made two cups of strong instant coffee. He sat in a chair stationed beside the fireplace and kept the same basic pose for three hours—head tilted, legs crossed, the fingers of his right hand either holding a cigarette or resting on his chest. The fireplace was littered with cigarette butts. Whenever he was tired of smoking he would fling his cigarette in that direction.

His answer to the first question did not please him. Several times he said: "Let's start again." But about five minutes into the interview he seemed to have forgotten that there was a tape recorder, or for that matter, an interviewer. He picked up speed and enthusiasm.

Brodsky's voice, which Nadezhda Mandelstam once described as a "remarkable instrument" is nasal and very resonant. His English is still heavily influenced by the mother tongue—the speech is liberally salted with "ya's."

During a break Brodsky asked what kind of beer the interviewer would like and set out for the corner store. As he was returning through the back courtyard one of his neighbors called out: "How are you, Joseph? You look like you're losing weight." "I don't know," answered Brodsky's voice. "Certainly I'm losing my hair." A moment later he added: "And my mind."

When the interview was finished Brodsky looked relaxed, not at all the same man who had opened the door four hours before. He seemed reluctant to stop talking. But then the papers on the floor began to claim his attention. "I'm awfully glad we did this," he said. He saw the interviewer out the door with his favorite exclamation: "Kisses!"

Interviewer: I wanted to start with a quotation from Nadezhda Mandelstam's book, *Hope Abandoned.* She says of you, "He is . . . a remarkable young man who will come to a bad end, I fear."

Brodsky: In a way I *have* come to a bad end. In terms of Russian literature—in terms of being published in Russia. However, I think she had in mind something of a worse denomination—namely, physical harm. Still, for a writer not to be published in his mother tongue is as bad as a bad end.

Interviewer: Did Akhmatova have any predictions?

Brodsky: Perhaps she did, but they were nicer, I presume, and therefore I don't remember them. Because you only remember bad things—you pay attention to them because they have more to do with you than your work. On the other hand, good things are originated by a kind of divine intervention. And there's no point in worrying about divine intervention because it's either going to happen or it's not. Those things are out of your control. What's under your control is the possibility of the bad.

Interviewer: To what extent are you using divine intervention as a kind of psychic metaphor?

Brodsky: Actually to a large extent. What I mean actually is the intervention of language upon you or into you. That famous line of Auden's about Yeats: "Mad Ireland hurt you into poetry—" What "hurts" you into poetry or literature is language, your sense of language. Not your private philosophy or your politics, nor even the creative urge, or youth.

Interviewer: So, if you're making a cosmology you're putting language at the apex?

Brodsky: Well, it's no small thing—it's pretty grand. When they say "the poet hears the voice of the Muse," it's nonsense if the nature of the Muse is unspecified. But if you take a closer look, the voice of the Muse is the voice of the language. It's a lot more mundane than the way I'm putting it. Basically, it's one's reaction to what one hears, what one reads.

Interviewer: Your use of that language—it seems to me—is to relate a vision of history running down, coming to a dead end.

Brodsky: That might be. Basically, it's hard for me to assess myself, a hardship not only prompted by the immodesty of the enterprise, but because one is not capable of assessing himself, let alone his work. However, if I were to summarize, my main interest is the nature of time. That's what interests me most of all. What time can do to a man. That's one of the closest insights into the nature of time that we're allowed to have.

Interviewer: In your piece on St. Petersburg you speak of water as "collected time."

Brodsky: Ya, it's another form of time . . . it was kind of nice, that piece, except that I never got proofs to read and quite a lot of mistakes crept in, misspellings and all those things. It matters to me. Not because I'm a perfectionist, but because of my love affair with the English language.

Interviewer: How do you think you fare as your own translator? Do you translate or rewrite?

Brodsky: No, I certainly don't rewrite. I may redo certain translations, which causes a lot of bad blood with translators, because I try to restore in translation even those things which I regard as weaknesses. It's a maddening thing in itself to look at an old poem of yours. To translate it is even more maddening. So, before doing that you have to cool off a great deal, and when you start you are looking upon your work as the soul looks from its abode upon the abandoned body. The only thing the soul perceives is the slow smoking of decay.

So, you don't really have any attachment to it. When you're translating, you try to preserve the sheen, the paleness of those leaves. And you accept how some of them look ugly, but then perhaps when you were doing the original that was because of some kind of strategy. Weaknesses have a certain function in a poem . . . some strategy in order to pave the reader's way to the impact of this or that line.

Interviewer: Do you get very sensitive about the way someone renders you into English?

Brodsky: My main argument with translators is that I care for accuracy and they're very often inaccurate—which is perfectly understandable. It's awfully hard to get these people to render the accuracy as you would want them to. So rather than brooding about it, I thought perhaps I would try to do it myself.

Besides, I have the poem in the original, that's enough. I've done it and for better or worse it stays there. My Russian laurels—or lack of them—satisfy me enough. I'm not after a good seat on the American Parnassus. The thing that bothers me about many of those translations is that they are not very good English. It may have to do with the fact that my affair with the English language is fairly fresh, fairly new, and therefore perhaps I'm subject to some extra sensitivity. So what bothers me is not so much that the line of mine is bad—what bothers me is the bad line in English.

Some translators espouse certain poetics of their own. In many cases their understanding of modernism is extremely simple. Their idea, if I reduce it to the basics, is "staying loose." I, for one, would rather sound trite than slack or loose. I would prefer to sound like a cliché . . . an ordered cliché, rather than a clever slackness.

Interviewer: You've been translated by some impeccable craftsmen—

Brodsky: I was quite lucky on several occasions. I was translated by both Richard Wilbur and Anthony Hecht—

Interviewer: Well, I was at a reading recently where Wilbur was describing to the audience—quite tartly, I thought—how you and Derek Walcott were flying in a plane over Iowa, re-correcting his translation of one of your poems—which did not make him happy . . .

Brodsky: True. The poem only profited out of that. I respect him enormously. Having asked him to do certain passages three, four, or more times, I merely felt that I had no human right to bother him with that one more time, I just didn't have the guts. Even that uncorrected version was excellent. It's more or less the same thing when I said no to Wystan Auden when he volunteered to translate some poems. I thought, "Who the hell am I to be translated by Wystan?"

Interviewer: That's an interesting reversal—the poet feeling inadequate to his translator.

Brodsky: Ya, well, that's the point. I had the same sentiment with respect to Dick Wilbur.

Interviewer: When did you begin to write?

Brodsky: I started to write when I was eighteen or nineteen. However, until I was about twenty-three, I didn't take it that seriously. Sometimes people say, "the best things you have written were when you were nineteen." But I don't think I'm a Rimbaud.

Interviewer: What was your poetic horizon then? Did you know of Frost or Lowell?

Brodsky: No. But eventually, I got to all of them, first in translation, then in the original. My first acquaintance with Robert Frost was when I was twenty-two. I got some of his translations, not in a book, again, from some friends of mine—well, this is the way you get things—and I was absolutely astonished at the sensibility, that kind of restraint, that hidden, controlled terror. I couldn't believe what I'd read. I thought I ought to look into the matter closely, ought to check whether the translator was really translating, or whether we had on our hands a kind of genius in Russian. And so I did, and it was all there, as much as I could detect it. And with Frost it all started.

Interviewer: What were you getting in school up until then—Goethe, Schiller?

Brodsky: We got the whole thing. The English poets would be Byron and Longfellow, 19th Century-oriented. Classics, so to speak. You wouldn't hear anything about Emily Dickinson or Gerard Manley Hopkins or anyone else. They give you two or three foreign figures and that's about it.

Interviewer: Did you even know the name "Eliot"?

Brodsky: We all knew the name Eliot. *(laughs)* For any Eastern European, Eliot is a kind of Anglo-Saxon brand name.

Interviewer: Like Levis?

Brodsky: Ya, like Levis. We all knew there was a poet Eliot, but it was very hard to get any stuff of his. The first attempt to translate him was made in 1936, 1937, in an anthology of English poetry; the translation was quite hapless. But since we knew his reputation we read more into the lines than there ever was—at least in Russian. So . . . immediately after the accomplishment the translators got executed or imprisoned, of course, and the book was out of circulation.

However, I managed to make my way through it gradually, picking up English by arming myself with a dictionary. I went through it line by line because basically at the age of twenty, twenty-three, I knew more or less all of the Russian poetry and had to look somewhere else. Not because Russian poetry ceased to satisfy me, but once you've read the texts you know them. . . .

Interviewer: Then you were translating too?

Brodsky: That was the way of making a living. I was translating all kinds of nonsense. I was translating Poles, Czechs, brother Slavs, but then I ventured across the borders; I began to translate Spanish poetry. I was not doing it alone. In Russia there is a huge translating industry, and lots of things weren't yet translated. In introductions or critical essays you would encounter the name of an obscure poet who had not been translated and you would begin to hunt for him.

Then I began to translate English poetry, Donne especially. When I was sent to that internal exile in the north, a friend of mine sent me two or three anthologies of American poetry . . . Oscar Williams, with the pictures, which would fire my imagination. With a foreign culture, a foreign realm, that you think you are never going to see, your love affair is a lot more intense.

So I was doing those things, reading, translating, approximating rather than translating . . . until finally I came here to join the original *(laughs)* . . . came *too* close to the original.

Interviewer: Have you lost any of the admirations you had? Do you still feel the same way about Donne, Frost?

Brodsky: About Donne and Frost I feel the same way. I feel slightly less about Eliot, much less about e. e. cummings. . . .

Interviewer: There was a point, then, when cummings was a very impressive figure?

Brodsky: Ya, because modernism is very high, the avant-garde thing, trickery and all that. And I used to think about it as a most desirable goal to achieve.

I lost a lot of idols, say, Lindsay, Edgar Lee Masters. However, some things got reinforced, like Marvell, Donne . . . I'm naming just a few but it deserves a much more thorough conversation . . . and Edward Arlington Robinson, for instance. Not to speak of Thomas Hardy.

Interviewer: When did you first run into an Auden poem?

Brodsky: In 1965. I was in that village, in that internal exile I had been sent to. I'd written several poems, a couple of which I sent to the man who did the translations of Frost that had impressed me so much—I regard his opinion as the highest judgement, even though there is very little communication—and he told me, "This poem of yours"—he was talking about "Two Hours in the Empty Tank"—"really resembles Auden in its sense of humor." I said, "ya?" *(laughs)* The next thing, I was trying to get hold of Auden. And then I did and I began to read.

Interviewer: What part of Auden's work did you first encounter?

Brodsky: I don't really remember—certainly "In Memory of Yeats." In the village I came across that poem . . . I kind of liked it, especially the third part, ya? That "earth receive an honored guest" kind of ballad-cum-Salvation Army hymn. And short meter. I showed it to a friend of mine and he said, "Is it possible that they write better than ourselves?" I said, "Looks like."

The next thing, I decided to write a poem, largely aped from Auden's structure in "Memory of Yeats." However, I didn't look into Auden any closer at that point. And then I came to Moscow and showed that friend of mine, the translator, these poems. Once more, he said, "This resembles Auden." So I went out and found Auden's poems and began to read him more thoroughly.

What interests me is his symptomatic technique of description. He never gives you the real . . . ulcer . . . he talks about its symptoms, ya? He keeps his eye all the time on civilization, on the human condition. But he doesn't give you the direct description of it, he gives you the oblique way. And then when you read a line like "The mercury was sunk in the mouth of the dying day—" well, things begin to change. *(laughs)*

Interviewer: What about your younger years? How did you first come to think about writing poetry?

Brodsky: At the ages of fifteen, sixteen, seventeen, I didn't write much, not at all, actually. I was drifting from job to job, working. At sixteen I did a lot of traveling. I was working with a geological expedition. And those years were when Russians were extremely interested in finding uranium. So, every geological team was given some sort of Geiger device. I walked a lot. The whole thing was done on foot. So you'd cover about thirty kilometers daily through pretty thick swamps.

Interviewer: Which part of Russia?

Brodsky: Well, all parts, actually. I spent quite a lot of time in Irkutsk, north of the Amur River on the border of China. Once during a flood I even went to China. It's not that I wanted to, but the raft with all our things on it drifted to the right bank of the Amur River. So I found myself in China briefly. And then I was in Central Asia, in deserts, as well as in the mountains—the Tien Shan mountains are pretty tall mountains, the north-west branch of the Hindu Kush. And, also, in the northern part of European Russia, that is, by the White Sea, near Archangelsk. Swamps, dreadful swamps. Not that the swamps themselves were dreadful, but the mosquitoes! So, I've done that. Also, in Central Asia I was doing a little bit of mountain climbing. I was pretty good at that, I must say. Well, I was young . . . so, I had covered a good deal of territory, with those geological teams and mountain climbing groups. When they first arrested me, in 1959, I think, they tried to threaten me by saying, "We're going to send you far away, where no human foot ever trod." Well, I wasn't terribly impressed because I had already been to many of the regions they were talking about. When they indeed sent me to one of those places, it turned out to be an area which I knew somewhat well, climactically anyhow. That was near the polar circle, near the same White Sea. So, to me it was some sort of déjà vu.

Interviewer: Still, there must be a pretty strong thread leading from the top of the mountain to your meeting Akhmatova.

Brodsky: In my third or fourth year doing geology I got into writing poems. I started because I saw a book of poems a colleague of mine had. The subject matter was the romantic appeal of all those spaces. At least that's what it seemed to me. I thought that I could do better, so I started writing my own poetry. Which wasn't really terribly good . . . well, some people kind of liked it, but then again everybody who writes finds himself an audience. Oddly enough, ya? All the literati keep at least one imaginary friend—and once you start to write you're hooked. Still, all the same, at that time I had to make my living. So I kept partaking in those travels. It was not so much that they paid well, but in the field you spent much less; therefore your salary was just waiting for you.

I would get this money and return home and live on it for a while. Usually by Christmas time or New Year's the money would run out and I would start to look for a job. A normal operation, I think. And in one of my last travels, which was again to the far eastern part of the country, I got a volume of a poet of Pushkin's circle, though in ways much better than Pushkin—his name is Baratynsky. Reading him forced me to abandon the whole silly traveling thing and to get more seriously into writing. So this is what I started to do. I returned home prematurely and started to write a really quite good poem, the way I remember it.

Interviewer: I read once in a book about Leningrad poets a description of your lair, the lampshade covered with Camel cigarette packs. . . .

Brodsky: That was the place where I lived with my parents. We had one big, huge room in the communal apartment, partitioned by two arches. I simply stuffed those arches with all kinds of bookshelves, furniture, in order to separate myself from my parents. I had my desk, my couch. To a stranger, to a foreigner especially, it looked really like a cave; you had to walk through a wooden wardrobe with no back, like a kind of a gate. I lived there quite a lot. However, I used every bit of money that I made to try to rent or sublet a place for myself, merely because at that age you would rather live someplace other than with your parents, ya? Girls, and so forth.

Interviewer: How was it that you finally came to meet Akhmatova?

Brodsky: It was in 1961, I think. By that time I'd befriended two or three people who later played a very big role in my life—what later came to be known as "the Petersburg circle." There were about four of us. One of them is still, I think, the best poet Russia has today. His name is Evgeny Rein; the name comes from the Rhine River. He taught me a lot in terms of poetic know-how. Not that he *taught.* I would read his poems and he would read mine and we would sit around and have high-minded exchanges pretending we knew a lot more than we did; *he* knew something more because he was five years senior to me. At that age it matters considerably. He once said the thing which I would normally say to any poet—that if you really want your poem to work, the usage of adjectives should be minimal; but you should stuff it as much as you can with nouns—even the verbs should suffer. If you cast over a poem a certain magic veil that removes adjectives and verbs, when you remove the veil the paper still should be dark with nouns. To a point I have followed that advice, though not exactly religiously. It did me a lot of good, I must say.

Interviewer: You have a poem which starts "Evgeny mine . . ."

Brodsky: Ya, it is addressed to him, within that cycle "Mexican Divertimento." But I've written several poems to him, and to a certain extent he remains . . . what's Pound's description: *"il miglior fabbro."* One summer, Rein said: "Would you like to meet Akhmatova?" I said: "Well, why not?" without thinking much. At that time I didn't care much for Akhmatova. I got a book and read through it, but at that time I was pretty much in my own idiotic world, wrapped up in my own kind of things. So . . . we went there, actually two or three times. I liked her very much. We talked about this and that, and I showed her some of my poems without really caring what she would say.

But I remember one evening returning from her place—it was in the outskirts of Leningrad—in a filled-up train. Suddenly—it was like the seven veils let down—I realized who it was I was dealing with. And after that I saw her quite often.

Then in 1964 I got behind bars and didn't see her; we exchanged some kind of correspondence. I got released because she was extremely active in trying to get me out. To a certain extent she had blamed herself for my arrest, basically because of the harassment; she was being followed, etcetera, etcetera. Everybody thinks that way about themselves; even I in my turn later on was trying to be kind of cautious with people, because my place was being watched.

Interviewer: Does that phenomenon give you a strange sense of self-importance?

Brodsky: It really doesn't. It either scares you or it is a nuisance. You can't derive any sense of self-importance because you understand a) how idiotic it is, and b) how dreadful it is. The dreadfulness dominates your thoughts. Once, I remember Akhmatova conversing with somebody, some naive woman, or perhaps not so naive, who asked, "Anna Andreyevna—how do you notice if you are being followed?" To which she replied: "My dear, it's impossible not to notice such a thing." It's done to intimidate you. You don't have to suffer persecution mania. You really *are* being followed.

Interviewer: How long did it take you to get rid of that feeling once you landed in Austria?

Brodsky: It's still around, you're cautious. In your writing, in your exchanges with people, meeting people who are in Russian affairs, Russian literature, etcetera. Because it's all penetrated, not necessarily by the direct agents of State Security, but by those people who can be used for that.

Interviewer: Were you familiar with Solzhenitzin at that time?

Brodsky: I don't think at that time Solzhenitzin was familiar with himself. No, later on. When *One Day in the Life of Ivan Denisovitch* was put out, I read it instantly. I remember, speaking of Akhmatova, talking about *One Day,* and a friend of mine said "I don't like this book." Akhmatova said: "What kind of comment is that—'I like it' or 'I don't like it'? The point is that the book ought to be read by 200 million of the Russian population." And that's it, ya?

I followed Solzhenitzin's output in the late sixties quite steadily. By 1971, there were about five or six books floating around in manuscript. *Gulag* wasn't yet published. *August 1914* surfaced at that time. Also his prose poems, which I found absolutely no good. But we like him not for his poetry, ya?

Interviewer: Have you ever met him?

Brodsky: No. We had one exchange in the mail. . . . I really think that in him the Soviet rule got its Homer: what he managed to reveal, the way he kind of pulled the world a little bit around, ya?

Interviewer: Insofar as any one person is able to do anything—

Brodsky: That's about it, ya? But then you have the millions of dead behind him. The force of the individual who is alive grows proportionately—it's not him essentially, but them.

Interviewer: When you were sent to the prison camp in 1965 . . .

Brodsky: It was an internal exile, not a camp. It was a village, fourteen people, lost, completely lost in bogs up there in the north. With almost no access. First I went through transitory prisons: Crosses.* Then it was Vologda, then Arkhangelsk, and finally I ended up in that village. It was all under guard.

Interviewer: Were you able to maintain an ongoing picture of yourself as someone who uses language?

Brodsky: That's a funny thing, but I did. Even sitting there between those walls, locked up, then being moved from place to place, I was writing poems. One of them was a very presumptuous poem—precisely about that, being a carrier of the language—extremely presumptuous as I say, but I was in the height of the tragic mood and I could say something like that about myself, to myself even.

Interviewer: Did you have any sense at that time that what had happened at the trial had already put you in the international spotlight?

Brodsky: No, I knew nothing about the international echo of that trial, nothing at all. I realized that I got a great deal of shit on my palate—on my plate—on my palate as well *(laughs)*. I had to do my stretch. . . . What's more, that was the time which coincided in an unfortunate way—but then

*Crosses is a prison in Leningrad.

again it was fortunate for me—with my greatest personal trouble, with a girl, etcetera, etcetera . . . and a kind of triangle overlapped severely with the squares of the solitary confinements, ya? It was a kind of geometry—with vicious circles.

I was more fired up by that personal situation than by what was happening to my body. The displacement from one cell to another, one prison to another, interrogation, all that, I didn't really pay much attention to it.

Interviewer: Were you able to stay in some sort of communication with the literati once you were sent into internal exile?

Brodsky: I was trying. Mailing things in a kind of roundabout fashion, or directly. Sometimes I even called. I was living in a "village." Fourteen little shacks. Certainly it was obvious that some letters were not read by my eyes alone. But, you know that you are up against it; you know who is the master of your house. It's not you. So therefore you're resigned to try to ridicule the system—but that's about as much as can be done. You feel like a serf bitching about the gentry, which has its own entertaining aspects.

Interviewer: But still a situation in which you must have been under extreme duress—

Brodsky: No, I wasn't. In the first place I was young. Secondly, the work was agriculture. My old joke is that agriculture is like public transportation in the U.S. It's a sporadic operation, poorly organized. So therefore you have enough time, ya? Sometimes it was pretty taxing, physically, that is; and also, it was unpleasant. I didn't have the right to leave. I was confined. Perhaps because of some turn in my character, I decided to get the most out of it. I kind of liked it. I associated it with Robert Frost. You think about the environment, the surroundings, what you're doing: you start to play at being almost a gentleman farmer. Other Russian writers, I think, had it much harder than me, much harder.

Interviewer: Did this life give you the rural sense that you have?

Brodsky: I love it. It gives you more than the rural sense . . . because you get up in the morning in the village, or wherever, and you go to get your daily load, you walk through the field and you know that at the same time most of the nation is doing the same. It gives you some exhilarating sense of being with the rest. If you look from the height of a dove, or a hawk, across the nation you would see it. In that sense it was nice. It gives you a certain insight into the basics of life.

Interviewer: Was there anyone with whom you could talk literature?

Brodsky: No—but I didn't need it, really. You don't really need it, frankly. Or at least I'm not one of that kind of literary person. Although I love to talk about those things. But once shorn of that opportunity, it's OK. Your democratic traits get set in motion. You talk to the people and try to appreciate what they're saying, etcetera. It pays psychologically.

Interviewer: Did you have many classics at that point?

Brodsky: Not really. Nothing, in fact. When I needed references I had to write letters to ask people's help. But I operate on a very basic level with the classics. That is, there's nothing very esoteric. You can find all of it in Bullfinch, ya? I'd read Suetonius and somebody else—Tacitus. But I don't remember, frankly.

Interviewer: At some point the classics must have been quite important. I don't mean specifically the classics, as much as the historical reach. . . .

Brodsky: Whenever you get in trouble you're automatically forced to regard yourself—unless you are self-indulgent—as a kind of archetypal character. So, who else could I think of being but Ovid? That would be the most natural thing. . . .

Well, that was a wonderful time, I must say. I'd written quite a lot and I think I had written rather well. I remember one breakthrough I made with poetry. I wrote the line "here on the hills, under the empty sky, on the roads leading on into the woods, life steps aside from itself and peers at itself in a state of bewilderment." This is perhaps not much, but to me it was important . . . it's not exactly a new way of looking, but being able to say that unleashes certain other things. You are then invincible.

Interviewer: You had no intimation that you would ever reach the West?

Brodsky: Oh, no. No Russian has that intimation. You're born to a very confined realm. The rest of the world is just pure geography, an academic discipline, not the reality.

Interviewer: When you left Russia you were going to Israel.

Brodsky: I had to go to Israel! I was given the walking papers to Israel. But I had no intention to go anywhere. I landed in Vienna and Carl Proffer from the University of Michigan, from Ardis, met me there. The first thing I saw when I looked out of the plane was his tall figure on the balustrade. We waved to each other. And the first thing he asked me as I walked up was, "Well, Joseph, where would you like to go?"

I said: "Jesus, I haven't the slightest idea." And I really didn't. I knew I was leaving my country for good, but for where, I had no idea whatsoever. One thing which was quite clear was that I didn't want to go to Israel. I didn't know Hebrew though I knew a little English.

Besides, I didn't have much time to think about that. I never even believed that they'd allow me to go. I never believed they would put me on a plane, and when they did I didn't know whether the plane would go east or west.

Interviewer: Was Carl Proffer trying to get you to come to the U.S.?

Brodsky: When I told him that I had no plans whatsoever, he asked, "Well, how would you like to come to the University of Michigan?" Other proposals came from London and from the Sorbonne, I believe. But I decided, "It's a big change, let's make it really big." At that time they had expelled about 150 spies from England and I thought, "That's not all of them, ya?" (*laughs*) I didn't want to be hounded by what was left of the Soviet Security Service in England. So I came to the States.

Interviewer: Was Auden actually in Vienna at the time?

Brodsky: Auden wasn't in Vienna, but I knew that he was in Austria. He usually spent his summertimes in Kirchstetten. I had a gift for him. All I took out of Russia was my typewriter, which they unscrewed bolt by bolt at the airport—that was their way of saying goodbye—a small Modern Library volume of Donne's poems, and a bottle of vodka, which I thought that if I got to Austria I'd give to Auden. If I didn't get to Austria I'd drink it myself. I also had a second bottle from a friend, a Lithuanian poet, Tomas Venclova—a remarkable poet, I think—who gave me a bottle of Lithuanian booze. He said, "Give this thing to Wystan if you seen him." So, I had two bottles, that typewriter, and Donne, along with a change of clothes, that is, underwear, and that was it.

On the third or fourth day in Vienna I said to Carl, "Wystan Auden may be in Austria—why don't we try to find him?" Since we had nothing to do except to go to the opera and restaurants, we hired an Avis car, a VW, got a map of Austria, and went to look for him. The trouble was there are three Kirchstettens. We went through all of them, I think—miles and miles between them—and finally we discovered the Auden-Strasse, and found him there.

He began to take immense care of me immediately. All of a sudden the telegrams in my name began to arrive in care of Auden, ya? He was trying to kind of set me up. He told me about whom to meet here and there, etcetera. He called Charles Osborne in London and got me invited to the Poetry International, 1972. I stayed two weeks in London, with Wystan at Stephen Spender's place.

In general, because in those eight years I was as well read in English poetry as in Russian, I knew the scene rather well. Except that, for instance, I didn't know that Wystan was gay. It somehow escaped me. Not that I care much about that. However, I was emerging from Russia and Russia being quite a Victorian country, that could have tinged my attitude toward Wystan. But I don't think it did.

I stayed two weeks in London, and then I flew to the States.

Interviewer: Your connections in the world of poetry have proliferated. You're friends with Hecht, Wilbur, Walcott—

Brodsky: I met Derek [Walcott] at Lowell's funeral. Lowell had told me about Derek and showed me some poems which impressed me a great deal. I read them and I thought, "Well, another good poet." Then his editor gave me that collection *Another Life*. That blew my mind completely. I realized that we have a giant on our hands. He is the figure in English poetry comparable to, well, should I say Milton? (*laughs*) Well, more accurately, I'd put him somewhere between Marlowe and Milton, especially because of his tendency to write verse plays, and his vigor. He's astonishing. The critics want to make him a regional poet from the West Indies, and it's a crime. Because he's the grandest thing around.

Interviewer: How about Russian writers?

Brodsky: I don't know really quite whom I react to most. I remember the great impact Mandelstam's poetry had on me when I was nineteen or twenty. He was unpublished. He's still largely unpublished and unheeded—in criticism and even in private conversations, except for the friends, except for my circle, so to speak. General knowledge of him is extremely limited, if any. I remember the impact of his poetry on me. It's still there. As I read it I'm sometimes flabbergasted. Another poet who really changed not only my idea of poetry, but also my perception of the world—which is what it's all about, ya?—is Tsvetaeva. I personally feel closer to Tsvetaeva—to her poetics, to her techniques, which I was never capable of. This is an extremely immodest thing to say, but, I always thought, "Can I do the Mandelstam thing?" I thought on several occasions that I succeeded at a kind of pastiche.

But Tsvetaeva. I don't think I ever managed to approximate her voice. She was the only poet—and if you're a professional that's what's going on in your mind—with whom I decided not to compete.

Interviewer: What was the distinctive element that attracted you but also frustrated you?

Brodsky: Well, it never frustrated me. She's a woman in the first place. But hers is the most tragic voice of all Russian poetry. It's impossible to say she's the greatest because other people create comparisons—Cavafy, Auden—but I personally feel tremendously attracted to her.

It is a very simple thing. Hers is extremely tragic poetry, not only in subject matter—this is not big news, especially in the Russian realm—but in her language, her prosody. Her voice, her poetry, gives you almost the idea or sense that the tragedy is within the language itself. The reason I decided—it was almost a conscious decision not to compete with her—well, for one thing, I knew I would fail. After all, I'm a different person, a man what's more, and it's almost unseemly for a man to speak at the highest pitch of his voice, by which I don't mean she was just a kind of romantic, raving . . . she was a very dark poet.

Interviewer: She can hold more without breaking?

Brodsky: Ya. Akhmatova used to say about her: "Marina starts her poem on the upper *do,* that edge of the octave." Well, it's awfully hard to sustain a poem on the highest possible pitch. She's capable of that. A human being has a very limited capacity for discomfort or tragedy. Limited, technically speaking, like a cow that can't produce more than two gallons of milk. You can't squeeze more tragedy out of a man. So, in that respect, her reading of the human drama, her inconsolable voice, her poetic technique, are absolutely astonishing. I think nobody wrote better, in Russian, anyway. The tone with which she was speaking, that kind of tragic vibrato, that tremolo.

Interviewer: Did you have to come to her gradually or did you discover her overnight?

Brodsky: No, it was from the very threshold. I was given her poems by a friend of mine. That was it.

Interviewer: In your own poems the speaking voice is so terribly solitary, without benefit of a single human interaction.

Brodsky: Ya, that's what it is. Akhmatova said this about the first batch of poems I brought her in 1962. That's exactly what she said, verbatim. I presume that's the characteristic of it.

Interviewer: As poems emerge are you conscious of the extent to which—for someone looking at them from the outside—they have a discernible line of development and movement?

Brodsky: No—the only thing I'm conscious of is that I'm trying to make them different from the previous stuff I've written. Because one reacts not only to what he's read, but what he wrote as well, ya? So every preceding thing is the point of departure. There should be a small surprise that there is some kind of detectable linear development.

Interviewer: You seem to write about places that don't appear to be the places where you've spent most of your time. Has there been anything on New York or Venice?

Brodsky: I don't think I've written anything about New York. You can't do much about New York. Whereas Venice—I've done quite a lot. But places like New England or Mexico or England, old England—basically when you find yourself in a strange place, and the stranger the place it is, to a certain extent, the better—it somehow sharpens your notion of your individuality, say a place like Brighton (*laughs*) or York in England. You see yourself better against a strange background. It's to be living outside your own context, like being in exile. One of the advantages is that you shed lots of illusions. Not illusions about the world, but illusions about yourself. You kind of winnow yourself. I never had as clear a notion of what I am than I acquired when I came to the States—the solitary situation. I like the idea of isolation. I like the reality of it. You realize what you are . . . not that the knowledge is inevitably rewarding. Nietzsche put it in so many words, "A man who's left by himself is left with his own pig."

Interviewer: I'll pay you the compliment of saying my immediate sensation of any place you're described in a poem is to never want to go there.

Brodsky: Terrific! (*laughs*) If you put it in writing I'll never be hired for an advertising job.

Interviewer: Is it deliberate that you've waited so long between books?

Brodsky: Not really. I'm not very professional as a writer. I'm not really interested in book after book. There's something ignoble about it, ya?

Interviewer: Does your family in the U.S.S.R. have any sense of what you're doing?

Brodsky: They have the basic idea, that I'm teaching and that I'm, if not financially, somehow psychologically, well off. They appreciate that I'm a poet. They didn't like it at the very beginning. For a good fifteen years they hated every bit of it, ya? (*laughs*)—but then why shouldn't they have? I don't think I'm so excited about it myself. Akhmatova told me that when her father learned that she was about to publish a book, he said, well, "Do please one thing. Please take care to not malign my name. If you're going to be in this business, please assume a pen name."

Personally, I'd much prefer to fly small planes, to be a bush pilot somewhere in Africa, than do this.

Interviewer: How do you feel about writing prose?

Brodsky: I love it, in English. To me it's a challenge.

Interviewer: Is it sweat?

Brodsky: I don't regard it as sweat. It's certainly labor. Yet it's almost a labor of love. If asked to write prose in Russian I wouldn't be so keen. But in English it's a tremendous satisfaction. As I write I think about Auden, what he would say—would he find it rubbish, or kind of entertaining?

Interviewer: Is he your invisible reader?

Brodsky: Auden and Orwell.

Interviewer: Have you ever tried writing fiction in any form?

Brodsky: No. Well, when I was young, I tried to write a novel. I wrote what I considered one of the breakthroughs in modern Russian writing . . . I'm awfully glad I never saw it again.

Interviewer: Does anything shock or surprise you? How do you face the world when you get up—with what idea in mind? "Here we go again," or what?

Brodsky: It certainly doesn't surprise me. I think the world is capable of only one thing basically—proliferating its evils. That's what time seems to be for.

Interviewer: You don't have a corresponding idea that at some point people will advance a quantum leap in consciousness?

Brodsky: A quantum leap in consciousness is something I rule out.

Interviewer: Just deterioration—is that the picture?

Brodsky: Well, dilapidation rather than deterioration. Well, not exactly dilapidation. If we look at things in a linear fashion, it certainly doesn't look any good, ya? The only thing that surprises me is the frequency, under the present circumstances, of instances of human decency, of sophistication, if you will. Because basically the situation—on the whole—is extremely uncongenial for being decent or right.

Interviewer: Are you, finally, a thoroughly Godless man? It seems contradictory. In some of your poetry I sense an opening.

Brodsky: I don't believe in the infinite ability of the reason, or the rational. I believe in it only insofar as it takes me to the irrational—and this is what I need it for, to take me as far as I can get toward the irrational. There it abandons you. For a little while it creates a state of panic. But this is where the revelations are dwelling—not that you may fish them out. But at least I have been given two or three revelations, or at least they have landed on the edge of reason and left their mark.

This all has very little to do with any ordered religious enterprise. On the whole, I'd rather not resort to any formal religious rite or service. If I have any notion of a supreme being I invest it with absolutely arbitrary will. I'm a little bit opposed to that kind of grocery store psychology which underlies Christianity. You do this and you'll get that, ya? Or even better still: that God has infinite mercy. Well, it's basically anthropomorphism. I would go for the Old Testament God who punishes you—

Interviewer: Irrationally—

Brodsky: No, arbitrarily. Even more I would go for the Zoroastrian version of deity, which is perhaps the cruellest possible. I kind of like it better when we are dealing with arbitrariness. In that respect I think I'm more of a Jew than any Jew in Israel. Merely because I believe, if I believe in anything, in the arbitrary God.

Interviewer: I suspect you've probably meditated a great deal about Eliot and Auden, the way they made these . . .

Brodsky: Flings . . .

Interviewer: Well, flings or final decisions.

Brodsky: Yes, I certainly did. I must say I stand by Auden's more readily than Eliot's. Although it would take somebody much smarter than I am to explain the distinction between the two.

Interviewer: From all the pictures you get, though, Eliot in his last days was a wonderfully happy man, whereas Auden . . .

Brodsky: Certainly he wasn't. I don't know. It denotes a lot of things. Basically, to arrange your life in such a way that you arrive at a happy conclusion is—well, perhaps I'm too romantic, or too young to respect this kind of thing; or take it seriously. Again, I wasn't fortunate enough to have had the structure laid out for me in childhood, as was the case with the both of them.

So I've been doing the whole thing essentially on my own. For instance, I read the Bible for the first time when I was twenty-three. It leaves me somewhat shepherdless, you see. I wouldn't really know what to return to. I don't have any notion of paradise. I don't have one that I derived from childhood which, first of all, is the happiest time, and is also the first time you hear about paradise. I went through the severe, antireligious schooling in Russia which doesn't leave any kind of notion about afterlife. So, what I'm trying to say, what interests me is the degree—the graspable degree of arbitrariness.

Interviewer: What are your highest moments then—when you are working in the depths of language?

Brodsky: This is what we begin with. Because if there is any deity to me, it's language.

Interviewer: Are there moments when you are writing when you are almost an onlooker?

Brodsky: It's awfully hard for me to answer. During the process of writing—I think these are the better hours—of deepening, of furthering the thing. You're kind of entitled to things you didn't know were out there. That's what language brings you to, perhaps.

Interviewer: What's that Karl Kraus line: "Language is the divining rod that discovers well of thought"?

Brodsky: It's an incredible accelerator of the cognitive process. This is why I cherish it. It's kind of funny, because I feel in talking about language I sound like a bloody French structuralist. Since you mention Karl Kraus at least it gives it kind of a continental thing to reckon with. Well, they have culture, we have guts, we Russians and Americans.

Interviewer: Tell me about your love affair with Venice.

Brodsky: In many ways it resembles my home town, St. Petersburg. But the main thing is that the place is so beautiful that you can live there without being in love. It's so beautiful that you know that nothing in your life you can come up with or produce—especially in terms of pure existence—would have a corresponding beauty. It's so superior. If I had to live a different incarnation, I'd rather live in Venice as a cat, or anything, but in Venice. Or even as a rat. By 1970 I had an *idée fixe* to get to Venice. I even had an idea of moving there and renting a ground floor in some palazzo on the water, and sit there and write, and drop my cigarette butts so they would hiss in the water. And when the money would be through, finished, I would go the store and buy a Saturday special with what was left and blow my mind (*puts his finger to temple and gestures*).

So, the first thing I did when I became free to travel, that is, in 1972, after teaching a semester in Ann Arbor, I got a round-trip ticket for Venice and went there for Christmas. It is interesting to watch the tourists who arrive there. The beauty is such that they get somewhat dumbfounded. What they do initially is to hit the stores to dress themselves—Venice has the best boutiques in Europe—but when they emerge with all those things on, still there is an unbearable incongruity between the people, the crowd, and what's around. Because no matter how well they're dressed and how well they're endowed by nature, they lack the dignity, which is partially the dignity of decay, of that artifice around them. It makes you realize that what people can make with their hands is a lot better than they are themselves.

Interviewer: Do you have a sense when you're there of history winding down. Is that part of the ambiance?

Brodsky: Yes, more or less. What I like about it apart from the beauty is the decay. It's the beauty in decay. It's not going to be repeated, ever. As Dante said: "One of the primary traits of any work of art is that it is impossible to repeat."

Interviewer: What do you think of Anthony Hecht's *Venetian Vespers?*

Brodsky: It's an awfully good book. It's not so much about Venice—it's about the American sensibility. I think Hecht is a superb poet. I think there are three of them in America, Wilbur, Hecht, and—I don't really know how to allocate the third palm.

Interviewer: I'm interested to know why you put Wilbur up as high as you do.

Brodsky: I like perfection. It's true that you don't hear the throbbings of the spheres, or whatever. However, the magnificence with which he uses the material compensates. Because—there is poetry and poetry. There are poets and poets. And Dick performs his function better than anyone else.

I think that if I were born here I would end up with qualities similar to Hecht's. One thing I would like to be is as perfect as Hecht and Wilbur are. There should be something else, I presume, of my own, but insofar as the craftsmanship is concerned one couldn't wish for more.

Interviewer: Is the communication between kindred spirits pretty close? Do you watch each other carefully? Walcott, Milosz, Herbert, yourself—poets sharing a certain terrain?

Brodsky: Not exactly that I watch Derek, but, for instance, I got two poems of his quite recently scheduled to appear in *The New Yorker*—an editor sent me the xeroxes—and I thought "Well, Joseph—" I thought, "This is something to reckon with the next time you write a poem." *(laughs)*

Interviewer: Who else is there to reckon with?

Brodsky: Oh, there are lots of shadows and lots of real people. Eugenio Montale would be one of the living ones. There is a German, a very good German, Peter Huchel. Nobody in France, to my knowledge. I don't really take that poetry seriously. Akhmatova has remarked, very wisely, that in the twentieth century, French painting swallowed French poetry. As for England, I'm certainly a great fan of Philip Larkin. I like him very much. The only complaint is the usual one—that Larkin writes so little. Also, Douglas Dunn—and there is a magnificent man in Australia, Les Murray.

Interviewer: What do you read?

Brodsky: Some books on disciplines with which I wasn't well acquainted, like Orientalism. Encyclopedias. I almost don't have time for such things. Please don't detect snobbery in this; it's merely a very grand fatigue.

Interviewer: And what do you teach? Does that affect your reading?

Brodsky: Only insofar as I have to read the poem before the class does *(laughs)*. I'm teaching Hardy and Auden and Cavafy—those three: it rather reflects my tastes and attachments. And Mandelstam, a bit of Pasternak.

Interviewer: Are you aware that you are on a required reading list at Boston University for a course entitled "Modern Jewish Writing"?

Brodsky: Well, congratulations to Boston University! Very good. I don't really know. I'm a very bad Jew. I used to be reproached by Jewish circles for not supporting the cause, the Jewish cause, and for having a great deal of the New Testament themes in my writing. Which I find absolutely silly. It's nothing to do with the cultural heritage. It's merely on my part the effect paying homage to its cause. It's as simple as that.

Interviewer: You are also listed in a book called *Famous Jews*—

Brodsky: Boy! Oh, boy! Well, *Famous Jews*—so I'm a famous Jew—that's how I'm going to regard myself from now on—

Interviewer: What about some of the people you most admire? We've touched on some of the ones who have died. How about the living, people whose existence is important to you, if only to know they are there.

Brodsky: Dick Wilbur, Tony Hecht, Galway Kinnell, Mark Strand. Those are just a few whom I know personally, and I'm extremely lucky in that sense. Montale, as I mentioned, would certainly be one; Walcott is another. And there are other people I like very much personally, and as writers. Susan Sontag, for instance. She is the best mind there is. That is on both sides of the Atlantic. Because, for her, the argument starts precisely where it ends for everyone else. I can't think of anything in modern literature that can parallel the mental music of her essays. Somehow, I can't separate people and writing. It just hasn't happened as yet that I like the writing and not the person. I would say that even if I know a person is dreadful I would be the first to find justifications for that dreadfulness if the writing is good. After all, it is hard to master both life and work equally well. So if you are bound to fake one of them, it had better be life.

Interviewer: Tell me what it was like to meet Lowell for the first time.

Brodsky: I'd met Lowell in 1972 at the Poetry International. He simply volunteered to read my poems in English as I read them in Russian, an extremely kind and moving gesture. So we both went on stage.

He invited me to come to Kent. I was somewhat perplexed—my English wasn't good enough. Also, I was somewhat worried about the railroad system in England—I couldn't make heads nor tails out of it. And the third, perhaps the primary reason why I didn't go, was that I thought it would be an imposition. Because, well, who the hell am I? And so, I just didn't do it.

Then in 1975 I was in the Five Colleges in Massachusetts, living in Northampton, and he called and invited me to come to Brookline. By that time my English was somewhat better and I went. The time we spent was in many ways the best time I can recall having while here in the States. We talked about this and that, and finally we settled on Dante. It was the first conversation about Dante since Russia which really made sense to me. He knew Dante inside out, I think, in an absolutely obsessive way. He was especially good on *Inferno.* I think he had lived for a while in Florence, or stayed there, so he felt more about *Inferno* than the other parts; at least the conversation revolved around those things.

We spent about five or six hours, more, and then we went for dinner. He said some very pleasant things to me. The only thing casting a shadow was that I knew that during Auden's last years they had had a row, kind of a lasting row. Wystan didn't like Lowell's extramoral situation, whereas Lowell was thinking that it was none of his business and was quite caustic about him as a poet.

Interviewer: That doesn't sound like something Auden would worry about very much—

Brodsky: In the sense that Wystan was a proper son of England, he would mind someone else's morality. I remember a remark he made. I asked him, "What do you think of Lowell?" It was on the first day I saw Wystan. I sat down and started to grill him in my absolutely mindless way. He said something like "I don't like men who leave a smoking tail of weeping women behind them." Or maybe it was the other way around: "A weeping tail of smoking women"—

Interviewer: Either way—

Brodsky: Ya, either way. He didn't criticise Lowell as a poet. It was simply kind of a commonplace morality at which I think he, Auden, enjoyed playing.

Interviewer: But it was Auden, after all, who would have God pardoning various people for writing well—

Brodsky: Ya, but he said that in 1939. I think, in a sense, that the reason behind all of this was that he insisted on faithfulness—in his own affairs as well as in a broader sense. Besides, he tended to become less flexible. When you live long you see that little things end up in big damages. Therefore, you get more personalized in your attitudes. Again, I also think it was kind of a game with him. He wanted to play schoolmaster and for that, in this world, he was fully qualified.

Interviewer: If you could get either or both of them back, what kinds of things do you think you'd talk about now?

Brodsky: Lots of things. In the first place—well, it's an odd question—perhaps about the arbitrariness of God. Well, that conversation wouldn't go far with Auden, merely because I don't think he'd like to talk about that heavy Thomas Mannish stuff. And yet, he became a kind of formal churchgoer, so to speak. I'm somewhat worried about that—because the poetic notion of infinity is far greater than that which is sponsored by any creed—and I wonder about the way he would reconcile that. I'd like to ask him whether he believes in the church, or simply the creed's notion of infinity, or paradise, or church doctrine—which are normally points of one's spiritual arrival. For the poet they are springboards, or points of departure for metaphysical journeys. Well, things like that. But mostly I would like to find out certain things about the poems, what he meant here and there. Whether, for instance, in "In Praise of Limestone" he really lists the temptations, or kind of translates the temptations as they are found in the Holy Book, or if they simply came out like a poem, ya? *(long pause)* I wish he were here. More than anyone else. Well, that's kind of a cruel thing to say, but—I wish three or four people were alive to talk to. Him, Akhmatova, Tsvetaeva, Mandelstam—which already makes four. Thomas Hardy.

Interviewer: Is there anyone you'd want to pull out from the ages?
Brodsky: Oh, that would be a big crowd. This room wouldn't hold them.

Interviewer: How did Lowell feel with respect to religion, finally?
Brodsky: We never talked about it, except ironically, mentioning it en passant. He was absolutely astonishing talking about politics, or writers' weaknesses. Or human weaknesses. He was extremely generous, but what I liked in him was the viciousness of tongue. Both Lowell and Auden were monologists. In a sense, you shouldn't talk to people like them, you should listen to them—which is kind of an ultimate existential equivalent for reading poetry. It's a kind of spinoff. And I was all ears, partly because of my English.

He was a lovely man, really lovely—Lowell, that is. The age difference wasn't that big between us—well, some twenty years, so I felt in a sense somewhat more comfortable with him than with Auden. But then again, I felt most comfortable with Akhmatova.

Interviewer: Did either one of them interrogate you in the way you wanted to be interrogated about yourself and your writing?
Brodsky: Lowell did. Akhmatova asked me several questions. . . . But while they were alive, you see, I felt as a young boy. They were the elders, so to speak, the masters. Now that they are gone I think of myself as terribly old all of a sudden. And . . . this is what civilization means, carrying on. Well, I don't think Auden would like rock music, nor do I. Nor Lowell, I think.

Interviewer: Do you have any close friends who are artists, painters, musicians, composers?
Brodsky: Here I don't. In Russia I had. Here the only person close to that is Baryshnikov. Composers, none at all. No, it's empty. The category of people I used to like most of all were graphic artists and musicians.

Interviewer: But you draw a lot of sustenance from those realms.
Brodsky: From music, yes. I don't really know how it is reflected in what I'm doing, but I certainly do.

Interviewer: What do you listen to? I notice that Billie Holliday is on the turntable now—

Brodsky: Billie Holliday's "Sophisticated Lady" is a magnificent piece. I like Haydn. Music is actually the best teacher of composition, I think, even for literature. If only because—well, the principle, for instance, of the concerto grosso: three parts, one quick, two slow, or vice versa. You know that you have to pour whatever you have into this twenty minute thing. Also, what can follow in music: the alternation of lyricism with mindless pizzicato, etcetera . . . they're like the shifts, counterpoints, the fluid character of an argument, a fluid montage. When I first began to listen to classical music, the thing that haunted me was the way it moves, the unpredictability. So in that sense Haydn is terrific stuff because he's so absolutely unpredictable. (*long pause*) It's so silly . . . I think how meaningless everything is, except for two or three things—writing itself, listening to music, perhaps a little bit of thinking. But the rest—

Interviewer: How about friendship?

Brodsky: Friendship is a nice thing. I'd include food then (*laughs*). . . . But other things that you're forced to do—paying taxes, counting the numbers, writing references, doing your chores—don't all those things strike you as utterly meaningless? It's like when we sat in that café. The girl was doing something with the pies, or whatever—they were in that refrigerator with the glass. And she stuck her head in and she was doing all those things, the rest of her out of the refrigerator. She was in that position for about two minutes. And once you see it there's no point in existing any more. (*laughs*) Simple point, ya?

Interviewer: Except that the minute you translate that into an image or a thought you've already taken it out of uselessness.

Brodsky: But once you've seen it the whole of existence is compromised.

Interviewer: It's coming back to time again—here because you're seeing the container with nothing in it.

Brodsky: More or less, ya. Actually I read in the front of Penn Warren's recent book (*gets up and rummages at his desk*): "Time is the dimension in which God strives to define his own being." Well, "strives" is a little bit kindergartenish. But there is another quote, this one from the encyclopedia: "There is, in short, no absolute time standard."

Interviewer: The last time I talked with you two things hadn't happened. How much of your time is filled with being preoccupied with Afghanistan and the hostage situation?

Brodsky: When I'm not writing or reading, I'm thinking about both. Of the two I think the Afghan situation is the most—tragic. When I saw the first footage from Afghanistan on the TV screen a year ago, it was very short. It was tanks rolling on the plateau. For thirty-two hours non-stop I was climbing the walls. Well, it's not that I'm ashamed of being Russian. I have felt that already twice in my life: in 1956 because of Hungary and in 1968 because of Czechoslovakia. In those days my attitude was aggravated by immediate fear, for my friends if not for myself—merely because I knew that whenever the international situation worsens, it's automatically followed by the internal crackdown.

But this is not what really blew my mind in Afghanistan. What I saw was basically a violation of the elements—because that plateau never saw a plough before, let alone a tank. So, it was a kind of existential nightmare. And it still sits on my retina. Since then I have been thinking about soldiers who are, well, about twenty years younger than me, so that some of them could be, technically speaking, my children. I even wrote a poem that said "glory to those that in the Sixties went marching into the abortion clinics, thereby saving the Motherland the disgrace."

What drives me absolutely wild is not the pollution—it's something much more dreadful. It's something I think when they're breaking ground to the foundation of a building. It's usurpation of land, violation of the elements. It's not that I am of a pastoral bent. No, I think, on the contrary, the nuclear power stations should be there—it's cheaper than oil, in the end.

But a tank rolling onto the plateau demeans space. This is absolutely meaningless, like substracting from zero. And it is vile in a primordial sense, partly because of tanks' resemblance to dinosaurs. It simply shouldn't be.

Interviewer: Are your feelings about these things very separate from what you write?

Brodsky: I don't believe in writing it—I believe in action. I think it's time to create some sort of International Brigade. It was done in 1936, why not now? Except that in 1936 the International Brigade was financed by the GPU—that is, Soviet State Security. I just wonder if there's anybody with the money . . . somebody in Texas who could financially back the thing.

Interviewer: What would you imagine the International Brigade doing?

Brodsky: Well, the International Brigade can do essentially what it did in

1936 in Spain, that is, fight back, help the locals. Or at least give some sort of medical assistance—food, shelter. If there is a noble cause, it is this—not some Amnesty International . . . I wouldn't mind driving a Red Cross jeep. . . .

Interviewer: It's hard to identify clear moral sides sometimes—

Brodsky: I don't really know what kind of moral sides you are looking for, especially in a place like Afghanistan. It's quite obvious. They've been invaded; they've been subjugated. They may be just backward tribesmen but slavery isn't my idea of revolution either.

Interviewer: I'm talking more in terms of countries.

Brodsky: Russia versus the U.S.? I don't think there is any question. If there were no other distinction between those two, it would be enough for me to have the system of a jury of twelve versus the system of one judge as a basis for preferring the U.S. to the Soviet Union. Or, to make it less complicated—because even that perplexes most people—I would prefer the country you can leave to the country you cannot.

Interviewer: You've said that you are fairly satisfied with your Lowell poem which you wrote in English. Is there any reason why you didn't just continue writing in English?

Brodsky: There are several reasons. In the first place, I have enough to do in Russian. And in English you have lots of terrific people alive. There is no point in my doing that. I wrote an elegy in English simply because I wanted to please the shadow. And when I finished *Lowell,* I had another poem coming in English. There were wonderful rhymes coming my way, and yet I told myself to stop. Because I don't want to create for myself an extra reality. Also, I would have to compete with the people for whom English is the mother tongue, ya? And, lastly, which is the most important, I don't have that aspiration. I'm pleased enough with what I'm doing in Russian, which sometimes goes and sometimes doesn't. When it doesn't, I can't think of trying it in English. I don't want to be penalized twice (*laughs*). And, as for English, I write my essays, which gives me enough sense of confidence. The thing is—I don't really know how to put it—technically speaking, English is the only interesting thing that's left in my life. It's not an exaggeration and not a brooding statement. That's what it is, ya?

Interviewer: Did you read Updike's piece on Kundera in the *New York Times Book Review?* He finished by referring to you, citing you as one who has dealt with exile by becoming an American poet—

Brodsky: That's flattering, but that's rubbish.

Interviewer: I imagine that he was referring not only to the fact that you have written a few things in English, but also to the fact that you were beginning to deal with American landscapes, Cape Cod—

Brodsky: Could be—in that case, what can I say? Certainly one becomes the land one lives in, especially at the end. In that sense I'm quite American.

Interviewer: How do you feel about writing something full of American associations in the Russian language?

Brodsky: In many cases you don't have the Russian word for that, or you have a Russian word which is kind of cumbersome; then you look for ways around the problem.

Interviewer: Well, you're writing about squad cars and Ray Charles's jazz—

Brodsky: Ya, that you can do—because Ray Charles is a name, and "squad car" has an expression in Russian, and so does the hoop on the basketball pole. But the most difficult thing I had to deal with in that poem had to do with Coca-Cola, to convey the sensation that it reminded me of *Mene Mene Tekel Upharsin,* that line Belshazzar sees on the wall that foretold the end of his kingdom. That's where the expression "writing on the wall" comes from. You can't say "Coca-Cola sign" because there's no idiom for that. So, I had to describe it in a rather round-about way—because of which the image rather profited. I said not "a sign," but something to the effect of the cuneiform or the hieroglypics of Coca-Cola, ya? So that it reinforced the image of "the writing on the wall."

Interviewer: What do you think happens psychically when you've brought the poem to a sort of dead point, to get beyond which you would have to go in a direction that you can't yet imagine?

Brodsky: The thing is that you can always go on, even when you have the most terrific ending. For the poet the credo or doctrine is not the point of arrival but is, on the contrary, the point of departure for the metaphysical journey. For instance, you write a poem about the crucifixion. You have decided to go ten stanzas—and yet it's the third stanza and you've already dealt with the crucifixion. You have to go beyond that and add something—to develop it into something which is not there yet. Basically what I'm saying is that the poetic notion of infinity is far greater, and it's almost self-propelled by the form. Once in a conversation with Tony Hecht at Breadloaf we were talking about the usage of the Bible, and he said, "Joseph, wouldn't you agree that what a poet does is to try to make more sense out of these things?" And that's what it is—there's more sense, ya? In the works of the better poets you get the sensation that they're not talking to people any more, or to some seraphical creature. What they're doing is simply talking back to the language itself—as beauty, sensuality, wisdom, irony—those aspects of language of which the poet is a clear mirror. Poetry is not an art or a branch of art, it's something more. If what distinguishes us from other species is speech, then poetry, which is the supreme linguistic operation, is our anthropological, indeed generic, goal. Anyone who regards poetry as an entertainment, as a "read," commits an anthropological crime, in the first place, against himself.

Exiled

CBS, *60 Minutes* / 1981

From CBS, *60 Minutes,* Sept. 13, 1981. Reprinted by permission of CBS.

Morley Safer: In our culture, the poets do not get the acclaim they get elsewhere. Here, they work in obscurity, their voices heard, their verses read by a small, scattered, dedicated few. In Russia, on the other hand, some poets are treated like princes—the poets they approve of. The others are treated somewhat more harshly—ignored, imprisoned, exiled. Joseph Brodsky, for example, is recognized to be among the greatest of living Russian poets. Seven years ago, after imprisoning him in labor camps* and mental institutions, the Soviets inflicted even crueler punishment: they exiled him. In effect, dispossessing him of his environment, language and culture, the tools of his trade. Brodsky is a non-practicing Jew who never wrote on Jewish or Zionist themes. He was never part of any dissident political movement. And still, he was exiled, perhaps simply for excellence. He said at the time that exile could be a test of his ability to endure.

At 40, he continues to write in his native Russian. He travels the American campuses giving readings, a relentless chant that has echoes of a Russia that has endured one kind of oppression or another for centuries.

Brodsky was never even officially published in the Soviet Union. His work was secretly mimeographed and circulated hand to hand. But when too many people began to read him, when the voice became too independent, he became an enemy of the people.

Brodsky: *Poetry is the supreme level of the language, you see, and people, somehow, are interested in that. Well, it's kind of a diversion from the usual obedient way of thinking. Inevitably, the man who says something different, he's a threat to the totalitarian state.*

Safer: A Russian and English typewriter are Brodsky's constant companions in his slightly schizophrenic world. Although the rhythm of the original Russian language may be lost in translation, the theme is understood—the Soviet poet as Soviet victim. In 1977 he wrote, "And when they would finally

*See note, p. 3.—*ED*

arrest me for espionage, / for subversive activity, vagrancy, for *ménage / à trois,* and the crowd, boiling around me, would bellow, / poking me with their work-roughened forefingers, 'Outsider! / We'll settle your hash!'—/then I would secretly smile, and say to myself, 'See, / this is your chance to find out . . . how it looks from the inside—you've stared long enough / at the outside—/so take note of every detail as you shout, "Long live our country!"'"*

Safer: His student audiences are intrigued by this fish out of his home waters. Naive, yet profound, questions: Must a Soviet writer avoid certain subjects?

Brodsky: Yeah. (Laughter) Actually, there are quite a lot of either forbidden themes or forbidden moods. You've got to stay away from explicitly religious themes, subjects. You'd better stay away from death; you don't talk about death. For instance, you're not supposed to use in your verses certain words like, say, "prison." As simple as that.

Safer: It's a familiar thing in the Soviet Union to take people they don't particularly like and, if not send them to a labor camp, send them for psychiatric examination.

Brodsky: Yeah.

Safer: What do they do? How do they treat you?

Brodsky: They give you all kinds of shots, all kinds of a medicine. They are extremely—sometimes extremely—painful. The sulfur, for instance, injections, when you can't move a finger without screaming out of pain. Or they just wrap you in the middle of the night into the sheet and plunge you into the cold bath. And then they would get you out and let that sheet on you dry up on you, and, well, the folds get into your skin, and it's extremely hurting. I remember I never could get angry with any of my interrogators, because he has a family to feed, and that he is a poor beggar—bugger—because, well, he has been that way, and it's a punishment in itself if he is that way.

Safer: Since his exile, he has been a teacher and poet-in-residence at the University of Michigan in Ann Arbor. One poem describes his life here with a blend of bitterness and wit.

> a spy, a spearhead
> for some fifth column of a rotting culture
> (my cover was a lit. professorship),
> was living at a college near the most

*"Vive la Patrie!" in the original and translated versions of the poem.—*ED*

> renowned of the fresh-water lakes; the function
> to which I'd been appointed was to wear out
> the patience of the ingenious local youth.

Brodsky: Very good, yeah . . .

Safer: Brodsky made the jump from exile to Ann Arbor through the efforts of Carl and Ellendea Proffer, who run a publishing house for Russian writers near the University of Michigan. They met him in Russia, where he haunted foreign libraries and exhibits.

Carl Proffer: Is it true you were a book thief at the American exhibit? (Laughter)

Brodsky: At the French exhibit.

Proffer: French exhibit.

Brodsky: The French exhibit, because of, I think, lots of friends of mine, lots of graduate students, academics, were committing theft from the library of the American Embassy. They would even steal the book without being able to read it. Well, in fact, I was stealing those books, and somehow, later on, at the later stage, I was looking into one and just perused through one, and something—well, I would recognize a dozen of words, and it would give me a boost.

Ellendea Proffer: Let me tell you, any decent, open society does not value a good poet in the sense that he's not going to be a bestseller. He's going to be a bestseller only in a closed society, where there is no real journalism, where you can't get the truth any other way. And so when these Americans go over in their condescending way and say, "Oh, you wonderful people, you're so poor, so noble, you all read," they don't know what they're saying. What they're saying is that they're living in a place where you can't read anything else. You can't read muckracking journalism. You can't read Tom Wolfe. You can't see *60 Minutes.* They don't have any other access, so the word is valued because the word is choked off.

Safer: Do you think you'll ever go back?

Brodsky: I don't think in flesh I will, but in paper I'm getting back quite frequently—that is, the manuscripts, the books, they're just floating there, floating or flying quite incessantly.

Safer: Do you hear from people who've read your work?

Brodsky: Oh, quite a lot, yeah. Yeah.

Safer: How does it get in there?

Brodsky: Well, there are channels. And I really wouldn't like to specify.

Safer: The sense of exile never leaves his verse. He reaches into antiquity. A letter from Odysseus to his son, Telemachus, expresses his own longing. He has a son, too, born out of wedlock 12 years ago, and still in Russia.

On tour, his poems are translated into English by an onstage associate.

> Telemachus, my son,
> all islands look alike when one has wandered as long as I have done.
> I can't remember how the war came out,
> even how old you are—I can't remember.
> Grow up, then, my Telemachus, grow strong.
> Only the gods know if we'll see each other
> again . . .

Safer: Do you hear from your family, from your son?

Brodsky: From my son, I don't. From my family, yes, I do. I'm trying to talk to them over the telephone from time to time. It's a pretty tough situation, but I've been trying to invite them for all these seven years just for a visit. They are too old to resettle, and I'm the only son. Well, as many times I tried, as many times they've refused.

Safer: You paint a very vivid picture of Leningrad, a very nostalgic portrait of the city and of Joseph Brodsky growing up in it.

Brodsky: Uh-hmm. Well, it's a nice city, incredibly beautiful, I think. Of what I've seen, I never saw anything that would parallel it.

Safer: You miss it?

Brodsky: Considerably so. I don't really know exactly what I miss. I think I miss the whole ambiance, the whole complex of things. What you miss, in the first place, your memories of this or that place, of this or that street. Many things have happened to me on those streets, and to have them not around to remind me about themselves, about those things, oh, it just almost like your past being kind of altered or edited.

Safer: You said you're in many ways lucky, but you're a man who's lost his home.

Brodsky: Uh-hmm. Yeah.

Safer: His family, removed from his family, his friends, his language, his—

Brodsky: That I haven't lost.

Safer: They have taken the tools of your trade away, to some extent.

Brodsky: So to speak, yeah.

Safer: That's almost a total loss.

Brodsky: The language, though, still, you have inside of yourself and, with it, you regain everything. As long as I write, I think I reconstruct all this missing castle.

Safer: When he's not teaching, he's trying to rebuild his castle in New York's Greenwich Village. There are echoes of Leningrad down here on the shores of the Hudson, and in New York, there are other closer reminders: his best friend, fellow immigrant and god of the ballet stage, Mikhail Baryshnikov. They are rivals for the women who, for some reason, throw themselves at both men, and it's a friendly rivalry, and both would rather praise each other than themselves.

Do you speak English to each other?

Mikhail Baryshnikov: Certainly, yes.

Brodsky: Why not? Especially when—if there is a girl who speaks English only.

Safer: Uh-huh.

Brodsky: Yeah, or somebody like you.

(Laughter)

You know, I'm just kidding.

Safer: That's all right. Well, when there is a girl, are you competitive?

Brodsky: No, well, from the threshhold, it's clear that I lost, yeah. So, no, there is no question about that.

Baryshnikov: Well, I don't say that. When we are sitting next to the table, it's the poet who is leading the evening, I'll tell you.

Brodsky: Well, for you I make an exception.

(Laughter)

Baryshnikov: I heard about him first time when I came to Leningrad, when I was 15, 16, and his poetry was not official poetry. Under the ground. You know, people was writing this poem or this—you know, poem just like that, you know, under—

Safer: By hand.

Baryshnikov: By hand under the table, and with locked rooms and locked windows. And then he left, and I was absolutely sure I will lose him forever. I will just hear some things. And it was very sad. It was terrible time, like to lose somebody who is very close to you, you know, maybe one of the closest people to something absolutely wonderful and decent and clean and honest and straightforward and—besides his genius—besides his genius as a poet.

Safer: And Brodsky replies:

How splendid late at night, Old Russia worlds apart,
to watch Baryshnikov, his talent still as forceful!
The effort of the calf, the quivering of the torso
rotating round its axis, start
a flight such as the soul has yearned for from the fates,
as old maids cherish dreams while turning into bitches.
And as for where in space and time one's toe end touches,
well, earth is hard all over; try the States.

The States has been kind to both. It heaps praise and wealth on one, mainly ignores the other, but allows him to speak and allows us to listen. Brodsky has been deprived of his source, his Russian environment, but the poet carries on, endures very well, thank you.

Brodsky: Thank you.

Safer: His latest collection, called *A Part of Speech,* will only sell four or five thousand copies, but not being on the bestseller list is to him a small price to pay for the right to write:

denied a chalice at the feast of the fatherland,
now I stand in a strange place. The name hardly matters . . .
here, I'll live out my days, losing gradually
hair, teeth, consonants, verbs, and suffixes . . .
If it gets hard, annoying,
I'll yell out: self-restraint is just dumb and morbid.
As for now, I can take a bit more of it.

(Safer and Brodsky standing on the shores of the Hudson)

Brodsky: You know, it really looks like the upper part of the right bank of Neva River in Leningrad, because there are factories, prisons—

Safer: Power stations.

Brodsky: Uh-hmm. Power stations, all those things, yeah. You just can't escape it. Well . . .

Safer: Are we that much different as people, do you think, Joseph, as worlds apart, as it mostly seems to me we are?

Brodsky: Well, you may take it as a flattery, certainly, but I think you are. You are better. In Russia, they don't have a Statue of Liberty, you see. Well, the concept of liberty is just not present. Well, they would talk about the social justice, about anything else, about the equal share for everybody, et cetera, et cetera, et cetera, which is not—well, but, no, that's a part—they won't talk about the liberty. That's the point.

An Interview with Joseph Brodsky

David Montenegro / 1986

From *Partisan Review,* 54 (Fall 1987), 527–40, republished in *Points of Departure: International Writers on Writing & Politics* (Ann Arbor: The University of Michigan Press, 1992). Reprinted by permission of the University of Michigan Press.

This interview took place on April 8, 1986.

DM: You've just published *Less Than One,* your first collection of essays. Do you find prose gives you a new latitude? What problems and pleasures do you find in writing prose that you don't find in writing poetry?

JB: Well, to begin with, I simply happened to write those pieces over the years. On several occasions, I've been commissioned for one thing or another, and I just wanted to do whatever was asked of me in each particular instance. What pleases me really about the book is that it's something that was never meant to be. Perhaps a collection or two of poems was in the cards, but a book of prose—especially in English—wasn't. It strikes me as something highly illegitimate.

As for the difficulties or differences, essentially the operations of prose and poetry are not so different. In prose, you have a more leisurely pace, but in principle prose is simply spilling some beans, which poetry sort of contains in a tight pod.

DM: You once wrote that prose is hateful to you because it doesn't have poetry's discipline.

JB: How shall I put it? To use an almost paradoxical term, that's one of prose's shortcomings. That's specifically what makes prose lengthy. What I value about poetry, if I can simply estrange myself to look with a kind of cold, separate eye at these things, is that in verse your mind—reader's or writer's—moves much faster, for verse is overtly final and terribly concise, it's a condensed thing. In prose there is nothing that prevents you from going sideways, from digressing. In poetry, a rhyme keeps you in check.

Basically, my attitude towards prose—apart from its being the vehicle of making a living because, in fact, prose is paid for, if not more handsomely, at least more readily than poetry—the thing that I can say in praise of prose is that it's perhaps more therapeutic than poetry. For poetry's risk, its uncertainty, well, its anticipation of failure is terribly high. And after a while one gets rather edgy or bilious.

In prose, I think, it's harder to fail. You simply sit and write, and as the day passes you've written several pages. Then the next day, and so forth. That in part perhaps explains why there are so many novels around. Prose gives a writer confidence whereas poetry does exactly the opposite.

DM: Efim Etkind, in his book *Notes of a Non-Conspirator,* called you a very modern poet. He said even when you were quite young you were presenting problems to yourself and dealing with problems presented to you by your times. What new problems does the modern poet face unlike those faced by the nineteenth-century poet, or even the poet prior to World War Two?

JB: That's a big question indeed. Now one of the main problems that a poet today faces—modern or not modern—is that the body of poetry prior to him—the heritage, that is—is larger, which makes you simply wonder whether you have anything to add to that body, whether you're simply going to modify some of your predecessors or whether you're going to be yourself.

But basically it's not so much the question asked at the threshold, whether you're going to modify somebody or not. You ask this subsequently, with the benefit of hindsight. It's a question you ask yourself because of the critics around. But it's precisely because you have such great people before yesterday who breathe on your neck, that you have to go a bit further, where theoretically nobody has been before. It simply makes it more difficult to write, because you are quite conscious of not wanting to be a parrot. And the people before you were quite great. To think that you can say something qualitatively new after people like Tsvetaeva, Akhmatova, Auden, Pasternak, Mandelstam, Frost, Eliot, and others after Eliot—and let's not leave out Thomas Hardy—reveals either a very enterprising fellow or a very ignorant one. And I would bill myself as the latter.

When you start writing, you know less about what took place before you. It's only in the middle of your life that you come to amass this knowledge, and it can dwarf you or mesmerize you.

That's one thing, one problem for the modern poet. The other is obviously that the modern poet lives in a world where what had been regarded as values, as virtues and vices, say twenty or thirty years ago, have, if not necessarily swapped places, at least been questioned or compromised entirely. A modern poet presumably doesn't live in a world which is ethically, let alone politically, as polarized as was the situation before the war. But I think the polarization is still quite clear. I don't really know what Etkind had in mind. Presumably, what he had in mind was a difference between the modern poet and a poet, let's say, of the turn of the century. Our predecessors perhaps had more to believe in. Their pantheon, or their shrines, were a bit more populated than ours. We are one way or another, in a sense, awful agnostics.

But there are agnostics and agnostics. I would say that the poet worships perhaps only one thing in the final analysis, and that has no embodiment except in words, that is . . . language. His attitude towards the Supreme Deity who is absent is more of a reproach for His absence than a pure jeering or else hosannas. Perhaps I am modern in that I am living in my own time and to some extent I reflect—what I write reflects—the sensibility of the people who speak my language towards their reality. In that respect, of course, I am modern. What else could I be? Old-fashioned? Conservative? Well, I'm conservative in terms of form, perhaps. In terms of content, in terms of the attitude towards reality, and the sensibility, I am fairly—well, I hope—*au courant.*

DM: You mentioned the polarization of good and evil. Do you think there's a blurring of those categories now?

JB: Not for an attentive eye, not for an attentive soul. But blurring the distinctions has become, indeed, an industry. It's done either deliberately by the forces of evil—for instance, by a certain political doctrine and its advocates, by its propaganda outfits—or it's done by honest, self-questioning people. But ultimately it's done by those who thrive on questioning and compromising things, the smart alecks who try to turn every idea, every reality inside out. And, of course, there's a great deal of gray area now. Well, that's fine by me. The greater the blur is, the more glory to you if you manage to sort it out. It's always been the case—the blur, that is. But today, given the population explosion, we have a quantum increase in devil's advocates as well. Doubt nowadays is more in vogue than convictions. To put it kindly—doubt is a conviction. Basically, we live in a period which is quite similar to certain stages of the Enlightenment.

DM: The scrutiny of all the preconceptions . . .

JB: . . . of all the preconceived notions indeed. Except, a Russian differs here. The results of scrutiny by a Russian may yield results totally different from those of his Western counterparts. For example, during the Enlightenment, scientific evidence led people to the denial of Supreme Being. Certain Russians—for example, Lomonosov and Derzhavin—were saying exactly the opposite, that the abundance of this evidence testified to the intricacy of the world, which is a divine creation.

DM: As a poet, you're conspicuous in that you often use religious imagery. Do you think it's still effective? Is it a common language?

JB: In my view, yes it is. At least it's common vis-à-vis my Russian audience. And I'm either generous or cynical enough to think that my Russian audience is not that qualitatively different in the final analysis from my English audience. But maybe that's wishful thinking on my part. I think it's still a language comprehensible to a certain percentage of people, and that's enough. For no percentage of the people is merely a small one. How small are, let's say, ten people, or six?

DM: Marek Oramus, while interviewing Zbigniew Herbert, said that Herbert *corrects* mythology. How do you approach it?

JB: You animate it, you try to make sense out of all of this, out of all that you've inherited. That's what you do. You're not really correcting it, you're making sense out of it. It's simply interpreted. It's the function of the species to interpret the Bible, mythology, the Upanishads, anything we have inherited, including our own dreams.

Basically, each era, each century, not to mention each culture has its own Greece, its own Christianity, its own Orient, its own mythology. Each century simply offers its own interpretation, like a magnifying glass, in a sense. We're just yet another lens. And it simply indicates the distance that grows between us and myths, and I think the attempt to interpret is essentially proportionate to the distance.

DM: You mentioned in one essay—and I'll just quote you—"At certain periods of history it is only poetry that is capable of dealing with reality by condensing it into something graspable, something that otherwise couldn't be retained by the mind." What are some other functions of poetry? What is the power of language through poetry?

JB: Poetry sells perhaps better as the record of human sensibility. To give you an example, the age of the Augustan poets. I think if we have a notion of Roman and of the human sensibility of the time it's based on Horace, for instance, the way he sees the world, or Ovid or Propertius. And we don't have any other record, frankly.

DM: This might not be pertinent at all since the poet's fascination with language isn't with its utility, but what does poetry now provide that prose doesn't, that religion doesn't, that philosophy doesn't? How strong is language in fending off a sense of chaos, in defending people or their sensibility from brutality?

JB: Well, I don't really know how to answer this, except by pointing out the very simple fact that speech is a reaction to the world, some kind of grimacing in the darkness or making faces behind the bastards' backs, or else controlling your fright or vomit. It's a reaction to the world, and in that sense it's functional. Protective? Does it protect you? No, more than likely not. It really *exposes* you. But it's quite possible that the exposure leads to the real test of your quality, of your durability. To say the least, producing something of harmony today is tantamount to saying in the face of chaos: "Look, you can't break me, not yet." And "me" in the language stands for everybody.

I don't really know what the function of poetry is. It's simply the way, so to speak, the light or dark refracts for you. That is, you open the mouth. You open the mouth to scream, you open the mouth to pray, you open the mouth to talk. Or you open the mouth to confess. Well, each time presumably you are forced by something to do so.

DM: When you first arrived in the United States in 1972, you said one fear you had was that your work would suffer a kind of paralysis because you would be living outside the environment of your native languge. But, in fact, you've been prolific. What effect *has* living here had on your poetry?

JB: I don't know. I guess what I was saying then simply reflected my fears. Prolific I was. I would imagine that I would have been as, if not more, prolific, with no less interesting consequences for myself and for my readers, had I stayed at home. I think that fear expressed in 1972 reflected more the apprehension of losing my identity and that self-respect as a writer. I think what I was really unsure of—and I'm not so sure today, as a matter of fact—was that I wouldn't become a simpleton, because the life here would require much less of me, not as subtle an operation on a daily basis as in Russia. And indeed, in the final analysis, some of my instincts have dulled, I think. But, on the other hand, by being apprehensive about that sort of thing, you're trying to make up your own mind. And, after all, you perhaps break even. You end up as neurotic as you would have been otherwise. Only faster, though you can't be sure of that either.

DM: You used the word stereoscopic before. Do you think being in another country gives you a sort of double vision?

JB: But, of course, if only because here a great world of information is available to you. I was talking not long ago with a friend of mine, and we were discussing the shortcomings of being away from our country. And we came to the conclusion that perhaps the usual apprehension of the individual as well as of his public or of his critics is that, once outside of danger, out of harm's way, one's instincts, one's pencil get duller. One's notion of evil becomes less sharp.

But, I think, on the contrary, in fact you find yourself really in a rather remarkable predicament vis-à-vis, let's say, the evil . . . well, vis-à-vis the dragon. That is, you can observe him, you can ascertain and assess him in a better fashion. You can see with greater clarity—precisely because of all the data available to you here which wasn't there—all his scales, all his spikes, all his teeth. On top of that, you are not mesmerized. Your attention is not clouded by the fear of being grabbed by that dragon at any time. So basically, if you are to take him on, you can find yourself as well armed as the dragon is. In fact, you establish a certain parity at this safe distance. And on top of that, you have always suspected that you are, perhaps, as bad as the dragon yourself, and given the chance you would be just as nasty and monstrous as he is. That is, you have always suspected there is more of a monster in you than of Saint George. It's not customary for a certain type of writer to regard himself as a fallen angel. One would rather regard oneself as a devil, as one of the devils.

And maybe the fact that I stayed, as you say, prolific reflects simply the availability of data. Maybe it reflects simply the realization that monstrosity is everywhere, while in Russia I thought of it as being our local specialty.

DM: It sounds as if you're implying an identification of the victim with the assailant.

JB: But of course. No, I would say simply your notion of the dragon becomes far more subtle. That is, you realize you may play Saint George *ad infinitum,* because the animal is everywhere. And in a sense, you become, your armor becomes, in the final analysis, your own scales. And clarifying these things on paper conspires to bring the subsequent charge of being prolific. Prose is a more natural medium for that sort of job, for pondering. And to answer your very first question, the thing that many fail to realize is that there is a great bond between a poem and essay writing. Both employ the technique invented, of course, in poetry by poetry, of montage. It's not Einstein, it's poetry. It's stanzas with those frame-like shapes.

DM: It's the parts trying to become the whole.

JB: Yes, exactly.

DM: In comparing two of your poems, "Elegy for John Donne," an early poem, and the more recent "Lullaby of Cape Cod," I was struck by how similar they are in many ways, but also how drastically different. Both are set at night, both are very solitary poems. The earlier poem seems to show a spiritual struggle. There's a definite battle going on. I think in the John Donne poem, you had the categories clearer: spirit, flesh, and so forth. And therefore the struggle was much more intense. But in the later poem, there's less certainty. There's a sense of exhaustion—maybe even a spiritual exhaustion. Instead of snow, there's the heat. You repeat the word "stifling." And also, there's the sheer weight of the material world. Despite the list of objects, in the earlier poem there's a sort of resurrection. In the later poem, everything seems to be drugged, heavy, as if it can't wake up. What do you think of this reading?

JB: There is some similarity, come to think of it. I never thought about it. I don't really know. Perhaps this is a valid comparison and a valid observation, and perhaps there is some sort of a genealogy of the kind that you're talking about. But I don't think so. I think the only thing it testifies to is, at best, not so much the evolution of the views as the consistency of the device.

I sort of like "Lullaby of Cape Cod." You should be aware of the fact that it's ninety-three lines longer in the translation than it is in the original. In the original, it's a bit more concise. And I think it's a far more lyrical work than "Big Elegy." In "Big Elegy" there is indeed a certain clarity of the spirit. It is a vertical job from the threshold. But "Cape Cod Lullaby" I was writing not as a poem with a beginning and end, but more as a lyrical sequence. It was more like playing piano than singing an aria. Actually I'd written that poem because it was the Bicentennial, you see, and I thought—well, why don't I do something? There is one image there, I think, where I use the Stars and Stripes.

DM: As you did with the word "stifling," you often use repetition and anaphora. It seems to me, your poetry is centrifugal. You start from a center and move outward, turning and separating different aspects of the subject. Whereas Akhmatova would be more centripetal.

JB: True, there is obviously a difference of temperaments. She seldom operates in big forms. She is a poet of great economy, and she's a more classical poet. Well, I wouldn't like to be compared to her.

DM: What gives you the least confidence now in poetry? Is there any particular problem that you're trying to solve?

JB: The poems are always particular when you are writing this or that one. I'm not trying to bill myself in any spectacular fashion, but I think as somebody who has always written in meter and rhyme, I do increase the purely technical stakes. Those two aspects, especially rhyme, simply are synonymous with compounding your own problems from the threshold, from the first impulse to write, which is fairly frequently a blissful one, in my case, or the sense of guilt. But I know what I'm going to do more or less from the moment I set out. That is, I more or less have the sense of form at the moment I'm starting with some sort of content, and the form gives you a great deal of headache.

DM: Like Auden, you have a fascination with form. Do you think structure itself sometimes leads you into new content?

JB: Presumably, because by and large it's very seldom that one knows at the outset where one is heading. Simply by virtue of being a citizen of a different era, you're *bound* to invest the ancient form, old form, compromised—if you will—form with a qualitatively new meaning. That creates contrast, it creates a tension, and the result is always new. It's bound to be new. And it's terribly interesting. Apart from anything else, sometimes you write about certain things precisely for the form's sake, in many ways. That's not to say that you're trying to write a *villanelle* and la-di-da to check whether your facility is still there. No, it's simply because, otherwise, to write about certain things wouldn't be as appetizing a prospect. After all, you can say only so many things, you can express only so many attitudes towards the reality of this world. In fact, all the attitudes in the final analysis are computable. And forms are not. Or at least the interplay of an attitude and the form in which it is expressed in writing increases the options.

DM: Some poets now don't use rhyme and meter, they claim, because they feel such form is no longer relevant to experience or experience doesn't have the continuity or structure that such form implies.

JB: They're entitled to their views, but I think it's pure garbage. Art basically is an operation within a certain contract, and you have to abide by all the clauses of the contract. You write poetry, to begin with, in order to influence minds, to influence hearts, to *move* hearts, to move people. In order to do so, you have to produce something which has an appearance of inevitability and which is memorable, so that it will stick in the mind of the reader.

You have to wrap it in such a fashion that the reader won't be able to avoid it, so that what you have said will have a chance of entering his subconscious and of being remembered. Meter and rhyme are basically mnemonic devices. Not to mention the fact to which Ezra Pound alerted us, I think way back in 1911 or 1915, by saying there's too much free verse around. And that was in the teens of the century.

DM: Or as Robert Frost said, free verse is like playing tennis without a net.

JB: Well, it's not tennis. And not cricket either.

DM: Are you getting together a new book of poems in English translation?

JB: That's somewhere on the horizon.

DM: Will it be by various translators, as was *A Part of Speech?*

JB: I would imagine so, because otherwise the book would be very slim.

DM: You're a translator yourself. You've done particularly difficult poets, John Donne, for example. Do you feel your work's been well translated into English?

JB: Sometimes it has, sometimes it hasn't. On the whole, I think I have less to complain about than any of my fellow Russians, dead or alive. Or poets in other languages. My luck, my fortune is that I've been able to sort of watch over the translations. And at times I would do them myself.

DM: Since Russian is an inflected language and phonetically very different from English, it must bother you that the sounds, the syntax, and the quality of the original can't be conveyed.

JB: Yes, but that's what makes translation intricate and interesting. Curlicue. Other people solve crossword puzzles; well, I have translations. Essentially the operation is like solving a crossword puzzle, except that the next day they don't print the answers. On the whole, though, the principles of assonance or consonance in English are not that drastically different from the Russian. A word is a word. A sound is a sound, after all.

DM: Are you translating anyone into Russian now?

JB: Not for the moment, no.

DM: If you object to the next questions, please tell me.

JB: Go ahead.

DM: I want to ask you about the trial.

JB: That was many moons ago. Nothing interesting about it.

DM: We can read the shorthand account of it, but what was it like from your point of view? It was a mock trial. It must have seemed absurd, though it was no joke. It must have made you angry.

JB: It didn't make me angry. In fact, it did not. Never. No, a joke it wasn't. It was dead serious. I can talk about that at length, but in short . . . how shall I put it? It simply was an enactment of what I knew all along. But it's nice when things are *enacted,* you know. I knew who the masters were, and I knew that I had no other choice, that one day sooner or later it was going to happen that I would be in that position. I didn't expect a worse position; I didn't expect a better position. It didn't surprise me in the least that it happened, and the only thing I was interested in was what kind of sentence I was going to get. It looked rather dreadful, because there were lots of people. It looked like what I've seen of a Nuremberg trial, in terms of the number of police in the room. It was absolutely studded with police and state security people.

It's funny how—looking back now with the benefit of hindsight—I didn't really pay very much attention to what was going on, because attention was exactly what the state would have liked you to display. Or feel, indeed. The state wants you to get . . . well, you don't allow yourself to get scared, and you just think about something else. You pretend it isn't happening. You simply sit there and, as much as you can, you try to ignore it. In fact, the only time I was moved during the whole thing was when two people stood up and defended me—two witnesses—and said something nice about me. I was so unprepared to hear something positive that I was a little bit moved. But other than that, no. So, I got my five years, and I walked out of the room and was taken to the prison, and that was it.

DM: You had already spent three weeks of interrogation in a hospital?

JB: It was more than that. It was the mental institution. But that wasn't for the first time. It wasn't the first arrest either. It was the third, I think. I'd been twice to mental institutions, three times to prisons. All that sort of thing. And since it wasn't terribly new or terribly fresh, I wasn't shocked then.

DM: Why did you feel that this would eventually happen?

JB: Because one way or another I knew that I was running my own show, that I was doing something which amounts essentially to private enterprise in what is otherwise a state-owned economy, so to speak. And I knew that one day I would be grabbed.

It's simply the different tonality, the different use of the language. In a society where everything belongs to the state, to try to speak with your own voice, etcetera, is obviously fraught with consequences. It's not so interesting. It's simply an idiotic situation, and you find yourself in the position of a victim, as a sort of martyr. Well, you find you're sort of ashamed of it. It's *embarrassing*.

DM: You said once that your months of forced labor near Archangel in 1964–65 were perhaps the most normal time in your life.

JB: True, almost two years of it.

DM: In fact, the people there, you said, treated you well, like a son.

JB: Well, a son . . . that was a bit too much. As one of their own, yes.

DM: You mentioned at one point that they were pleased to have a poet among them.

JB: What they were pleased with, if they were, was simply another pair of hands, and also because I knew a little bit of medicine and could assist them. They were highly uneducated people, and the closest medical help was about twenty-five miles away. So, I was simply helping them as much as I could and they were just nice to me, not in exchange, but basically because they were normal people and had no axe to grind with me.

DM: And you continued to write and to study English?

JB: Yes.

DM: And translate?

JB: Well, as much as I could. I had to work in the field, etcetera, but there you get this normal life, a hired hand sort of thing. Perhaps a little bit more work sometimes, and you're not being paid. But essentially it was okay.

DM: In 1965 you were released and you remained in Russia until 1972. You did a lot of writing during that period also. Were you interfered with by the authorities?

JB: Not very much. They would interfere with publication, but with life as such, no. Several times there would be subpoenas for interrogations and this and that. . . .

DM: When you first came to the United States, what surprised you most? It's been said that you drew some of your expectations from reading Robert Frost, that you felt America would be more rural than you found it.

JB: Not more rural, but I thought that the people would be less vocal, less hysterical, more reserved, more prudent with their speech.

DM: Could we talk a minute about current politics?

JB: Be my guest.

DM: What do you think Gorbachev's effect will be in certain areas of the world, in Afghanistan, in Poland and just on United States–Soviet relations in general? Do you think he'll make drastic changes?

JB: When Gorbachev became General Secretary, Derek Walcott asked me what I thought of him. Well, frankly, I said, nothing, and I hope it's mutual. Since then, I haven't changed my opinion.

DM: Let's go on to two other people probably more pleasing for you to talk about. You knew Auden and Akhmatova, and they seem to have been very important to you. Could you say something about Auden and also about Akhmatova, how they struck you or how they affected you?

JB: I can tell you how. They turned out to be people whom I found that I could love. Or, that is, if I have a capacity for loving, those two allowed me to exercise it, presumably to the fullest. To the extent that I think—oddly enough, not so much about Akhmatova but about Auden—sometimes that I am he. That shouldn't be reported, perhaps, because they would fire me everywhere.

Essentially, what do you love in a poet like Auden is not the verses. Obviously you remember, you memorize, you internalize the verse, but you internalize it and internalize it and internalize it until the point comes when he occupies in you more of a place perhaps than you yourself occupy. Auden, in my mind, in my heart, occupies far greater room than anything or anybody else on the earth. As simple as that. Dead or alive or whatever. It's a tremendously strange thing, or maybe I'm freaking out, or maybe I freaked out at a certain time, or maybe I've just gone mad. I simply think about him too often. In a sense, I can go as far as to say that, if I could supply an index to my daily mental operation, I think Auden and his lines would pop up more frequently there, would occupy more pages, so to speak, than anything else. And similarly Akhmatova, though to a lesser extent, oddly enough, I must confess. Well, I shouldn't pretend.

Both of them I think gave me, whatever was given me, almost the cue or the key for the voice, for the tonality, for the posture towards reality. In a sense, I think that their poems to a certain extent—some of Akhmatova's and quite a lot of Auden's—are written by me, or that I'm the owner. That is, it doesn't matter what I do in my attitude towards people, in my attitude towards what I'm writing. I know that I'm myself, that gender distinguishes me from both of them, I would say, in many ways. But I sort of live their lives. Not that I'm a postscript to either one of them. Both would rebel against that. But to myself it's more sensible or more pleasant perhaps to think that I'm a postscript to them than that I'm leading my own life. I happen to think of myself as somebody who loves Auden or loves Akhmatova more than myself. It's obviously an exaggeration, but it's an exaggeration I feel comfortable with sometimes. I know quite clearly one thing about both of them: that they were both better than I in all possible respects. And that's enough. You simply think about people who are better than you are, and you spend your life sort of—how shall I put it—thinking about everybody you bump into.

DM: In your poem "Nature Morte," is there an echo—maybe it's because of the shortness of the lines—of "September 1, 1939"?

JB: No, no. That's not true. I know what makes you feel that way. It's the opening of "Nature Morte." Well, there is that. There are other poems perhaps which have strong echoes of Wystan's, but I think at that time I was more under the influence of MacNeice than of Auden. That poem is an old one.

DM: You've stressed several times in your writing how language outlives the state. But, in our precarious age, the life of the state may in fact be the life of the language.

JB: No, not at all. No.

DM: What I'm getting at is the nuclear threat.

JB: Yes, I know.

DM: A sense of the continuity of language is so important, not to mention confidence in the future, which may seem very fragile or even nonexistent to some. Does this have an effect?

JB: No, I don't think that the future's fragile or nonexistent. I think we are in very good shape. That is, I don't think nuclear disaster is to occur. The greater the proliferation of all that nonsense, the safer we are, if only because the machines will try to control one another and the sense of command, the sense of responsibility is going to be far more diffused. Today it already takes two to launch a missile. So, eventually it will require three, four.

DM: Nobody can do it.

JB: Yes, nobody can do it and so forth. It's of course a little bit silly, but something along those lines sort of instills hope in you. But should the worst come, should the worst happen, I don't think that will automatically mean the end of the language. In the first place, I think whatever the destruction inflicted by the states upon one another, something will survive. And language obviously will survive because the funny thing about language is that it knows better than anything or anyone what it means to mutate. The language's ability to mutate is terrific. It's a bit like roaches.

DM: A last question. Absolutes are something you deal with a lot in your prose. What absolutes would you say we have to live by if our sense of good and evil is somewhat oversophisticated perhaps, or sophisticated to the point of paralyzing us? What other types of absolutes are there, if any, or do we need them?

JB: Well, there is one. It's kind of a funny thing to be asked. And it puts me immediately in a position where I am tempted to proselytize, to a certain extent. But, first of all, one shouldn't really allow oneself into that situation where one's sense of good and evil gets so, as you say, sophisticated. Basically there is one criterion which nobody with sophistication would refuse: that you should treat your own kind the way you would like to be treated yourself. It's a tremendous idea offered to us by Christianity, in a sense. It's a terribly selfish idea, and it finally established the bond.

DM: It turned the urge toward self-preservation into a social value.

JB: But of course. Frost said once, to be social is to be forgiving. And that's basically the requirement, to forgive because you would like to be forgiven yourself, not only by the Almighty, but by your fellow beings. And I thought the other day—well, I looked—now it's going to be a little bit maudlin, but then in effect I prove my profession—out of the window and I saw a star. Then I thought, that star over there, presumably, with some help, is the domain of the Almighty, all the stars, etcetera. Then it occurred to me that this thought about loving your neighbor as yourself travelled here from quite afar. I thought, how appropriate is the origin. That is, the stars being the origin of this idea. For a star to like its neighbor, it takes something, yes? It's kind of interesting to think about, to think it through. I don't really know. . . . I don't think any magazines will want this interview.

DM: Do you think they won't swallow it?

JB: No, it's not that they won't swallow it. They'll probably find it too lyrical.

Interview with Joseph Brodsky

Missy Daniel / 1988

From *Threepenny Review,* 11 (Fall 1990), 23–24. Reprinted by permission of *Threepenny Review.*

This conversation between Nobel Prize–winning poet Joseph Brodsky and Missy Daniel took place in New York City in 1988.

Missy Daniel: You called your latest book *To Urania.* Of the nine muses, why do you write to Urania, the muse of the heavens? What is a poet's relationship to a muse?

Joseph Brodsky: I don't think I can answer this in any coherent fashion. Basically, Urania is the muse of astronomy, of geography, and also, according to some interpretation, the muse of love. She has several properties. And the title of the book was actually initially *Homage to Urania,* simply because it was after Auden. The trouble, though, was that I didn't have a poem of comparable consequence to "Homage to Clio." So therefore I omitted *Homage* and I left it *To Urania.* And that's all. Well, I simply think that Urania is indeed older than Clio.

It's simply—how should I put it?—well, it's the name of the whole thing, the name of the universe, if you will. Look at Dante's *Purgatorio,* Canto XXIX, verses 41–42: "O most holy virgins, if fastings, cold, or vigils I have ever borne for you, need drives me to ask you for reward; now must Helicon pour forth for me and Urania help me with her choir to put in verse things hard for thought."

Daniel: Auden wrote that poetry makes nothing happen. It can move you, it can change you, perhaps it can save the world. Yet it makes nothing happen.

Brodsky: It's nonsense. So many people simply misquote the author. The line goes, "Poetry makes nothing happen: it survives." It purifies the language, it does lots of things. It's a terrific mental acceleration, to begin with. It shortcuts a great deal of matter, a great deal of rational or even irrational matter. In my view, it is the most efficient tool of cognition very often. It lives its own life. It has its own dynamics. It has its own past, its own pedigree, its own present, and its own future. It's not necessarily parallel to life, of course, like art is not exactly parallel to life. It's also, I think, in absolutely mundane terms, the supreme form of human locution, and as such it's the species'—in my view—anthropological goal, genetic goal, whatever it is. It's not simply an entertainment, it's not a "read." If what distinguishes us from the rest of the animal kingdom as a species is speech, then poetry is our biological imperative. It's the most succinct form of uttering this and that.

Daniel: You said in your Nobel Prize speech that if you have read Dickens, you will somehow be more inhibited from taking a shot at someone than if you haven't. What gives you that faith?

Brodsky: Well, because I think had I not read Dickens or Dostoyevsky or anybody or Balzac, etc., etc., I would be a rather different man. I would be—well, I don't necessarily pride myself on what I am, but I think at least that osmosis alone doesn't teach you to care for another human being. We need some help there. And the laws themselves don't prevent you from being nasty towards other members of your species. Literature is, apart from anything else, a sentimental education. If only because of that, it makes us a little bit more gentle.

Daniel: It seems that even that isn't enough to make human beings good.

Brodsky: Well, that would be enough, at least in the society where the ecclesiastical authority is down, the political authority has never been of any consequence—and rightly so—in the society where philosophy doesn't enjoy a great deal of vogue. It's only history and literature that can curb our bestiality. They have sort of a mitigating effect on our instincts, yeah?

Daniel: From time to time.

Brodsky: That's frequent enough for me.

Daniel: Another man who won the Nobel Prize for literature, St.-John Perse, said, "It is enough for a poet to be the guilty conscience of his time." Is that enough?

Brodsky: Sounds sort of dramatic—melodramatic. I don't take myself that seriously. Actually, it would be enough, but that's not enough, obviously. Well, you can settle for that job, but in poetry it's not enough. Poetry is not a didactic enterprise, to begin with. That is, it has a didactic aspect, of course, but it's not only that. It's first of all the aesthetic endeavor, and basically it improves one's aesthetic perceptions. And with that comes a great deal in attendance, yeah? When man is more aesthetically, so to speak, developed, to say the least, he is less susceptible to all sorts of—well, how shall I put it—social idiocies.

Well, he's less susceptible to demagoguery, he's less susceptible to self-congratulatory postures, including the aforementioned, he's less susceptible to that sort of a universal call for basking in our sense that we are victims of this or that circumstance. Aesthetics builds human dignity. The man becomes more resilient, more indestructible in many ways, yeah? A good poem does something to you. It sets you in a state you wouldn't arrive to otherwise.

Daniel: You wrote in an introduction to the poetry of Osip Mandelstam that writing poetry is an exercise in dying. In what sense?

Brodsky: Oh, in so many senses. To give you one, simply you think, does it have anything to outlast me? Suppose I'm gone, will I be ashamed of what I have said? And how will it go over when I'm gone, yeah? Will it hold some water? Well, that's one way.

Another aspect of it, well—the sense of futility of what you are doing, yeah? There are all sorts of—the sum of all those sentiments attendant to production of anything. Besides, the poem itself sort of gravitates towards the finale.

Daniel: You're getting to the end all the time, you mean, the end of the line, or the end of the stanza—

Brodsky: Yeah. End of the stanza and end of the poem, of its world.

Daniel: So it's about endings more than beginnings.

Brodsky: Yes, more than beginnings, to say the least, yeah.

Daniel: Does it also have something to do with your being quite mindful of the dead when you write?

Brodsky: But of course, of course. Once I had my students write a paper. I was teaching Hardy at that point, at Mount Holyoke. The funny thing about Hardy is that one-third of his poems are set—well, it's a recurrent thing in him—in a graveyard. They deal with some sort of posthumous set-ups, effects of one's life, etc. It's always graveyards, twilight, whatever it is, and he ponders, looks at the slabs, and whatever. Well, I asked my students why this subject is so frequent in our man's work. Is it simply Victorian taste, *weltschmerz,* you name it, etc., etc., etc? One of my students was a young girl, 21 or 20, I guess. She said, "Well, it's all of those things. Also his training as an ecclesiastical architect, this and that, etc., etc. But I think it has to do with the medium itself, with poetry, because it's moribund." By definition, a poem is moribund.

Daniel: And you agree?

Brodsky: Well, to a certain extent I do. Like we all are.

Daniel: You've said that you have been given two or three revelations in your life.

Brodsky: Yeah, well, two or three, yeah. Well, it's actually a private matter, obviously. Fancy me talking about revelations. The reason I never told about them to anyone is simply because I thought, "Well, next thing will happen to me is I'll be locked up." Also, they took place when I was rather young, well, I was 22, 23. And I thought, "Well, if I'm going to mention that, well, some Jeanne d'Arc deal will . . ."

Daniel: This is certainly an age that doesn't put too much stock in people who claim to have revelations.

Brodsky: Stupid of them, of the age.

Daniel: What does one know after a revelation that one doesn't know before?

Brodsky: Ah. Sensible question. One gets certain that one is doing right. Because affirmation comes from so far away, it's almost like—how shall I put it?—it's simply that somebody cares to instruct you from the bowels of the universe. You sense that somebody bothered about you out there in that great infinity. Actually, both times that I had those moments which I regard as revelations, I had some sort of astronomical illumination, yeah? And I guess I'm actually rather distressed that they cease to, that nothing of the sort has happened in quite a while. But I guess the reason for that, that they haven't happened in quite a while, is in a sense the profession or the occupation in which I am engaged, because, one way or another, I'm deliberately fishing there, yeah? Had I not been fishing there, or poaching or whatever it is, maybe I would be issued something, yeah? That's all I can say about it. Well, I guess up there it's arbitrary. Or maybe there are too many of us, and now it's someone else's turn. . . . I think simply when it happens you hear it. You can't really deny it. You try to be as rational as you can be, but, well, it doesn't work. In fact, I think one of the prerequisites for that is—well, it normally arrives when you are indeed at the end of your rope.

There was a great Russian philosopher, Lev Shestov. He was just the cat's pajamas, I think, in that field. He maintained there are three methods of cognition. One, by analysis, another by synthesis—that is, intuitive synthesis, so to speak, which is not parallel, for instance, to analysis, but is the one that absorbs analysis, and then adds something on top of that—and the third one is the method, if you will, that was available to the biblical prophets, that of revelation. That's a form of cognition. And according to him a revelation normally occurs when reason fails.

Daniel: You are a great admirer of Robert Frost. His reputation as just a pastoral New England poet is only partial—

Brodsky: Yes, well, that's another nonsense, another silliness. Mr. Frost is the most petrifying, most terrifying poet this earth ever bore. And if he is 100 percent American, it's in that sense: Americans *are* that way.

Daniel: Petrifying?

Brodsky: Well, I mean, they sort of have all that in themselves, yeah.

Daniel: Yet Americans are optimists, always looking on the bright side, never wanting to end anything on a note of gloom.

Brodsky: Yes, the tenor is life-affirming, positive, but that's the tenor of any society, basically. That's the tenor. Life also has its bass, and when it speaks in bass, you see a shrink.

Daniel: You know about Frost's life in great detail, beyond the Lawrance Thompson biography—details even about his high-school days with his wife—

Brodsky: The way I came upon it was rather interesting. In itself, it tells you something about the country. It was many years ago, I think 1975 or 1974, I was flying from New York to Detroit, I think—American Airlines—and there was an in-flight magazine. In that magazine I saw an excerpt from Lesley Frost's memoir about her father, and that's where she told the story. (There is a book by Lesley Frost, though I haven't seen it.) I just remember that well. Funny. But you see, that's the whole point about this country. You *can* find that sort of story in an in-flight magazine.

Daniel: That's what makes America great?

Brodsky: Yes, that's why. You won't find it, let's say, in the pages of *TLS* or *New York Review of Books,* or, I don't really know, whatever it is, *Criterion.* I don't really know where. That's where it sits. That's where it hides.

Daniel: You have said that you even played a bit at being the gentleman farmer, thanks to Frost.

Brodsky: Yeah, well.

Daniel: But wasn't it a posture, a pose—

Brodsky: At that time, it wasn't, although I think I failed miserably, both as a gentleman and as a farmer. Whatever I was—or am—I don't think I would come up with, volunteer, a definition, nor would I accept anyone else's.

Frost is the greatest poet America produced in this century. To me he is so un-European, and his stuff is indeed an addition to the species' record of itself. Frost is a poet of terror, he is not a tragic poet. Tragedy has to do always with a *fait accompli.* Terror, with the anticipation. And Frost is a poet of negative anticipation. He's a poet of the human negative potential, if you will. I think he is about as significant to our comprehension of ourselves as Dostoyevsky, for instance. Perhaps even more, in many ways, in some ways, because, well, at least his verse is not encumbered with sort of ecclesiastical connotations, etc.

If you think about great—how should I put it—not about great poets, but about great contributions made by poetry in this century to our cognitive abilities, again, to the record of human sensibility, which is what literature is, Frost would be at the top of my list, because there's something rather unprecedented. I would cross out Eliot, of course, because in a sense that sensibility, in English, to say the least, in an English poet, has been predated by someone like Thomas Hardy. I would cross out Yeats, because it's but a wrinkle on a Homer lyric. I would just leave Frost. I really don't know. I would be hard-pressed to suggest somebody else. What matters here is not sublimity but gravity. I would add Auden also. I would put Auden there. Wystan imparts to that gravity its great intelligence, ability for great intelligence.

Daniel: One of your favorite lines from Frost is "to be social is to be forgiving."

Brodsky: Yeah, from "The Star Splitter." There's another one of his that I like best. If this knight would have had a motto it would be from "A Servant to Servants." There's that line a woman says, actually she quotes her husband, who is her oppressor: "Len always says, 'The best way out is always through.'"

Daniel: Why do you like that even better?

Brodsky: Because there are no other ways out, indeed.

Daniel: There is also Auden's line about loving your crooked neighbor—

Brodsky: Yeah, with your crooked heart. And also, "Life remains a blessing although you cannot bless." It's from the same poem: "O look, look in the mirror, O look in your distress; Life remains a blessing, although you cannot bless." It's actually a summary of his posture towards reality, I think.

Daniel: And yours? Is it a summary of yours?

Brodsky: I'd say that, yeah, I'd say that. Well—sometimes I can.

Daniel: Sometimes you can?

Brodsky: Yeah. Sometimes I delude myself that I can, yeah.

I think now I'll go immodest full speed. There is one line, I think, which I've done, but I don't really know how it comes off in English. "The soul in the passage—" well, "in the course of a lifetime, acquires mortal features." It's from a long peace ["Gorbunov and Gorchakov"] in *To Urania,* at the end. Actually, let me see, let me find it. It should be here. Actually, it's watered down: "I think the soul while living in this place assumes the features of its mortal frame." Well, it's not "in this place." It's just simply thrown in for the rhyme by the translator. "While living in the course of life, acquires mortal features."

Daniel: That's the summation—

Brodsky: Yeah. I think the soul in the course of a lifetime acquires mortal features. Well, that's perhaps my better line. Perhaps there is some truth to it.

Daniel: I'd like to ask about you and Shakespeare.

Brodsky: Me and Shakespeare? Yeah, me and God. Go ahead.

Daniel: The importance of Auden and Frost and Donne for you is well known. But what about Shakespeare? Has he also been an influence?

Brodsky: Well, this is just— *[Brodsky picks up a postcard he's written to someone and reads:]* "King Lear: How old art thou? Kent: Not so young, sir, to love a woman for singing. Not so old to dote on her for anything. I have years on my back 48." That's what I am.

Daniel: Shakespeare gives you material for postcards, you mean?

Brodsky: Yeah, kind of.

Daniel: Anything other than that?

Brodsky: There is plenty other. To travel and to regret all things—well, basically, how should I put it—you do with that whatever you like. How should I put it best? Of course, I can start by the melodramatic—that the fates willed me to two cultures. That's nonsense, and yet there is something to it. Somehow my only reproach to providence is that I wasn't brought up with Shakespeare so that he would be in my bloodstream. Of course, I read all I could read, yeah—indeed, all I could read. But still I never was an English-speaking child, and this is what I am sort of sad about. I wish I had that language when I was a kid. It's neither here nor there, because one is born when one is born, etc., etc. But it's sort of regrettable that I—that the cadences of my speech or of my English haven't been, how should I put it?

Daniel: Informed?

Brodsky: Informed, yeah, well, shaped by Shakespeare. I arrived to him in fairly rational or rationalistic fashion. I was reading him since I was 16 or 17, first in Russian. To answer your question more pointedly and less sentimentally, the play I like best is *Antony and Cleopatra,* and a great deal of the sonnets—

Daniel: Because?

Brodsky: Because it's a play about obsession, yeah. I also like *Cymbeline.* If you ask me because of what, I wouldn't be able to tell it. Well, (a) because it's a play about obsession, and also because of the verse in it. I like the Chronicles, and I like *Lear.* I don't know why. But if I would put a hierarchy into place, I would say *Antony and Cleopatra,* and Chronicles, because they're tremendous fun, *Cymbeline, King Lear, Tempest,* I guess. I don't really know. It sounds like hierarchy, but it's simply—

Daniel: And you mentioned the sonnets—

Brodsky: Yeah, and many of the sonnets, although Donne's sonnets I prefer, of course. But it's a different cup of tea.

Daniel: You have said that if someone must choose between a good life and good work, fake the life and produce the good work. Why? Is there any level of achievement in poetry that would merit the human wreckage in some poets' lives—like Robert Lowell's, or even Frost?

Brodsky: What troubles me with somebody like Lowell is that the quality of the work doesn't justify the wreckage to Lowell, or the magnitude of the wreckage. . . . But I think a man is capable of a very limited kind, form, and volume of damage. And it's in all of us, yeah? Well, the point is not what we can do in life. Life invites cliché. In art one can avoid it. That's why we read. Work rejects it. That's why we work. What art, in the final analysis, tells you is, don't use cliché. It's what we can do on paper. That's where distinctions should be drawn, yeah? No, I'm not trying to defend any one of them, nor do I try to implicitly say anything palatable about myself. Well, I guess I don't measure up to Frost, but I think I measure up to Lowell. And in comparison to Lowell, I think I'm a much milder guy. Life is always a disaster, one way or another. Even the successful life is a disaster. So I don't see any point in squaring it with the work. This way you are not going to ascertain anything.

Daniel: When Richard Wilbur was asked how many active, writing poets a country needed in order to be healthy, he said fifty. What do you think?

Brodsky: Well, I don't know how many it does need. Well, as many as it can get. But what's interesting is a country never can afford at any given time or at any given generation more than one great poet. It can't afford two or three.

Daniel: Why?

Brodsky: It's simply because if there's more than one, if there are two or three, then reading poetry becomes a full-time occupation, and the country doesn't want it to happen. So it elects one, appoints one, and proceeds merrily in its own despicable ways, that's all.

Daniel: A country can only cope with one, otherwise reading poetry would take over too much.

Brodsky: Yeah. Otherwise, it would have to become a different country.

Daniel: You were asked once in Dublin about what responsibility a poet might have as a healer, and you said, "If a priest can't take a stand for the Ten Commandments, at least a writer can."

Brodsky: Yeah. I said something more over there.

Daniel: Does a poet have that responsibility, even more than—

Brodsky: Of course. What's more, I think a poet can increase the list, increase the number of commandments.

Daniel: What would you add? The admonition to love your neighbor as yourself?

Brodsky: Yeah, well, also, think about the distance from which that instruction traveled to us. Suppose it's coming from stars, well, if the residence of the deity is up there. Then this idea to love your neighbor as you do thyself has something rather interesting, because, can you imagine what is the neighbor of a star? A star has for a neighbor another star.

So it means not only so much as "love they neighbor," but love something that is very distant as yourself.

Daniel: Isaiah Berlin, in his book about Tolstoy—*The Hedgehog and the Fox*—uses the ancient line, "The fox knows many things, but the hedgehog knows one big thing." Are you a fox or a hedgehog?

Brodsky: At the risk of displeasing Isaiah, I think I would refuse to answer the question within the offered framework.

Daniel: Tolstoy was both, he said.

Brodsky: Well, so was Homer, so was Shakespeare. So was Faulkner, so was Frost.

Daniel: You don't find this categorization useful?

Brodsky: Well, maybe I'm a fox, to go along with this. But I think I know something that a hedgehog does. Or perhaps I'm a foxy hedgehog.

Esthetics Is the Mother of Ethics

Grzegorz Musial and Tomislav Longinović / 1989

From *Periplus: Poetry in Translation,* edited by Daniel Weissbort and Arvind Krishna Mehrotra (Oxford University Press, 1993), 37–50. Reprinted by permission of Oxford University Press, New Delhi, India. The interview took place in 1989, when Brodsky visited the University of Iowa to give a reading of his poetry.

Grzegorz Musial: This is the magazine I'm working for, *Res Publica,* a monthly formerly published underground, but openly since 1986. It is the leading magazine for the younger generation of the independent Polish intelligentsia. Every issue is devoted to a special problem. This is the Prague Spring issue, this is the Viennese issue. Vienna is the symbol of the end of Europe, fin-de-siècle decadence. The question is whether we are faced with a new decadence of culture at the end of this century. So the question of spirituality arises, moral values. Of course there is no need for me to repeat something you know very well, but I would just like to emphasize that in the non-violent Polish revolution, the question of spirituality was a crucial one, because the Cross was placed in the middle of this revolution as a symbol of the readiness to forgive, the readiness to bear witness to the times, to suffer, to make sacrifices. So that is why I would like to ask the great poet about. . . .

Brodsky: Quit the epithet, O.K.?

Musial: O.K.

Brodsky: So, what is your question, simply . . .

Musial: What is your attitude to religion? The same question you were asked a half-hour ago at the question and answer session at the University, and which you refused to answer. You even added: "This is one of those questions one is not supposed to ask, or to answer."

Brodsky: I, I don't think, well, for one thing, in my view, religion is a highly ecclesiastical persuasion, so to speak, is a highly personal, not only personal, an intimate matter, well, and you don't talk about your intimate concerns in public. That's to begin with. Secondly, to talk about them in public very often amounts to proselytizing, and one very easily slips into that mode, which may be good for society, but for the individual is almost invariably bad, even if you bring to the audience what you consider the ultimate truth, even if you are convinced that it will be better for them. I don't believe that one should proselytize. One should simply leave these things for people to decide on their own. Faith is a matter of arrival, well, people arrive to faith, they don't receive faith, in my view. Life generates that in them, and nothing can substitute for the efforts of life. It's actually the job that is best left, and best executed, obviously, by time. In part my reserve here is also the product of living in a country, which embraces or is embraced by several creeds. It's not a homogeneous country like Poland, and to, say, carry a cross in America, it may produce rather unpleasant echoes, say, in the mind of some, Ku Klux Klan. Secondly, some people who are of different religious persuasions may feel somewhat offended. This place is very much like Alexandria in the second or third century B.C., a marketplace of religions. Well, in a sense, it is all very well for the Poles to be Catholics or new Catholics. But in so far as you are within the confines of your community, it's fine. The moment you spill over the borders you find all sorts of things, and a great number of conflicts, very bloody conflicts, in the human history, precisely were religious wars, so one should bear that in mind. Now, we can return obviously to the question of religion, but before I forget your initial point about the decadence of culture. Culture decays only for an individual. Talking about the decadence of culture is to promote a solipsistic view of reality. It's like ethics dying for a lecher. If you are a lecher, ethics is dead. If you are not and you are living next door to a lecher, your ethics are in full bloom. So I think it's a little bit premature and melodramatic to talk about the decadence of culture and, especially, the new decadence, et cetera. And I'd be terribly careful with all this. Indeed, what's happening in the culture is rather peculiar, well, culture is not an exception from other aspects of existence, though we all become now—it's my firm view—the victims of a new demographic situation in the world. There is a huge increase of people. There is an old educational structure, however, surviving intact. That is, the old educational structures in society haven't adapted themselves as yet to the new demographic realities. And for that reason, a great number of new arrivals are facing very old tenets. Speaking of culture, for instance, in the last, let's say, twenty or thirty years, in literature, very little qualitatively new has happened. However, the population of the globe has doubled in the last twenty years, so the net result of it is that the new arrivals, the new generations, are dealing, or are exposed to at best, material which is dated from their point of view. That is, the new generations don't seem to have produced something qualitatively new. So, therefore, the new generations are living off the old ties, the old cultural ties. Unquestionably, that creates either thirst or neglect on the part of the general population. In the West it's always a matter of distribution, because there is a great deal of wonderful words, even produced fairly recently, but they're not distributed. It's a capitalist country and you go by profits, and the man who tries to make a profit, as a rule, has a very limited version of what the market is like. He goes for certainties, not for the possibilities, and that's what limits him. Well, he simply does not assess the importance of these losses, and so on and so forth, and presumably very often he cannot. In the East . . . in the East, also for a variety of reasons, it has been regarded as prudent and useful to assert old values, which is quite all right, of course, and very often it serves as a kind of good for the intellectual, or cultural glue for the society, except that I don't think that this glue is terribly solid. I would think that the trouble—and now we're getting back to religion—the trouble with religion and with that sort of new Catholicism of yours is to remember where it was in the non-violence in Poland, et cetera, et cetera. The problem with those things—how shall I put it? is that in the final analysis they are ethical issues, and ethics, by itself, can't keep society together. You need something else, and I think ethics can be easily faked. There is nothing easier than to fake high principles. I think in order to make society indeed survivable, you ought to give society esthetics, because esthetics can't be assimilated. That is, a man has to become an esthetical being first. Esthetics, you see, in my view is the mother of ethics. And good though the Church may be about ethical matters, it can't produce art. To say the least, the treatment by art of ecclesiastical matters is very frequently far more interesting than the treatment of ecclesiastical issues by the Church itself. For instance, the version of afterlife given by Dante in his *Commedia Divina* is far more interesting than what you can find even in the New Testament, not to mention St. Augustine, not to mention other Fathers.

Musial: I think the definition of the standards which the Church is trying to activate in Poland now relates rather to the question of morality than . . .

Brodsky: Well, what you in the end have is somebody stressing morality, and what is the basis for that morality? Well, the basis for that is obviously the notion of God. And we've been living in a world which has been very busy negating the existence of any supreme being. Therefore, the people have to take morality or ethical principles on faith, which is fine and dandy, but it can be easily challenged. As I said, I think that esthetics is the mother of ethics, and the ethical principles emerge from the esthetics, and esthetics is tangible, it is more palpable, in a sense, than the subject of your faith.

Musial: I guess that you refer more to the moral teaching of the ancient, pre-Christian philosophers like Marcus Aurelius, for example, and to others like . . .

Brodsky: Let's not name names. What I'm trying to say is this, the human being makes his or her choice first on an esthetical rather than on an ethical basis. Take a child, take a baby, a one-year old who doesn't speak, whose experience of the world is zero. Well, mother holds up baby in her arms, the parents are having a party, and the baby smiles at somebody and cries at another. Well, in other words, he likes this person and doesn't like that person. That is, the child exercises an esthetical choice. Or his judgement is an esthetical judgement, see, but that is, esthetics do precede ethics, that's what I'm trying to say. And I think esthetics is a more sound basis to build a society, or civil society, upon, because in the end, you have to, when it comes to the moral choices—if it's based on the Church, on the faith, on the religion—then you in the end have to legislate, whereas esthetics make you a decent human being without legislation.

Musial: Where do you place the metaphysical experience then, the spiritual experience of a single person, the knowledge which goes with that kind of experience?

Brodsky: Well, I place it above the Church. The Church, or religion, is one of the many manifestations of the metaphysical potential of human beings. The reason I do this, and I have to get a little bit personal here . . . Well, I don't want to take too much of your time or of your page, but what happened to me was that my life went round such a course that I've read the Bhagavad-Gītā, the *Mahābhārata,* the Upanishads, became acquainted with them before I got acquainted with the Old and New Testaments, and it's simply because the Bible wasn't available in Russia for my generation. I came to read the Bible only at the age of twenty-two or twenty-three. So, I read those things and they provided me with terrific metaphysical horizons, indeed, horizons. With Hinduism, let's say, to put it sort of vaguely, you get indeed a sense of tremendous spiritual Himalayas, one reach after another, et cetera, et cetera. Still it was clear to me that it wasn't my cup of tea. That is, simply, well, how shall I put it, biologically not mine, because though I could practice, and loved to practice, self-negation—not self-detachment, even, but self-negation—I practiced that for purely defensive reasons, because when you're grabbed by the police, et cetera, and beaten up—well, I think that's an extraordinary hell—they can't really get you, because you think you are not your body. Still, in the end, I felt it wasn't mine, and when I read the Old and New Testaments, and I read them one after another, well, I don't separate them the way it's done, for instance, in this country and the way it's presumably done in Poland too . . .

Musial: No, not any more, it disrupts the unity . . .
Brodsky: So, one thing I immediately sensed, that while the Old Testament is more congenial to me, partly because I'm a Jew—but it's not because I'm a Jew, it's simply a frame of mind, certain experiences—still I remembered the metaphysical horizons offered to me by Hinduism, and I realized that, metaphysically speaking, the Old Testament, not to mention the New Testament, is inferior to the metaphysical possibilities offered to you by Hinduism. This is why I always find myself in a difficult situation when somebody starts to talk about this or that particular church, because I think human metaphysical potential very seldom—well, that's my conviction—very seldom is fully exercised by this or that particular creed.

Musial: On a certain level of religious experience one comes to a similar pattern of moral values. When you go through the deep experience of Catholicism, for example, you go through the same steps of metaphysical experience, exactly seven steps—a seven-step mountain Thomas Merton called it—as you do in Buddhism, right . . .
Tomislav Longinović: Eight in Buddhism.

Musial: Eight in Buddhism.
Brodsky: Good to see you gentlemen counting. But I'm more interested, well, how shall I put it, in matters of principle here. I spoke not so long ago about that to Milosz, and in literature you very often, a writer very often finds himself in sort of a double bind. That is, partly as a writer, as an active writer—well, writing, editing, correcting, correlating the things that he's saying to more or less the reality of society, et cetera, or trying to influence the society—he finds himself squarely in the Western tradition, in the tradition of the control of the will, in fact, a personal lyricism, imposing that upon the society or altering the society, whereas at the same time, simply by virtue of his occupation, he finds himself very much in the Eastern bind as well, in the self-negating position. So, one way or another, a writer is a cross between those two, and in fact, the value of literature, the value of poetry in particular, for a reader, for a general population, is precisely this, precisely that breech or that fusion of the self-negation and will. That's why literature is so, in a

sense, attractive to us, or poetry in particular. So, I'm not interested in the seven types or eight types of ambiguity, because there are more than that.

Musial: André Malraux said that the twenty-first century will be either spiritual or it will not be at all.

Brodsky: It may be . . . Well, Malraux said so many things. The French are very fond of making up reasons, ever since La Rochefoucauld, and presumably before, I don't know. Milosz thinks that we are entering, the world is entering an entirely nihilistic stage. I am not so sure of that, although on the face of it, reality doesn't conform to any ethical standards, as we see it. It's getting rather paganistic. I think what may emerge—and this is one of my greatest apprehensions—what may emerge is a tremendous religious strife, not exactly religious, between the Moslem world and the world that is vaguely Christian. The latter won't be able to defend itself, the former will be terribly assertive. It's simply for the numerical reasons, for pure demographic reasons, that I perceive the possibility for such a strife. I am not a sage, I am not a prophet, I can't presume to say what the twenty-first century is going to be like. To say the least, I am not even interested in what the twenty-first century is going to be like. Well, I am not going to be there, for one thing, so why should I bother . . . And it was easier for Malraux, it was clear that he wouldn't be there, so it was easy to fantasize . . . The foreseeable future, that is, foreseeable by me, which again can be terribly erroneous, is precisely the conflict of the spirit of tolerance with the spirit of intolerance, and there are all sorts of attempts to resolve that conflict now. The pragmatists try to suggest that there is some equivalence between these principles. I don't believe that for a minute. I think that the Moslem notion of universal order should be squashed and put out of existence. We are, after all, six centuries older than the Moslems spiritually. So, I think we have a right to say what's right and what's wrong.

Musial: I'd like to come back to the idea of my last question—I don't want to take too much of your time. On a more personal level, while listening yesterday to your poetry reading, I was very moved by the way you read. I felt it was more like a moan, more like a cry . . .

Brodsky: It wasn't a moan, it wasn't a cry, it simply has to do with the prosodic nature of the Russian language.

Musial: Which I understand, but with the exception of what you do with your reading.

Brodsky: Well, maybe . . .

Musial: Rhythmically, it's very . . .

Brodsky: But it has to do with the meters presented, with the prosodic aspects of the poem, of this or that particular poem. But all literature that we have in Christendom—and Russian literature belongs in Christendom squarely, poetry especially—is a spinoff of the liturgical services, of the liturgical practices, of the hymns, if you will. So, there is this tremendous carryover of those, and poetry is an art of assertion, it's not an art of self-effacement. And the difference, of course, between the English delivery, delivery of that stuff in English, and the delivery of that stuff in Russian is simply a cultural difference now, because it's considered *mauvais-ton* in the English tradition to be assertive. It all kind of started about a century ago and so forth. *Bon-ton* means to be self-effacing. But I think it's a little bit ridiculous, because poetry is not an art of self-effacement. If you want to be self-effacing, you can take the next logical step and completely shut up.

Musial: I see.

Longinović: I think one question which is connected to Russian religious philosophers at the end of the nineteenth and the beginning of the twentieth century—Shestov, Solovyov, Berdyaev, who thought that we were in a way entering the new Middle Ages with the Age of Communism—do you see any connection with the apparent dissolution of monolithic communism?

Brodsky: Well, you see . . . how funny . . . in a sense, they were right, because—well, Shestov never said anything of the sort, it was Berdyaev's idea—in a sense they were right, merely because looking into the future they couldn't see anything but darkness. But like all those prophesies, especially Berdyaev's prophesies, well, it's basically easy to make a prophesy because we have so few options in general. Now it's seventy years later and I don't think it's going to be the Middle Ages. I don't want to sound overly optimistic, but communism, well, it's curtains for communism, for any sort of ideological society, in my view, at least in Eastern Europe. In the Orient, perhaps, and in Latin American countries, for perhaps the next thirty or forty years, and perhaps in the Far East, there is some possibility of some ideological society. But for the Europeans, it's over, so I think the societies now are going to evolve along a more pragmatic line, which is also nothing to cheer about. But one thing about a pragmatical principle is that it considers all the options and, therefore, it doesn't rule out the religious or metaphysical option, or won't legislate against those options. In that respect, we should not forget about one thing. We shouldn't say that the religious man is better than an atheist, though perhaps in our hearts and in our minds he is, and it's a more interesting, infinitely more interesting existence. But I think the root of all evil is when one person says, "I'm better than the other."

Musial: You mentioned the importance of Milosz in your life, the influence he had on you. Could you say something more about this? I guess it's a kind of spiritual experience of the sort we were talking about before.

Brodsky: Milosz is simply, well, a tremendous presence. I am fortunate to know him personally. First of all, I've translated some of his poems. Secondly, he helped me enormously. He wrote me one letter, a very short letter exactly at the moment of my arrival in the United States, which indeed took instant care of a great many insecurities that I harbored at that time. He said in that letter, among other things—he was talking about translation, et cetera, et cetera—he said I understand that now you are worried about being capable of continuing to write in a foreign country, et cetera. He said, if you stop, if you fail, there's nothing wrong about that. I've seen that happening to people. It's perfectly human, et cetera. Well, it's perfectly normal for a human being to be able only to write within his own walls, or in his context. However, he said, should that happen, it will show your real value, that you are good on the domestic. There's nothing wrong with that. But when you read that sort of thing—no! And for that reason, I'm awfully grateful to him. But aside from that, I am envious, well, I have a terrible envy of him having lived such a long life. I wish I were there in the twenties and the thirties. I wish I had the same experiences. But ultimately I simply admire his mind. It's a Manichean bent. We make war about this and that, but there is nothing better than an argument with Milosz, it enriches you enormously. It's not only cultural differences or cultural material, baggage that he carries, it's the methodology of his mind, the entire predictability of it. It's great to talk with him about esthetical matters, about, for instance, matters of absurdity, of the absurd in literature, better than to talk about ethics, which is a much more stale discourse in the end.

Musial: Have you ever had another deep experience with Polish literature or a Polish writer?

Brodsky: Norwid.

Musial: Norwid, I see. And contemporary writers, Gombrowicz, for example, who's had a tremendous influence on the young Polish intelligentsia . . .

Brodsky: That's understandable, but I think for me, Gombrowicz, much though I like *Ferdydurke,* and what's the other one? I forgot.

Musial: —*Cosmos, Pornographia.*

Brodsky: Much though I like those, I still think Gombrowicz, by the virtue of circumstance—not virtue, by the vice of circumstance—has come to make a big deal out of himself, for himself. That is, he was indeed a literary person, that is, temperamentally, he is quite the opposite, well, of me personally, because I don't write that much. I don't make literature out of everything. I used to, not exactly pride myself on it, but I used to regard myself more as a gentleman who occasionally occupies himself with composing a poem, or writing a piece, whereas Gombrowicz was indeed, well, his life was literature, and also he took himself and the unpleasantries [sic] of his existence a bit too seriously, in my view. But that's my view, that in no sense detracts from Gombrowicz. It's simply my personal view of him. Well, now, for other Polish writers, I think the greatest boost I ever got in my life was from Norwid. I translated Norwid into Russian. Not much, about six or seven lengthy poems, and I don't think there is any greater poem in any language that I know of than "Bema Pamięci Raport Załobny" [A Mournful Report in General Bem's Memory]. I happen to know that by heart, too, but that's one. It is simply the vector of tragedy in his voice. To me, he is a more important poet than Baudelaire, of the same period, a far greater thing, though I don't really care for his long dramatic poems. But the poems, some of them, are absolutely remarkable, terribly far ahead of his time. I don't place a great deal of value on that sort of thing, but it's stunning to find this sensibility in the nineteenth century. You know, in Rome on the Via Sistina there are two houses, they are door to door, and there are two memorial plaques. On one it says here from such and such—and it's the same years practically, well, with one or two years' difference, they're almost overlapping—here lived Norwid, and the next door, here lived Nikolai Gogol.

Musial: What do you think of Herbert's poetry?

Brodsky: Well, I translated Herbert. I like Zbigniew enormously, and you are tremendously fortunate in Poland to have in one century, or rather in one half-century, poets of this magnitude, Milosz and Herbert. I would throw in for good measure also Szymborska, and not Szymborska entirely, but she has tremendous poetry, tremendous poems. I wish I were assigned to make a selection of her poems. But speaking of Herbert and Milosz, I can't really say one is better than the other, et cetera, because at those heights there is no hierarchy. However, in a sense, because Milosz's operation is huge, you can make the argument that Milosz includes Herbert's idiom, whereas Herbert doesn't include Milosz's. But there is no hierarchy at those heights, it's not even a qualifier here. I would say Milosz is a greater metaphysical event for me than Herbert, although I wouldn't like to live solely with Milosz's poetry and without Herbert's. It in fact makes me appreciate Milosz more and the presence of Milosz makes me appreciate Herbert more. He is in the final analysis, Zbigniew, a great esthetician, a great esthete. He is exactly the man who made his preferences, his choices, on the basis of taste, not on the basis of morality, on this and that. He said something to that effect himself.

Musial: He wrote a poem, the famous one, "The Power of Taste."

Brodsky: Yes, "The Power of Taste." I don't follow Polish poetry right now very closely, and I don't see now . . . Well, I used to, but for the last ten or fifteen years I've been somewhat out of touch . . . I don't really know who in general is what. I don't know who are the followers of Milosz, let's say. But at least I know who is the follower of Herbert. Zagajewski seems to me to represent a development of Herbert's idiom in many ways. He's an absolutely remarkable poet, and the most important discovery for me in Polish poetry for the last ten or fifteen years, and in fact, we're friends with Adam, and it's one of the better friendships that I've had in my life. That's all.

Musial: Thank you.

Joseph Brodsky: The Poet and the Poem

Grace Cavalieri / 1991

From *American Poetry Review,* 21 (November/December 1992), 51–54. Reprinted by permission of *American Poetry Review.* This program was recorded at the Library of Congress, October 1991, and was originally broadcast on *The Poet and the Poem,* public radio station WPFW-FM in Washington, D.C. Poet Grace Cavalieri produces and hosts the program. The series is distributed nationally by the Pacifica Program Service.

Joseph Brodsky is a native of Leningrad, now St. Petersburg. His poetry has been published in twelve languages. Joseph Brodsky has lived in the U.S. since 1972 when he was exiled from the Soviet Union. He is the recipient of the John D. and Catherine T. MacArthur Foundation Award. His essay collection, *Less Than One,* was awarded the 1986 National Book Award for criticism. Winner of the 1987 Nobel Prize for Literature, he is one of only five Americans to win the award during the past thirty years.

Grace Cavalieri: Your initial address at the Library of Congress (October 1991) was also published in *The New Republic.* Here you present yourself as an activist for poetry, an enthusiast . . . "The poetry consultant as the poetry activist." Is that how you wanted to be received?

Joseph Brodsky: It's fine if people feel that way but the main point is simply I honestly regard that this job, being paid by the Library of Congress in Washington, makes me the property of the public for this year. It is in the spirit of the public servant. My concern is the public's access to poetry which I find very limited, idiotically so, and I would like to change it if I can.

GC: Do you think you can?

Brodsky: It takes more than a speech preaching to the converts here at the Library. It takes publishers, entrepreneurs to throw money into the idea.

GC: In addition to wanting more poetry published and distributed you bring a new view to American poetry. Would you tell us some of your feelings about this country's poetry?

Brodsky: Basically, I think it's remarkable poetry, a tremendous poetry this nation has and doesn't touch. To my ear and my eye it's a nonstop sermon of human autonomy, of individualism, self-reliance. It's a poetry hard to escape. It has its own faults and vices but it doesn't suffer malaise typical of the poetry of the continent—Europe—self aggrandisement on the part of the poem, where the poet regards himself as a public figure . . . all those Promethean affinities and "grand-standing." Those things are alien to the generous spirit of American poetry, at least for the last century. The distinction of an American poet from his European counterpart, in the final analysis, is a poetry of responsibility . . . a responsibility for his fellow human beings. This is a narrowing of the ethical application of poetry. What a European does—French, German, Italian, Russian—is move his blamethirsty finger. It oscillates 360 degrees all the time, trying to indicate who is at fault, trying to explain his and society's ills. An American, if his finger points at anything, it's most likely himself or the existential order of things.

GC: And you call this a sermon of resilience?
Brodsky: Yes if you like.

GC: You were exiled from Russia in 1972, having previously been sentenced to five years hard labor at an Arctic labor camp. Did the efforts of Russian intellectuals and writers win your release?
Brodsky: Not only those. People abroad too. One person who interceded in my behalf was the father of the H-bomb, Edward Teller.

GC: And you then accepted the invitation to come to this country?
Brodsky: I was put on a plane going only in one direction with no return ticket and a friend of mine from the University of Michigan, now dead (Carl Proffer), a great man, a professor of Slavic languages, met me and asked how I would like to come to the University of Michigan as poet in residence.

GC: That young man, all those years ago . . .
Brodsky: Almost twenty.

GC: He was such a brave stubborn independent man. Do you feel that he's still with you? Do you know that man now?
Brodsky: He is still within me. Those years in Michigan are the only childhood I ever had.

GC: In reading the transcripts of your trial I was struck with how unafraid you sounded. How did you feel?
Brodsky: I don't really remember. I don't think I was afraid. No. I knew

who runs the show. I knew I was on the receiving end so it didn't really matter. I knew what it would boil down to.

GC: I was wondering when watching the Thomas hearings recently how you might feel while watching them . . . the way they were doing business . . . having been on the hot seat once yourself, and watching something so vastly American and unwieldy as those hearings. In a way it could only happen in America.

Brodsky: I felt very upset with a bad taste in my mouth. It wasn't really a court case. I felt it was utterly ridiculous and people often find themselves in the predicament choosing between two things where neither one is good.

GC: I would have liked to see a poet as questioner. We would have gotten a different approach.

Brodsky: I wouldn't question Judge Thomas. I know enough about the transaction between the opposite sexes not to question him on that score.

GC: Do you write poetry primarily in English now?

Brodsky: Poetry I write primarily in Russian. Essays, and lectures, blurbs, reference letters, reviews, I write in English.

GC: How much are we missing? We see and hear English translations of your poems and some are called brilliant in any language.

Brodsky: You can't say you are missing much. You can't say you are missing the prosody of another language. You can't miss the acoustics of another language. That of course you can't have and you're not missing it. You can't miss something that you don't know.

GC: We can get a good lyrical poem anyway that is matchless.

Brodsky: That's what it is if it works in English. You have to be a judge of solely how it is in English.

GC: We shouldn't feel we're getting only ninety percent of something which is absolute.

Brodsky: You get a poem in English, good or bad. You can't fantasize about what it'd be like in the original.

GC: I was watching you recite recently without looking at the page. Can you recite every one of your poems in Russian?

Brodsky: By heart? I don't think so. Not any longer. Until I was forty I knew them all.

GC: Do the translations usually please you.

Brodsky: It's a very peculiar sensation when you receive the translation of your own poem. On one hand you're terribly pleased that something you've done will interest the English. The initial sentiment is the pleasure. As you start to read it turns very quickly into horror and it's a tremendously interesting mixture of those two sentiments. There is no name for that in Russian or in English. It's a highly schizophrenic sensation.

GC: There isn't a word for joy and terror.

Brodsky: Jerror.

GC: Your devotion to the craft as well as to the spirit of poetry is well known. You're famous for your reverence to the forms, the metrics, the structure. Since you are a man who champions individualism, I have to ask whether you believe there could be some poet's experience which would not fall within a formalistic structure?

Brodsky: Easily so. I'm not suggesting a straitjacket. I'm just thinking that when the poet resorts to a certain medium, whether it is metric verse or free verse, he should be at least aware of those differences. Poetry is of a very rich past. There's a great deal of family history to it. For instance when one resorts to free verse, one has to remember that everything prefaced with the epithet "free" means "free from what." Freedom is not an autonomous condition. It is a determined condition. In physics it's determined by the statics. In politics it's conditioned by slavery, and what kind of freedom can you talk of in transcendental terms. Free means not free but liberated, "free from"—free from strict meters, so essentially it's a reaction to strict meters. Free verse. An individual who just resorts to it has to, in a miniature manner, go through the history of verse in English before liberating himself from it. Other than this you start with a borrowed medium—how should I say this—a medium that is *more* not yours than are strict meters.

GC: Do you teach creative writing?

Brodsky: No, I don't. I teach creative reading. My course at Mt. Holyoke is described as teaching "the subject matter and strategy in lyric poetry"—What's the poet after; How's he doing it; What's he up to?

GC: Reviewers attribute all sorts of things to you regarding craft . . . moral, social forces embodied in craft.

Brodsky: All those things are there.

GC: I am also very interested in your plays and I wonder if you think they're getting enough notice.

Brodsky: I don't think they are but I never expected them to get much.

GC: *Marbles* was produced just once?

Brodsky: Once or twice here, but all over the place in Europe.

GC: This reminds me of Howard Nemerov. His dramatic literature is among the best written in English, and it scarcely could get produced. When I read *Marbles* I thought I saw another side to your writing.

Brodsky: It's actually the same.

GC: The themes are but you get a little wilder on the stage.

Brodsky: It's very natural for someone who writes poetry to write plays. A poem, and especially the poem saddled with all those formal hurdles of rhyme and meters, is essentially a form of dialogue. Every monologue is a form of a dialogue because of the voices in it. What is "To be or not to be" but a dialogue. It's a question and answer. It's dialectical form, and, small wonder that a poet one day gets to write plays.

GC: Do you like the theater?

Brodsky: To read but not to go to. Often it's been an embarrassment.

GC: You start with an instinctive knowledge of the elements of theater—the containment of the prisoners within a cell *(Marbles)*.

Brodsky: The poet in a poem is a stage designer, a director, the characters, the body instructor, etcetera. Take for instance "Home Burial" by Robert Frost. It's a perfect little drama. It's also a ballet piece. Even Alfred Hitchcock would like it. There's a banister which plays a substantial role.

GC: And we should mention the compression of action of stage. The poem itself is compression of space. The word "marbles" brings forth many meanings—the colloquialism, the game, the actual statues on stage, all those. What was the word in Russian which carried all those nuances?

Brodsky: The same. Marbles. But it carries less nuance in Russian than in English.

GC: You have in your poetry humor, irony, wryness. But in theater you do some high jinx. I think it's much more spirited and you have a chance to break free a little bit more.

Brodsky: Possibly, but I don't think I'm freer in prose than in a poem.

GC: When you heard that you won the Nobel Prize for Literature that must have been quite a moment for you.

Brodsky: It was funny. I was in the company of John Le Carré in a restaurant in London and a friend ran in with the news.

GC: Your acceptance speech is one of the finest essays you have ever written. I thought it must have been a pleasure to be able to write that—to be given the opportunity—the chance to say everything that you stand for. It might even have been easy for you to write, because you had this one opportunity to say everything you believe and to tell who you are. What do you think is the one thing which resonates from that speech?

Brodsky: I don't really know what does. I would advise to a writer to prepare it beforehand for when it happens, when you are awarded the Nobel Prize, you have only a month to write it and all of a sudden you don't know what to say and you're under the gun. I remember I was rushing to write it and it was darn difficult. I was never more nervous than then.

GC: So you think all writers should write an acceptance speech for the Nobel prize just to have on hand?

Brodsky: Yes, just in case.

GC: Well it isn't a bad idea to have a credo.

Brodsky: To begin with.

GC: Even if no one wants it.

Brodsky: You can use it for yourself.

GC: Are you pleased with the acceptance speech?

Brodsky: Yes, I'm pleased with several points.

GC: You delivered it in Russian.

Brodsky: At the last moment. As I entered the room (I made up my mind). I had two versions of it, the Russian and the English.

GC: And at the last moment you felt more comfortable with the Russian. It was then published in *The New Republic.* We should reprint that one.

Brodsky: That would be nice because it's a good speech.

GC: What it says is that poetry is the only thing that counts.

Brodsky: Perhaps the most valuable remark made there is that there are two or three modes of cognition available to our species: analysis, intuition, and the one which was available to the biblical prophets—revelation. The virtue of poetry is that in the process of composition, you combine all three, if you're lucky. At least you combine two: analysis and intuition—a synthesis. The net result may be revelatory. If you take a rough look at the globe and who inhabits is . . . in the West we have the emphasis on the Russian now, on "reason." A premium is being put on it. And the East has reflexiveness and intuition. A poet, by default, is the healthiest possible specimen—a fusion of those two.

GC: Do you know Václav Havel?
Brodsky: No, I've seen him twice.

GC: Did you speak?
Brodsky: No. It took three quarters of a century for the Czech Declaration of Independence to wind up in the right hands.

GC: Have you received an invitation to return to your native land?
Brodsky: No I have not. Who cares?

GC: You haven't been back since '72. Last summer I concentrated on Russian history. But somewhere I stopped taking notes on current affairs simply from fatigue. You must feel that way.
Brodsky: For the first time I'm somewhat proud for the country I was born in. It finds itself in a tremendous predicament. Nobody knows what to do. Nobody knows how to live. Nobody knows what steps to take and, yet, for the first time in its long history, it doesn't act radically facing this confusion. In a sense that confusion reflects the human predicament par excellence, simply because nobody knows how to live. All forms of social and individual organization, like the political system, are simply ways to shield oneself and the nation from that confusion. And for the moment they don't shield themselves . . . their faces. Thomas Hardy once said the recipe for good poetry, I paraphrase badly here, "One should exact the full look at the worst," and that's what takes place right now in Russia so maybe the results will be attractive. I'm not terribly hopeful here because there are 300 million people. No matter what you do, there are no happy solutions for that amount of people. One should be cognizant of that. If I were at the helm, near the radio, near the mike, that's what I'd tell people. It's not going to be glorious for everybody. Freedom is no picnic. It's a great deal of responsibility, a great deal of choices and a human being is bound to make some wrong choices sooner or later. So it's going to be quite difficult for quite a number of people. The entire nation, at this point, needs something like vocational training be-

cause lots of people have been put in jobs wrong for them. They relied on the state—on the paternalistic structure. There is terrific inertia from always relying on somebody and not taking individual responsibility.

GC: How will the Russian poet reflect this?

Brodsky: I don't think we can say art depends on history or social reality. It's a Marxist idea, or Aristotelian I think, that art reflects life. Art has its own dynamics . . . its own history . . . it's own velocity . . . its own incomprehensible target. In a way it's like a runaway train upon which society boards or doesn't board. And when it boards, it doesn't know which direction it'll go. The train started a long time before. Literature (poetry) is older than any existing political system, any system of the government or any social organization. A song was there before any story. And so basically it evolves, develops, and continues along its own lines sometimes overlapping with the history of the state or the society or the reality of society—sometimes not. One shouldn't subordinate art to life. Art is different from life in that it doesn't resort to repetition and to the cliché, whereas life always resorts to clichés in spite of itself because it always has to start from scratch.

GC: One remark you've made about the Augustan era, the Roman time on earth, is that the only record we have of human sensibilities is from the poets.

Brodsky: Yes I think the poets gave us quite a lot more than anything else, any other record.

GC: What do you think the future will know about us from what we say?

Brodsky: It will know pretty little about ourselves. It will judge us by what literature we leave.

GC: By what literature remains.

Brodsky: A millennium hence . . . I don't know if people will still exist but if they're interested in the twentieth century they'll read the books written in the twentieth century.

GC: You've taught at the University of Michigan. You've been a visiting professor at Queens College, Smith College, Columbia University, and Cambridge. You've been awarded honorary doctorate degrees from Williams College and Yale University.

Brodsky: And some other places . . . The University of Rochester, also from Oxford, England, among others. We should just mention those—not that I'm shaking my medals.

GC: At each time do you make a speech?
Brodsky: Regretfully, yes.

GC: Should they be collected in a book?
Brodsky: Well, no.

GC: Does Joseph Brodsky have any poetry that is not published?
Brodsky: Plenty.

GC: Is there anyone who'd reject a poem?
Brodsky: Yes, that's healthy. Nothing changes that way.

GC: How do you write your poems? Do your poems gather themselves? Do you walk along collecting images until the time to release?
Brodsky: I don't deliberately or knowingly collect things. The poem always starts with the first line, or a line anyway, and from that you go. It's something like a hum to which you try to fit the line and then it proceeds that way.

GC: Mystics say the very beginning of the human species came through sound, the vibration of sound.
Brodsky: That's nice of them.

GC: With the poet as well. With you the vibration is first?
Brodsky: Some tune . . . some tune which has oddly enough some psychological weight, a diminution and you try to fit something into that. The only organic thing that is pertinent to poetry, is like the way you live. You exist and gradually you arrive at a certain tune in your head. The lines develop like wrinkles, like grey hair. They are wrinkles in a sense, especially with what goes into composing . . . That gives you wrinkles! It's in a sense the work of time upon the man. It chisels you or disfigures you or makes your skin parched.

GC: So it's eroding you and you carry it around?
Brodsky: You do with sentences what time has done to you.

GC: In the formation of it, are you carrying parts of the stanzas around with you also?
Brodsky: Of course you do, yes.

GC: And the mechanics . . . You use longhand first?
Brodsky: Yes, I don't have a computer. Then I type with one finger. Computers have no use to me.

GC: Which finger.

Brodsky: Index finger, right hand.

GC: I saw a poem of yours in *The New Yorker* last January and I wondered how many poems you get published a year in periodicals.

Brodsky: It varies. For the last year I published about ten.

GC: Ten new poems in one year. That's quite a bit.

Brodsky: Yes if you're lucky. I spent half the year in Ireland and published several poems in *TLS (The Times Literary Supplement).*

GC: It is said that when you were in a work camp at the time of Eliot's death you were able to write your verse to him in twenty-four hours.

Brodsky: Two or three days, yes.

GC: So you are extremely focused but he also meant a lot to you. That helps.

Brodsky: It did. Also, extraordinarily, under the circumstances, I had a form or shape for that poem. I borrowed from W.H. Auden's poem, "In Memory of Yeats." I made some changes. I made the first part a slightly different rhyme scheme.

GC: And you learned English by translating poetry?

Brodsky: By reading it and translating it.

GC: Line by line by line. How do you think your English is now?

Brodsky: I don't know. Sometimes even I am satisfied but often I don't know what to say. I am at a loss.

GC: Don't you think we are in any language?

Brodsky: With a mongrel like me it's perhaps more frequent.

GC: Do you think and dream in both languages?

Brodsky: People think in thoughts and dream in dreams. They collate these in language. When we grow up we become fluent in this and for that reason we believe that we think in languages.

GC: Do you ever use material from your dreams?

Brodsky: Frequently. Several times I composed poems when I just woke up. W.H. Auden suggested to keep a pad with a pencil to jot a few tings, but mine came out as jibberish.

GC: Dreams are not always useful except for the feeling load.

Brodsky: The subconscious is a source but a composition is a highly rational enterprise in many ways. You may think of the dream as inspiration but then you type it down and then you begin to correct it. You replace the words. It is an invasion of the reasoning. Poetry is an incurably semantic art and you can't really help it. You have to make sense. That's what distinguishes it from other arts . . . from all other arts.

GC: You call it the highest point of human locution.

Brodsky: That's what it is.

Joseph Brodsky: An Interview

Mike Hammer and Christina Daub / 1991

From *Plum Review* (Spring/Summer 1992), 45–61. Reprinted by permission of Mike Hammer and Christina Daub.

Joseph Brodsky was born in Leningrad in 1940 and came to the United States in 1972, an involuntary exile from the Soviet Union. Since then, he has published in English several volumes of poetry and a collection of essays, *Less Than One,* which won the National Book Critics Circle Award in 1986; his five volumes of poetry in Russian are unavailable in his native country, although he is widely regarded as its preeminent living poet. Mr. Brodsky was awarded the Nobel Prize for Literature in 1987. He currently serves as the poet laureate of the United States.

This interview was conducted 31 October 1991 by M. Hammer and Christina Daub at the Library of Congress.

Q: You began writing at 18 or 19. Could you tell us the story behind this beginning?

A: There's no story behind it. One day you find yourself scribbling . . . writing some poems. I guess I read some, and I thought it could be done better. It was many years ago. I was working with geological teams in the summer—field work—and I saw a collection of poems by somebody who was a geologist, and I simply thought they were nice poems, but that something more interesting could be done about it. That was more or less the topical thing.

Q: What has sustained your writing?

A: I don't really know (laughs). Well, it was interesting to write poems, more interesting than doing anything else. Composition is a tremendous mental exhilarator. You make connections that you didn't expect to make, to say the least, and once you've done that, once the connections have been made, you get hooked. You want to do more.

Q: Are your feelings about writing poetry different than your feelings about writing essays or plays?

A: Oh, yes. I hate prose. Plays are not that different, because the nature of a poem is in a sense a discourse, a dialogue, even with yourself as it were.

It's a dialogue with yourself. The fact that poets frequently find themselves writing for the theater is natural, because the nature of a poem as a medium is dialectical. If you think about how poetry started, you think of Augustan poets, like Romans, they all went through rhetorical training. They were all trained in the argument. The very phenomenon of the couplet . . . so it's a small wonder that one lapses into writing plays. As for prose, I don't like it very much. Not at all, in fact. It's mostly out of necessity. It's prostituting yourself.

Q: There is a line in one of your essays: "The school is a factory is a poem is a prison is academia is boredom, with flashes of panic." Is this biographical?

A: What do you think it is? I invented it. Essentially, it's one and the same thing. No matter what you do, you are in that state.

Q: The state of boredom and panic?

A: A fusion of boredom and panic, yes. A mixture of boredom and panic. Don't you think it is?

Q: So you're bored and panic-stricken at the same time?

A: Uh-huh.

Q: Now, as we speak?

A: Even now as I speak.

Q: Is it different since you came to the U.S.?

A: It's no different, no. Not at all, because I never taught in Russia, you see. It's a continuum.

Q: Teaching contributes to . . .

A: Of course. One thing is another, basically. Well, that is . . . well . . . God, it's so simple. You barely can distinguish a certain trait of your character from another.

Q: And there's nothing that can change that?

A: Not much does, no. Well, you may deviate here or there, but it's a temporary diversion. Those characteristics are the most frequent, the most permanent.

Q: When you write, are you in a state of panic?

A: No.

Q: Are you in a state of boredom?

A: No. I don't know what state I'm in. I don't really know. I'm not really self-aware that way. At least I know that I'm doing something that interests me.

Q: In an interview you gave a few years ago, you said you consider yourself an American citizen but a Russian poet.

A: Yes.

Q: How do you feel, as a Russian poet, being the U.S. poet laureate?

A: Well, there's not that much of a collision over it in the minds of quite a number of people. I didn't want to take this job. I argued against it. The people upstairs suggested it. I said you must be out of your gourds, you don't need a person with an accent here. They said, they don't have a problem with that at all. Well, I said, I do. There were additional extenuating circumstances which made me say yes. And I don't feel at tremendous odds, in fact I feel quite proud. There's an element of pride here for me, if only because, how should I put it to you, this is something which wasn't supposed to happen, which wasn't in the cards at all, and that certainly is a pleasure. I like when unpredictable things take place. Well, I belong to a generation of Russians, maybe "generation" is too rich here, maybe I should narrow it a little bit, for whom, for a variety of reasons, partly as a reaction against the communal realm, the literature was the main art. We embraced the notion of individualism, of human autonomy, the notion that you are on your own in a big way. In that respect, we were more American than Americans themselves appeared to be. Well, that's what I discovered. We are the generation that were brought up on a diet of Faulkner and Frost.

Q: Which were accessible in Russia?

A: Yes, in translation. Some were satisfied by the translation. Some of us took a further step to learn English, for that express purpose, to read that stuff in the original. So, it's only natural for me to do this, that is, subjectively it's somewhat natural. I wish I didn't have an accent, but even that doesn't disturb me much.

Q: Were you able to read poetry while you were in prison?

A: No, but write it, yes. I composed in my mind, because you couldn't have paper or books. A prison is a prison. Your cot and your bars, floor, ceiling four walls, the door.

Q: Were there other poets in the same prison?
A: No, no it was an average prison. It wasn't a prison for poets. It was a prison for prisoners.

Q: Were you in there for what you had written?
A: Well, I suppose so. I don't really like talking about all this. It's really like dropping names. It's melodramatic stuff. All my life, I was trying to avoid melodrama. I've been to prison three times, mental institutions twice, but it didn't in any way influence what I write. It has no bearings. It's part of my biography, but biography has absolutely nothing to do with literature, or very little. We can spend twenty-five years in the camps or survive a Hiroshima bombing, and there's not a single line. So biography has very little consequence.

Q: What about the need to survive?
A: I don't really know about that. I never rationalized about it. You either survive or don't. And you don't call it survival. You act like a dog. You sort of sniff to see if it's dangerous or not, and some other dog's pee is there by the post, so you realize it's not your post.

Q: Do you ever intend to go back to Russia?
A: I don't know. I may, I may not. You can't return to a childhood. You can't step twice into the same little river. It would be like returning to your first wife, about as rewarding as that. Not that I had a first wife . . . (laughs)

Q: How did your own poetry first appear in Russia?
A: It wasn't published underground, because the underground never had presses. What the underground had was the typewriter. You make five or six copies and give it to somebody, and he makes more, this kind of thing.

Q: Is it a small readership?
A: It had a substantial readership, because, I think . . . the net amount of copies . . . it's impossible to estimate. Nobody will ever know that for a fact. There are no statistics, and they kept no records, because of the nature of the venture. A poet would have 20, 30, 40 thousand bundles of his work circulating.

Q: Just from the typewriter?
A: Yes, sometimes within one city, you'd walk into somebody's apartment, and he or she would show you a bundle of your work.

Q: We always hear stories of the great audiences for poetry in Russia, filling stadiums. Is that true?

A: Well, it used to be the case. But it's not a great audience, nor for that matter is what the audience gets that great. I don't believe in that at all. I don't believe in performances. In fact, I don't believe in readings, so much, because it's very hard as a rule to follow what the poet delivers from the pulpit. What you have to do is to read from the paper, from the page. Although there are some people who manage to sway you and to make an impression upon your life with the manner of their delivery.

There used to be those stadium gatherings, etcetera, mainly in two cities of the empire, and they would be quite infrequent. Whereas, take this country: there are, of course, fifty states, an abundance of schools and poetry societies, and this and that, that sponsor readings every given night in the territory of each state. You have a bunch of readings. Per capita, I think the exposure to poetry in the United States is comparable to what you've got in Russia. Not to mention medium quality, which is somewhat high in these parts.

Q: Don't you think poets are treated differently in Russia?

A: Both yes and no. There are lots of poets who toil in utter obscurity. There's a handful who caught or who catch the public eye or the state's eye or the watchdog's eye. It always happens simultaneously. You can be treated nastily. You can be treated with a great deal of authority. The public's view of a poet in Russia is a somewhat exalted view. It's partly because of the absence in Russia of history. Very often the literature may involve a critic of society and, as it were, society's conscience. Well, in these parts, you don't have that sort of thing. It's not incumbent upon a poet, because there are institutions, the church, the agendas, there are all those people. In Russia, the poet will take it upon himself to perform all these jobs, which is a good thing for a poet, but also it is dangerous, because it can hit you on the head. Very often a critic of some ill or evil assumes by criticizing something that he is good himself. So this is a tremendous misconception that is very radical in this profession, and I don't think it's healthy. There's also vanity involved when the nation looks up to you. Soon you may forget your job. Your job is to write well.

Q: Do you think the situation in poetry is better now in Russia?

A: Well, I think it's far better, because for the first time in history, the poets can be left alone there. They are not, anymore, the public spokesmen.

They are not going to publish an extraordinary number of copies. They are not going to enjoy stadiums any longer. Russia enters the twentieth century. It's the end of the Victorian era. Now it's going to be like every other place. My colleagues in Russia complain to me that nobody reads them any longer. Nobody reads poetry any longer. Everybody reads journalism, which is good, actually. You have to get off the high horse. That is, not only by fire or by water, you have to be baptized by vulgarity of the human heart, of the masses.

Q: What is vulgarity of the human heart?

A: Vulgarity of the human heart is when you think that you are better than somebody else. That's the root of all evil.

Q: How do you see your position as poet laureate now?

A: Well, I don't really know. I don't see it in any clear-cut manner. I simply regard myself as a public servant. What I regard as my responsibility here is to try to enlarge the audience for poetry in this country. I try to do all I can. I can't do much. I can write an article, make a speech, etcetera, etcetera.

Q: Do you propose a public poetry or poetry for the people?

A: I do not propose a poetry for the people. I am proposing poetry, as it is, being distributed to the people.

Q: Made accessible.

A: Made accessible, not in terms of content, which is accessible enough in my view, but accessible in terms of the physical facility of the average man to open a collection of poems.

Q: In your mind, it's a matter of distribution.

A: Well, I'm talking about distribution, not adjusting the standards of poetry to the level of its customer.

Q: Education?

A: It's not education, you don't need any education. We're all literate, and every literate person can read. The idea that poetry enjoys a limited audience comes from the times when literacy was a privilege of the few, whereas now literacy is practically universal, how should I put it, property, if you will. Nearly everyone is fairly literate and is capable to read.

Q: Is it possible to have that kind of appreciation and respect for poetry in the United States with the media and . . .

A: Forget the media! Of course it's possible, of course it's possible. The publishing world has been terribly, how should I put it, inert. I think it's stupid, idiotic, dangerous. But, still I think it can be fixed.

Q: How?

A: How? Well, you just simply distribute more widely.

Q: But don't you think that's a fault of capitalism, in a way, because the publishers are going to publish what sells, and what sells are the Tom Clancy books and Stephen King.

A: That's quite true, but you can sell something which doesn't sell if you sell it cheaply. The price of an average book of poetry is something like fifteen bucks. Who wants to do that? But if you publish it cheaply, if you put it in a paperback, if you don't go for the hard cover to begin with, if you print it cheaply, you could price it for something like two bucks each. You could sell 200,000 for two dollars instead of selling 20,000 for fifteen. And I think you can get even better returns that way.

Q: Do you think that would change poetry?

A: I don't know what it's going to do. I don't really know if it's going to change poetry. It will simply increase access. I think people are fully capable of reading poems. It's a shortcut very often, tremendous compression, condensation, and you don't need that bloody full novel. You can do it within a smaller space. The returns for poetry are far greater and more needed.

Q: Perhaps the way it's taught intimidates people.

A: But, in a sense, just as well. The failure of education here is a good thing, in a sense, because it doesn't interfere with the masses' appreciation of language. The whole point is, as long as you are capable to read what a man should write, you don't need an intermediary. You don't need an intermediary to read a book. You see, this is ultimately a highly intimate, highly idiosyncratic process, reading a book, you see. And it's good, in a sense, that in high school you people have been taught very poorly, because the academic categories never become an intermediary of interference between your own sense, your own appreciation of the language. In that sort of a shortcoming, there's a virtue there.

Q: Did you have any regrets when you left high school?

A: Well, yes, I did. I regret practically everything that I do.

Q: But you wouldn't change that?

A: Well, you can't really change.

Q: You can choose not to regret.

A: You may choose not to regret, but that's a matter, not so much of a choice, but of a temperament.

Q: Whom do you write for?

A: You know what Stravinsky said to that? He was very cute. There is a book of interviews with Stravinsky by Robert Craft, and he puts the same question to Stravinsky and he says "for myself and for the probable alter ego."

Q: You don't write your poems in English?

A: No, I do. Not that many, though, a small percentage really, but sometimes I do.

Q: But you write your prose in English.

A: Mainly. All those prose pieces with a few exceptions were commissioned pieces, and when you are commissioned something, you are given a deadline. Of course, I could have written them initially in Russian and then translated them into English, but that's one hell of a way of meeting a deadline.

Q: Is the Russian language better for your poetry?

A: I don't really know whether it's better. It's a more organic thing for me to do. It's simply more immediate if you will. I like that language for its euphonic powers. It's tremendously rich euphonically. The average length of a Russian word is something like three or four syllables, and that alone makes for a euphonic or acoustic event.

Q: As opposed to monosyllabics . . .

A: Yeah, as opposed to monosyllabics. Well, basically what Russian does by the means of vowels, English does by the means of consonants.

Q: What do you like about the English language?

A: Clarity. In Russian or in German or in French what matters is the combination of words, whereas in English what matters is the meaning. It's the difference between playing chess and playing tennis. In chess, what matters is the complexity of the moves. In tennis . . . well . . . it's how you win the game, or lose more often (laughs). Whereas in English, the ball immediately flies back into your face. It's immediately back in your court. The main question the writer of a Russian sentence asks himself is whether it's a good sentence, whatever that means. Whereas in English, the first question he asks himself is whether it makes sense.

Q: What about free verse?

A: What about it? I don't like it that much, frankly. Because . . . well . . . everything that is prefaced as *free* immediately introduces a question mark in my mind, free from what? Freedom is not an autonomous category. It's a conditioned category. In physics, it's conditioned. In politics, it's conditioned by slavery. When we're talking about free verse, essentially, we're talking about freed verse, liberated from the constraints of strict meter. In order to be able to manage it, to master it, to write it well, you ought to know what you've rid yourself from. You ought to know about the constraints. In a sense, free verse is a historical development, mainly a reaction in the last century and in the beginning of ours, to the strict verse. Therefore, for a poet, a young man or woman or whomever it is, if he is about to practice it, what he has to do in a sense, in miniature, is repeat the process his literature went through before it arrived at free verse. That is, you have to be able to write in meter and rhyme, and abundantly. Whereas, when you start immediately from the threshold, as many people do, writing free verse, it's not so much free verse, because every freedom is your personal adventure, your acquisition of freedom. Every personal acquisition is personal, syncretic, etcetera, otherwise what you do is simply borrow somebody's else's form, which is not filtered through your own system, which means simply that you borrow not so much a form, as a formlessness. And a great deal, 99 percent of it is, in a sense, total garbage. People have no sense of their own language, or they don't have any sense of cadence. All you get in the majority of free verse is, at best, a story line. That's where it stops. The whole point is, poetry should be memorable, and internalized, in a sense. Very often I do the following with my students: I give them a poem in free verse. They read it, and then I turn it upside down, and I ask them to quote me a line from it, and very often the result is nil. In the case of somebody who has had the experience of the formal verse, and then switches to free verse, he knows the gravity of the word within the sentence. Take Eliot. Eliot's lines are memorable oddly enough. Not all of them, but they are. Eliot is one example, but one of few.

Q: Why are Eliot's line memorable?

A: Simply because, how should I put it to you, he knows what makes a line. What makes a line is its cadence. What you borrow is cadences from the speech. So what one hears is the intonation, and intonations are reproduceable, they're memorable.

Q: Essentially, it's an American idiom?

A: Not exactly an American idiom, not in Eliot's case. It's what Frost said about "sentence sound," which is the basic principle of free verse. You ought to have a very good ear for those things, for sentence sounds. The way to develop your ear is to write English in a formal verse. That's what I think. You ought to know where to end the line. You do it simply by ear, not simply for the sake of the graphics.

Q: Truman Capote called that typing.

A: Very often it is.

Q: When you started writing, did you start with very formalized verse?

A: As a matter of fact, not. When I think I was 18, 19, 20, 21, I wrote *vers libre.* But I quit. Well, actually at 18, I had written about ten to twenty poems of a very intricate nature. But then I wanted to be modern. Everybody else in civilization, in our culture wrote free verse, so I tried, and I did. But I was the first person to dislike that. It's not so much my choice, it's my ear. I love the sound. I love the meters. I love rhymes. I think I'm a pretty good rhymer. And I wouldn't give it up. What for?

Q: Are you pleased to see the neo-formalists in the United States?

A: As long as people don't get shrill and dogmatic, it's fine. It's like a pendulum from one extreme to another.

Q: Is there an interest in Russia in American poetry?

A: There is a fashion, there always was. It started I think, in a big way, sometime in the 30s and 40s. They had tremendous anthologies of American and English poetry that started in 1956, 1957, and every five or ten years there is an anthology of American poetry.

Q: Who are the upcoming poets in Russia?

A: Oh, there are several, the numbers are huge. There is a tremendous upsurge now, that is in quality.

Q: Do you see a dramatic change in the work of the young writers?

A: The quality is much higher.

Q: Do you think that's a result of the declining audience?

A: No, no, no, no, no. It's simply a result, if it's a result of anything, it's a result of many things that became available to them now. They know what's been done in Russian poetry over the last century, and now they can draw on it and they can bounce against it, etcetera. Whereas, previously they worked artificially within the confines of two or three idioms. Now they can experiment as much as they care to. They can be daring. I still think about your question, about the young poets. I don't think there is anyone singular that I can . . . it became to my eye almost a demographic phenomenon. There are plenty of them. It wouldn't be fair to say this or that. It's simply a very high quality. I'm very envious, but then, maybe I'm envious of their youth.

Q: What about young American poets?

A: There are two or three that I live very much. There are two women that I like. One is Melissa Green. She is from Boston, from Winthrop to be more exact. Another is a wonderful girl, Gjertrud Schnackenberg.

Q: What do you admire about their work?

A: Two things. Tremendous intensity and tremendous intelligence. In the case of Ms. Green, I think it's a tremendous facility. She's a tremendous rhymer. There's a collection of hers called *Squanicook Eclogues,* wonderful eclogues, I think. Virgil would be proud of those. Tremendous rhyming, tremendous texture. And as for Ms. Schnackenberg, there is one poem I wish I had written, but she did, it's called "Supernatural Love." It's a tremendous poem, written mainly about her father. So are, oddly enough, the *Squanicook Eclogues.*

Q: Do you ever translate the work of other poets?

A: Very seldom, very infrequently. I think there are people far better qualified to do that.

Q: Some of the translators that have worked on your work . . . do they speak Russian?

A: I think in translation, what matters is your ability to handle your own language . . . English in this case, the second thing is congeniality. I found working with Walcott that his intuition is stunning. He knows no language, but he knew what I was doing.

Q: Who do you think is the better translator of your work? You or—

A: I wouldn't say. I wouldn't be able to make a blanket judgment here. It all depends . . . The success in translation is always the matter of a fluke. Sometimes it's a matter of luck, of chance really. One thing I can say is the reason I translate myself is simply . . . it's not because of vanity or enthusiasm for my own work. Quite the contrary. It's simply because very often it quickly develops into a great deal of bad rub, especially if the man is older than yourself. Whereas, you can correct the translator, you change the poem once, twice, three times, a fourth time. People would say, it's lousy English, but in the original it's great. In order to avoid that association, I decided to do it myself, so I could be blamed. I would take the responsibility. I would rather reproach myself than by what some other gentleman would say.

Q: Isn't it frustrating writing the poem in your native language and then translating it yourself?

A: It's not only that. It's not a simultaneous process. What's frustrating here is that your peers and friends judge you on the basis of something which has been done a long time ago. Translation is by definition, how should I put it . . . the consequence, the effect, not the cause, so therefore, you shake hands with people who have formed their opinion about you on the basis of something that has been written five or ten years ago. That prompts you in a sense to write occasionally a poem in English to show the boys who you are or who's in charge.

Q: In one sense, then, your American readers are behind the times.

A: Well, essentially, yes.

Q: So you catch them up every now and then.

A: From time to time.

An Interview with Joseph Brodsky

Blair Ewing / 1993

From *Maryland Poetry Review* (Spring/Summer 1994), 47–50. Reprinted by permission of Blair Ewing.

The following interview was conducted on December 10, 1993 at the Café Maurizio, in Mr. Brodsky's new home in Brooklyn Heights, and in his car on the Brooklyn Bridge on the way back to Greenwich Village in New York City.—Blair Ewing

[Part I: Café Maurizio]

BE: Late last year (1992) you published a poem ("Bosnia Tune") and an op-ed piece in the *New York Times* on the vast tragedy occurring in what was once Yugoslavia. In the poem you limned the senselessness of the violence and death ("By and large not knowing why / people die.") but in the op-ed piece you strongly criticized President Clinton for inaction and at the end of your essay even raised questions about our self-image as a moral nation. Please comment on your future as a dissident and the relationship between your political views and your poetic craft.

JB: I have no future as a political dissident, nor do I have a past as a dissident. Now, you better ask more pointed questions, you know you can. Now, what is it you are asking?

BE: Well, I'm asking about your role as a citizen, *and* as a poet.

JB: Well, that's exactly what it is. That's the role of the citizen—I was willing to speak my conscience and I did. That's all. And I hope it carried some weight. That's why I proceeded to do it. The saddest things about the poem and the essay you mention is that had to be written, and that they had to be written by me.

BE: Did you write "Bosnia Tune" in Russian first and then translate it into English?

JB: No, I wrote it in English.

BE: Do you still write primarily in Russian and then translate your work into English?

JB: Primarily poems I write in Russian, yes.

BE: How is your crusade on behalf of poetry coming? I've heard of great victories recently* . . .

JB: Well, there are lots of victories, and lots of good press, and lots of positive sentiment floating around, but it doesn't somehow translate into what is required for the success of that project—namely, the cash. The project is being carried forward out of pocket, in miniscule amounts.

BE: I thought I read that 100,000 copies of the anthology you put together had been bought by the Book-of-the-Month club to be distributed in hotels . . .

JB: Well, I think the figure is an exaggeration. I was in Washington recently, a week ago, I think, and saw Andrew Carroll. He is more informed about the day-to-day transactions with the hotels. One chain has, I know for a fact, signed up. Because they get letters from their customers, etc. . . .

BE: They do? That's great!

JB: Yes, but on the large scale, we are still courting foundations to support it. And the publishers—we find that their resistance is something of a paradox, to put it mildly, because the publishers are the ones who stand to gain from it. But they move no finger . . .

BE: Not even your publisher?

JB: No, not even my publisher. It's all rather piecemeal, but it grows.

BE: This seems to be a major, long-term commitment on your part . . .

JB: Yes, it is—well, I don't really know, as long as I exist. Perhaps that's not so terribly long.

BE: But this does seem to be a distinct activity, separate from your actual work on your poetry.

JB: No, not such a distinct activity—a telephone call, a letter, that sort of thing. Blair, do you smoke?

BE: No.

JB: Good man. Here, take these, would you?

---

*Interviewer's note: Mr. Brodsky and his partner Andrew Carroll have collaborated to create the American Poetry and Literacy Project to spread the gospel of poetry by passing out books of children's poetry, and placing anthologies in hospitals and hotel rooms, etc.

BE: Okay. I know this game.

I'd like to ask you about the performance of your poetry. In the past you've expressed real ambivalence about giving readings, but this doesn't come across when you perform. I've seen quite a few poets read, and you are definitely one of the most dynamic—so why the resistance? Isn't this also a good way to spread the gospel?

JB: It is. But I have reservations about my English pronunciation, and that's what really gets in my way—but I have become more confident in my pronunciation the longer I have been on the circuit.

BE: But your delivery in Russia is also impressive: even though I don't understand the words, I know it's a poem. Others in the audiences seemed to feel the same way. When you perform, you always seem to read "Letters from the Ming Dynasty" and "Slave, Come to My Service." Are they part of a semi-permanent performance repertoire?

JB: Not really—you simply coincided. But I do like that poem ["Letters . . ."] to begin with, and it was well-liked by a Russian friend of mine who died. Also, another friend of mine from the days of yore, Derek Walcott, translated it into English.

BE: In terms of the advice you've given to poets in the past—you believe aspiring poets should first recapitulate the history of poetry in some sense before they write free verse only—but you have also advised poets to use lingo.

JB: Yes, there are enormous resources there. For instance, normally people resort to free verse because they deem the traditional means as already employed by others, and therefore compromised, in a manner of speaking. One must try to "beat" the forms, not simply do them. Lingo and colloquialisms can help.

BE: You once remarked that one of the benefits of being sent to prison was that the argot of criminals became available to you.

JB: Yes, indeed, it was. In Russia that didn't give one that much of an edge because the language of society is sufficiently criminalized. It's simply a matter of means—you're writing "1 a.m." and wondering, what am I going to rhyme this with? Everything appears to be stale, until you come across something like "I am . . ." though this example has nothing to do with argot.

BE: I've also meant to ask you about "sense of place" in poetry—it seems as though many poets develop and enunciate a strong rootedness, whereas others need to escape their place of origin to find their voices . . .

JB: Well, there is no law here. It all boils down to one's temperament. For some it is imperative to stay in one place, with their set of references. For others, it is certainly the departure that matters. Lots of people made a universe of their lapels, while others built their universe out of dislocation. An example of the first would be Robert Frost, the example of the latter would be Rilke.

BE: But it also seems to me that once the dialectic of art and life is engaged, that certain rules of development do seem to exist . . . What do you think?

JB: Exactly what I've said before. A poet is not a man of action. His existence, his qualities, are not defined by his actions, but by what he makes. He is a maker. The crucial thing for the maker is the material. You may lead whatever life you like: insurance salesman, nuclear submarine captain, whatever it is. It doesn't really matter. You can do something totally unrelated to this other activity. And for that reason we have these biographies of poets, which is a totally ridiculous thing. You can have biographies of submarine captains or politicians simply because their métier is action. The poet's métier is words, making words, language. So, if you are of a mind to write a biography of a poet, you have to write a biography of his verses . . .

BE: Do it the reverse of the way it's been done?

JB: Practically, yes. I was once very much struck by a very peculiar development. I saw a biography of Marcel Proust in which the biographer spent hundreds and hundreds of pages trying to prove that Alvertine was in fact Albert—this is fine and dandy. But the whole point is that Proust wrote the entire novel in order to actually obscure that. In other words, the biographer's pen was moving in the diametrically opposite direction to his subject's.

BE: But what about those poets who deliberately attempt to intertwine their art and their life? Like the Beats, for example—is this legitimate?

JB: Legitimate, illegitimate: it all boils down to the results. In the case of Ginsberg, there were some nice results. As for their method—how shall I put it to you?—I can put it to you very nastily: your ability to live, to exist, to create something out of the fabric of life is far more limited than your ability to create something out of the fabric of the language. So, if you are bent on this sort of combination, you may end up with very little.

BE: How does one define a poetic "success"? One great poem? Two? An outstanding book?

JB: It is not the one who defines success. It's the public that defines your success. Or the readers who define your success. Basically, the postures available to any individual within the context of his existence are fairly limited. The postures available to you linguistically are infinite. Hence, your answer. I really don't know how to define success.

BE: Is success the ability to be retained in the memories of one's readers?

JB: I would imagine that would be as good a definition as any. Well, perhaps a better one.

BE: Something many of my friends wanted to ask you—what are you reading these days? Who are you reading these days?

JB: Oh, I'm reading all sorts of things. Last night, for instance, I was reading a collection of poems by Christopher Middleton. Very good poet, very much neglected, yeah? It's a bit here and there, on the tedious and tragic side, but I like that. I also like histories, historical writing because, out of necessity, they economize on space.

BE: You have written some interesting poems about historical figures: Tiberius, Mary Queen of Scots . . .

JB: There are more to come. It is simply that a historian has to deal with paradoxes, all the time. How shall I put it to you? Herodotus, at the very beginning of his history, in the first paragraph said something like this about paradoxes with respect to the origins of the Trojan War—according to some, the reasons for the outbreak of the Trojan War were these, according to others, those. I [Herodotus] personally think the reason was this. So he gives you alternative theories. Thucydides and subsequently Plutarch turned that variety of opinions into an art of paradoxical writing. The variety is then given to you not in three different paragraphs, but within one sentence. It was this type of writing that gave us literature, basically—well, the beginnings of literature.

BE: Not poetry?

JB: Yes, well, poets gave us some, yeah, but basically it was the historians who gave us the literature we know—our literary language, if you will.

BE: You mentioned more to come. When are your next books coming out?

JB: According to my publishers, they are due out next fall [fall '94], but I could have done them yesterday. But they have their own plans.

BE: Turning to the question of influences, you've always mentioned Auden, Milosz, and even Eliot as . . . poets who have influenced you. What about [other] influences?

JB: Ah, that's a good question! [long pause] I should try to answer this. You see, all my life I've been influenced by somebody. And I imagine I am still influenced, one way or another, but not in such a palpable way, as to be detectable to myself. I don't think anybody influences me, well, it's not that there's no one to influence me; I just think I have ossified, one way or another. Perhaps it's that my susceptibility to influences have become arthritic—you can be influenced by somebody you've read but before you go to implement it, it's gone. Well, the inspiration that I get, normally, I get from the dead, oddly enough, and not because of the morbidity of my predilections, but because it is they who sort of call you, "Do this, do that." I'm not influenced by any contemporary poet, although I fancied myself somewhat influenced by [the Italian poet] Montale. But I recognized that when I found myself thinking about Montale, it wasn't exactly Montale, but my fantasy of Montale. I recognized in him what I saw in no one else: working out of the civilization in a sort of oblique way, because Italy is synonymous, in my mind anyway, with civilization. And he was just taking byways and sideways, travelling in the peripheries of civilization, yeah? It's not so much Montale, as my fantasy of him.

BE: You seem to have a real affinity for Italy, and Venice in particular. You recently published a collection of essays about Venice *[Watermark]* . . .

JB: That town I indeed love, and I wish I never stopped writing that book.

BE: And yet, your poems—I haven't read very many with Italian subjects.

JB: I was thinking the other day of compiling an edited selection of my "Italian" poems, and I realized there are 15 to 20 such poems. It could be a book, but not a long one . . . *[laughter]*

BE: In the early 70s you went to Mexico for a brief time . . .

JB: That was in 1975.

BE: 1975. And there were some poems that issued from that. Mexico is very much on our minds these days. Any plans to go back?

JB: Well, life is a matter of contingencies, as you probably already know, and it simply has to do with the opportunity, not with the desire.

BE: You once said you felt that the elegy was the most fully developed form in our language . . .

JB: Let's go, ok? Take your machine, and let's get the car and we'll continue . . .

[Part II: Mr. Brodsky's new home in Brooklyn Heights. The interview proceeds in English as the poet supervises workers in Polish and Russian . . .]

BE: Sorry I locked your keys in your car . . .

JB: It's too late for that! [laughter] Anyway, it's their job at the garage to fix it . . .

BE: Now that some time has passed since your stint as poet laureate down in Washington, do you have any additional thoughts on that experience?

JB: Ah, no—I think all the thoughts I have on that subject have already been voiced.

BE: The reason I ask is this: the post of U.S. Poet Laureate is a relatively new and particularly American thing. Do you still consider yourself, after that experience, a Russian poet, but an American citizen?

JB: Well, I don't ask myself questions of this nature, and I don't know of what use these definitions are. What I think about myself is of no consequence—what matters is what I manage to do. And that's not for me to define.

BE: I guess I persist in this line because in recent discussions of and articles about the leading American poets and the contemporary poetry scene to my dismay your name is often left out.

JB: Well, how do we define a poet? Basically, by their language or by their nationality. If you want to define me by language, I am obviously a Russian poet. But if you want to define me according to citizenship, I am an American poet.

BE: Well, again, another reason I bring all this up is that the emphasis in your poems on the individual, individualism and human autonomy seem quite American to me.

JB: Yes, to me too. But they've always been that way. Presumably, in that sense, I always was totally American.

BE: As a former Nobel winner yourself, do you have any thoughts on the recent award of the Nobel to Toni Morrison?

JB: No, I have no response to that whatsoever.

BE: Did you attend the ceremony?

JB: Certainly not. The ceremony is for her, etcetera . . . I haven't read anything by her. I've seen a few essays here and there, which I thought were pure garbage. But I would hate to form my opinion based on that . . .

BE: I've wanted to ask you about a poem you wrote in 1968, "Gorbunov and Gorchakov." It's a long poem, containing several long, lyrical soliloquies and dialogues between these two characters, who are ostensibly confined in a mental institution.

JB: Basically, yes, that's the plot.

BE: It seems to me that this "dramatic" poem is the one most like the plays you have written *[Marbles, Democracy!]*

JB: Well, perhaps. Actually the most interesting aspect of that work is that it was done in decima, and the story is indeed a discourse on the matter of executions, actually about Easter time, so it's the Passions, basically. The most interesting aspect to me at the time was that I was writing in decima, and decima has a completely mind-boggling effect upon the reader, not to mention upon the writer. When you have six pairs of the same rhyme, you have the sense of excess, even redundancy, madness. So, the whole point was to bring the dialogue, both in terms of the subject matter and the stylistic means to the point where it was impossible to continue, and yet to continue. That's what I was up to there, I would imagine . . .

BE: Have you ever performed that poem?

JB: Not in its entirety. Well, some of the units, to entertain my friends, that sort of thing. But it's difficult: you need two voices there.

BE: That's what I thought as I reread it, and that's what reminded me of your plays. The image I got was of these two men on some sort of stage or set.

JB: I think maybe this should be a radio play. *Marbles* is more in the same vein. It's also basically a dialogue, with choruses here and there. As for the poem: in Russian it's a remarkable job, I am still quite puzzled about being able to pull it off. I did.

BE: How many lines is it, exactly?

JB: I think it should be 1300 lines.

BE: Is it your longest poem?

JB: Yes, it's the longest single piece.

BE: What about the future of your efforts at playwriting? Do you envision more of that kind of writing?

JB: Right now, no. I envision no plays. Right now I am trying to translate some poems I have written, and to write some essays on the side, which I wish I didn't have to do. Basically, I would like to publish a couple of books next year.

BE: I see. How many poems would you say you publish in magazines every year, on average? 10? 12?

JB: I honestly don't know. As many as they take.

BE: Do you still have poems rejected?

JB: Of course. To give you an estimate on the number I publish in magazines, I would say 10 to 15.

BE: And about how many poems per year would you say you produce?

JB: It varies and it depends, mainly on your working pace and your luck. I would say between 20 and 40 pieces a year.

BE: How do you decide when you are writing something, how do you reach a conclusion, This [poem] is no good" Is it obvious?

JB: [laughing] Of course it's obvious!

BE: Well, okay. I'm just not sure it's so obvious to everybody. I see lots of bad poetry published, and I've written quite a few bad ones myself.

JB: Well, I'll tell you one thing, and it's not exactly a parable, it's my memory. I was, I think, an aspiring poet until the age of twenty-five or six. At the age of twenty-six, something happened: I developed a professional instinct. I remember I had written a poem which I liked very much, it was a wonderful poem, etcetera, and yet, and yet, and yet, something in me sensed that the sonic mass of the poem was not sufficient, and it was a pretty long poem, at that. I felt I needed one more stanza of eight or twelve lines. And I was thinking and thinking and thinking and I had no such stanza in me. But at one point I got it, and when I got that stanza, I thought the poem had finished. What I was saying in that stanza was presumably developing the theme or story of the poem further, but I felt the need to write it because there was a sonic vacuum that I had to fill. And that instinct, that knowledge, that criteria, I never had that before, so at a certain point, I think I found myself in a position in this world where I started perceiving poems as sonic entities. And gradually I knew, better and better, the volume. Now can I get a ciggy? Just, just a few puffs . . .

BE: Okay.

[Part III: In Mr. Brodsky's car on the Brooklyn Bridge, returning to the Village]

BE: Recently I read an article, I can't recall the author, about how Frank O'Hara helped promote the early work of John Ashbery . . .

JB: Frank was a very different sort. He could make an event out of going around the corner for some cigs. He loved life.

BE: I mention Ashbery because reading his work, especially "Self-Portrait in a Convex Mirror," helped me continue, gave me some confidence . . .

JB: Well, I believe the duty of poet is to make things clearer, and John makes things fuzzier. The Queen is naked.

BE: I meant to ask you before what you think of Rita Dove's idea about poetry videos? Could this also be a good way to stimulate interest, participation, reading?

JB: Yes, of course, but I am suspicious of anything that moves away from books, the printed page.

BE: Why?

JB: Because if someone sees poetry video, they might well want to see another video, but I would prefer to stimulate interest in a book. Reading a well-written poem is a mental adventure that takes the reader further and deeper than a video. We should keep in mind that we humans are the vibrating fringes of the masses of inanimate matter.

Joseph Brodsky Answers *Argotist*'s Questions

Nick Watson / 1995

From *The Argotist* (March 1996), 33. Reprinted by permission of *The Argotist* (Liverpool, England).

Shortly before his recent death, the Nobel Laureate Joseph Brodsky spoke briefly to *The Argotist* about poetry, memory, and exile . . .

A.: You comment on the value of "estrangement" to developing first an individual perspective and second a writer's perspective. Is the one a necessary prerequisite of the other and how much are you using Shklovsky's concept of "estrangement", if at all?

J.B.: The former is surely necessary for the latter, and the other way round I am afraid is also. Hence the answer to your Shklovsky question.

A.: "Appearances are all there is" *(Less Than One).* David Hockney has said "all art is surface" and that surface is "the first reality". Are you talking about the same thing and what depths are negated by privileging surface?

J.B.: There are no depths. Appearance is the summary of phenomenae.

A.: In *Less Than One* you deny the hegemony of the "linear process", yet immediately follow this with a (linear) paradigm—"A school is a factory is a poem is a prison is academia is boredom, with flashes of panic." Again, shortly after arguing that narrative, like memory, should be non-linear (i.e. digressive), you assert that history is cyclic (a linear image). Would you comment firstly on the nature of these contradictions and secondly on the problematic of linearity in your writing?

J.B.: Cyclic is not linear! See your laundry machine or dishwasher. I don't believe I have "the problematic of linearity" in my writing. But having said that I must admit that stanzaic composition indeed possesses the kind of morphology similar to that of crystals growing.

A.: *Selected Essays* is, it seems to me, self-consciously aphoristic: self-conscious in poetic rather than prosaic decision-making (e.g., "The more indebted the artist, the richer he is."). Can you expand?

J.B.: 1) Do you expect a writer to be unaware of what he is doing?

2) One gets aphoristic for reasons of economy.

A.: How completely do oppressive political regimes destroy individualism? I am thinking that individualism may find alternative modes of expression, that it is not something which can be cultured or suppressed but is an innate predisposition. Similarly, in a "free" society, expressions of "individualism" are often no more than a reclothed lumpen consciousness.

J.B.: Innate disposition is subject to the outward mental diet. The latter can be reduced, thus conditioning the former. So you may find yourself disliking, say, Mao instead of Wittgenstein. In a free society you can do both; in a free society you have a better chance to define your true enemy, which is the vulgarity of the human heart.

A.: You glibly put Sholokov's Nobel Prize (1965) down to "a huge shipbuilding order placed in Sweden" *(Less Than One).* How credible do you find the "All Literature Is Politics" argument?

J.B.: It's bullshit.

A.: Postwar poetry in the USSR and the USA has vast stylistic/thematic differences. First, are you now looking to become part of the American tradition and second, how (critically) constrained do you feel in relation to American culture?

J.B.: I have no such aspiration. Nor do I aspire to the contrary. As for the American culture, some of it I find revolting, some awe-inspiring. Its diversity rules out a possibility of total approach.

A.: In the preface to *A Part of Speech* you mention reworking translations of your work to bring them closer to the original in terms of content rather than form. Has this forced choice, emphasising content over form, caused you to rethink your attitude to language in any way?

J.B.: No, it hasn't. You can sacrifice this or that aspect of a poem while translating but not in the process of composition.

A.: How is poetry best read—aloud to an audience or silently to oneself?

J.B.: Both, but not one without the other.

A.: Although memory fails to adequately reconstruct the past (in "A Room and A Half") has poetry allowed any successful reconstruction?

J.B.: No. Nothing can do this. That's what time's passage is all about.

A.: When Publius says, "Home! . . . where you won't be back ever." *(Marbles),* is this Joseph Brodsky speaking to us directly or is it facile to draw comparisons between an author and his characters?

J.B.: No, it's not facile, and yes, it's my own attitude.

A.: Your work draws on many other literary sources making for more or less esoteric writing. What is your attitude towards the accessibility of your work?

J.B.: I couldn't care less about this sort of thing, although I am finding your remark highly surprising. If my stuff strikes you as being esoteric then something is really off with the City of Liverpool.

An Interview with Joseph Brodsky

Elizabeth Elam Roth / 1995

From *South Central Review,* 14 (Spring 1997), 1–9. Reprinted by permission of *South Central Review* and Elizabeth Elam Roth.

I came to Joseph Brodsky's work via his good friend Mikhail Baryshnikov, about whom I frequently wrote in my capacity as a freelance dance critic before enrolling in the M.A. English program at Southwest Texas State. In 1991, when Mr. Brodsky was Poet Laureate, I read his "Immodest Proposal"[1] suggesting that poetry, like the Bible, should be placed in every hotel nightstand in America—and in factory lunchrooms, doctors' offices, airports, anywhere people had time to kill. Although whimsically made, the suggestion was taken seriously by Andrew Carroll, then an undergraduate at Columbia, who contacted Mr. Brodsky and, with the poet's support, founded the nonprofit American Poetry and Literacy Project, of which I am now assistant director. To date, the APL project has given away over 30,000 volumes of poetry. Knowing of my position with the Project and that my master's thesis, then in progress, compared aspects of Mr. Brodsky's poetry with Robert Frost's, the SWT Department of English invited Mr. Brodsky to be their Lindsey Lecture Series guest, 2–3 November 1995—or approximately ten weeks before his death in January 1996.

I have made this interview as syntactically correct as possible while retaining Mr. Brodsky's speech patterns, removing many but not all of his familiar stammerings as he searched for the correct English word, as well as his idiomatic "etcetera, etcetera, etcetera" and "yeah?" *("ja")* with which he ended many of his sentences. Words in brackets denote my interpretations of omitted information important to the comprehension of the sentence; parentheses indicate words not understood—or responses, such as laughter. In all probability, Mr. Brodsky may have addressed, in one way or another, several of the topics brought up at this question-and-answer session; but, to my knowledge, he had never publicly declared the debt he owed Hinduism when measuring the success of his poetry, nor had he revealed the fact that he considered himself a Calvinist. Additionally, his discussion of the linguistic polemics between the Soviet Union (in relation to the Russian language) and other European countries (to German and Italian) is unique. It was clear to us that Mr. Brodsky tired easily and was unwell; he frequently took nitroglycerin tablets. The audience at his reading the day before this Q & A session was a mixture of Southwest Texas State undergraduates, graduate students, faculty, and the general public. This Q & A session was attended mostly by SWT Department of English faculty and MFA students, who, with me, were the questioners.

Joseph Brodsky comes into the classroom and takes a seat at the front of the room, greeting certain people he had met at the departmental reception or at lunch or dinner the day before. He nods to strangers, saying, "I'm Joseph."

Q: I was wondering what your religious background was.

A: Well, basically, I would say my religious background, well, it never existed. I have none. I have been brought up in a very secularized society in a family that practiced nothing of the sort, no religion. It's actually an understatement; the state or the country I grew up in was atheistic and [practicing religion] would result in some sort of backlash, and one would be curious about what was banned. I was not an exception. I was quite curious about Christianity, Judaism, all those things. But the Bible came to my hands late; I was about twenty-three. So in the absence of that, in the normal process of reading things, I came across the Hindu literature, and the first books of the sacred (divination?) I read were things like Bhagavad-Gita, Upanishad, Mahabharata, that sort of thing. Through my circle of friends, I got interested in Hinduism and kept reading on, so now of course, that would have required practicing some sort of yoga to get serious about it. That I couldn't manage. I couldn't stand on my head (laughter) or concentrate, so I read; and I must say that the physical horizons of Hinduism are absolutely astonishing. You have a sense of spiritual Himalayas looming one ridge beyond another, beyond another, beyond another. However, I knew, one way or another, partly because I couldn't practice it [yoga], it is not exactly for me. So the pursuit was largely intellectual. At the age of twenty-two or twenty-three, I came across the Bible, that's Old Testament and New Testament; and mind you, in Russia, people don't do a separation—Old Testament, New Testament. One is read as a sequel to the other. So in a sense, I recognized that this is civilization or the culture or plane of spiritual regard which is presumably my own. In a sense, I had to make a choice, as it were. The choice was not in terms of the church or in terms of the practice but in terms of the orientation, I suppose, or drift. And I got quite absorbed in all that, and I read quite a lot about the Bible, but I never practiced any of it. Well, presumably in some sense I did, but not in the traditional institutionalized manner. However, that encounter with Hinduism served me in great stead, because when I've dealt with Judaism in my mind or Christianity, I am constantly aware, I still am, of a relative narrowness of those two doctrines in comparison to Hinduism. In this line of work that I have been pursuing some thirty years, that awareness proved to be quite beneficial, at least in my view. No matter how wonderful the insight that I may obtain in the process of work, something in me tends to throw it against those backdrops of those horizons of Hinduism. . . . Does it stand well or doesn't it? And if it doesn't, depending on the strength or the weakness of my psychological state at the moment, I will discard this work or insight, or I allow it to exist, yeah? (Laughter)

Since you asked me about my religious affiliation—not affiliation, but proclivity—I will speak about that reluctantly. I would say now, today, that I regard myself as a Calvinist: that is, one who fears severe judgment of one's own views, one's own endeavors. It is an easier, I suppose, way of handling matters, ethical matters, simply because . . . I came at some point to think that if the Supreme Being that the creed offers is capable of forgiving me, for this and for that, I'm not interested in that Supreme Being. I *can* be forgiven. It's a matter of hubris, of course. But it's also the full recognition, a substantial degree of recognition of what I have done or what I do. That, I don't possess, that sort of infinite mercy toward myself. . . . I just can't dream it myself, to rely on somebody who is going to say to me, for all my shortcomings, it's okay. The better way to describe myself is along the Calvinist lines. (Deep sigh)

Q: How do you view the soul? Can the language of the soul be political or ironic?

A: On the question of soul, I have to get back to the Bible, I suppose. Well, the natural question that arises in everybody who hears about that sort of thing is: What is the seat of the soul in the human body? And I remember reading in Leviticus that remarkable passage. I think it was in Leviticus, which was describing the sacrifice; and it was an instruction to the people, after the sacrifice of the animals: You can eat the meat of the animals, but as for the blood, don't drink the blood because in their blood is their soul. So I came to view the blood as the seat of the soul; so much so that once, when I had substantial surgery and underwent a blood transfusion, I was concerned with what kind of blood I was going to get. Whose? (Laughter) Well, that is neither here nor there; it doesn't answer your question. I don't believe in this . . . no, I'm not going to use that . . . I'm a little bit tired of this dichotomy, soul and body. I don't really believe that those things should be (sigh) separated. . . .

Q: (interrupting) I guess what I mean is the self, a deeper self, not separate from the body or anything.

A: There's a fusion—well, as long as we're alive, we can't separate those things. . . . And I don't believe it's good for our body, and vice versa. (Laughter) In terms of writing, etc., etc., if you find something offensive intellectually or bodily, you obviously have to act accordingly, defensively. I don't know how else to describe it. So, I think we need a more clear-cut question. We need to first agree about terms. Rephrase it, please. Think of the kind of conduct, from your point of view, that is reprehensible, and then ask the gentleman [JB] what he thinks about it. (Laughter)

Q: You talked yesterday about the dangers of writing a political poem, that you have to go further, you have to step further down into yourself to get to the heart of it.

A: I was quoting Frost, who said irony is a descending metaphor—there are ascending metaphors and descending metaphors. And irony is a kind of wonderful thing, because it immediately wins you cheers and the disposition of your public, etc., yeah? Technically speaking, irony is innovation, revelation, or epiphany; well, let's use a technical term: let's use "elevation." The lower you get in your daily practice, the more difficult it is to elevate yourself. It's like, when you are on the second floor and the building has twenty stories. . . . and you have to climb to the twentieth floor, and it's a bit easier to do it from the second or third floor than the basement. With irony, you deprive yourself of the basement. It's attractive, it's fun, in the basement; but each next time you have to go up, you have to begin at the lower rung of the ladder. And that's what I mean about relying on [. . .] economy in this line of work. It's very true that from a supreme ironist you can't, by and large, get a revelation. And as you know, about literature, one gets immediately aware of that sort of thing, and one wonders, what way am I going to do? It's tempting and it's easy to crack a joke.

Q: Yesterday you spoke about anger and persecution. Could you speak about the nature of catharsis in poetry, your poetry?

A: To tell you the truth, I don't apply the category. And speaking generally about catharsis in art, you shouldn't really believe that it can be brought about by simple adherence to this or that. A work of art or poem can bring catharsis to somebody through secondary or tertiary aspects of it, through a certain rhyme; and you feel release, you are free. It is in the domain of *means,* basically. You may be a virtuous soul, superb and saintly, except that what you write would be of very minimal consequence for your reader. There are good examples; perhaps the best example would be the current Pope. He writes poetry. It's not bad poetry, but it doesn't do anything, not even for his compatriots. (Sigh) So I think spiritual integrity is not enough in art. . . . There should be something in your fingers, something. . . .

Q: Poets in our country choose to write in free verse and express the idea that it's more authentic to the poetic impulse than form. What do you think about that?

A: It is not authentic to obey the poetic impulse. When they write, they *feel* authentic—and when it's finished [they feel authentic]. But it remains a part of their own biographies, because authenticity is only one tenth of the game. We are all out to write authentically, aren't we? Well, one way or another. So the whole point is not to compete in the degree of authenticity; we have to compete in the degree of the artifice which we can produce. Free verse is a marvelous medium sometimes, but anything that is practiced is not acted "free." The main question, then, is free from what, yeah? In the world of transcendence, freedom is the last judgment, yeah? (Laughter) It's not an autonomous category. It's a liberation. The technical term for free verse is *vers libre,* liberated verse, but liberated from what—from strict meters, from standard, conservative forms. So in order to write free verse, you have to write a hell of a lot of the conventional verse and only then, as a reaction, to break away from. As long as, I believe, 1911, Ezra Pound said there's too much free verse around. I don't have in general an argument against it, when it is occasional, when it is a departure. But when it is the only trick available, I get a little bit. . . . The problem with the free verse is simple to me: You may write something terribly authentic, terribly wonderful, or maybe not even authentic, maybe something terribly artful, with great imagery and this and that, etc., etc. And you read it, and you are tremendously entertained. But the moment you turn the page, you don't retain anything. And the whole point about art is precisely its retentive quality. The job of a poet is to make a memorable utterance, or have, apart from its substance, a sense of linguistic inevitability. To that end, there are various means: meter, rhyme, God knows what. You may spend your entire life doing an authentic job, but nobody will remember a single line of yours. Then what? It's a hard thing! In terms of art and life, they're not identical. They are different mediums. Art has its own history, its own dynamics, its own philosophy, and its own future. It's your decision: am I going to produce art or am I going to do something therapeutic for my—whatever it is—system?

Q: In *The New Yorker* article you wrote about Frost, "On Grief and Reason,"[2] you made the distinction between tragedy and terror, and defined the continental tragic hero. Are there these elements in your work, and do you consider yourself a continental tragic hero?

A: I'm less than Frost. I'm less a poet than Frost, no question about that. I think I may have my redeeming qualities. I'm more . . . I don't really know. What I can say subtly about myself will strike you as a false humility, so I'd rather avoid saying that. By the virtue of biographical circumstances, I'm basically continental. I think my work has integrity, but not the integrity of Frost's. I will speak about myself, just for one second. And I will tell you the reason that I allow myself to do this. Assuming I am continental, I will show you the continental weaknesses and continental virtues. The weaknesses are obvious: the posture of the tragic hero, if you will, as suffering. I try very hard to avoid that sort of thing. I don't believe the sensibility of the victim is what emerges from my work. We all try to be honest. We think that is all . . . all in the human interplay—there's a great deal of human interplay. But it's not enough in art. By and large, I think the continental tradition is more interesting in terms of the artifice, yeah? It gives it flowers, and those flowers are not idle flowers. It is a beauty in which a man can tell another man what man is capable of. It shows you the emphasis on aesthetics—in the continental tradition. It shows a man his positive potential, his artistic potential. A man who is in touch with the continental tradition will, in the end, make choices that are more aesthetically informed. (Deep sigh)

Q: Most of us only have access to your work in translation. English is more closely related to German, French, and so on, than to Russian. Do you think there is more a barrier between us and Russian literature than between us and French—harder for a translator to make a translation from a more distantly related language?

A: (Noise of agreement) English is more closely related to the Germanic and Romance languages; no question about that. It is more a matter of the translator who does the job. However, having said that, I have to point out something simple, so simple that . . . first of all, Russian culture is a part of

Christendom culture; that is, we are just one aspect of it and our set of values not to mention many of our practices are quite similar. Therefore, I don't believe the language creates such a barrier. What creates the barrier is some historical reality, which for most of the century was politically different from the reality of the realms of the Romance and Germanic languages. That explains in many ways the popularity of the Russian nineteenth-century literature and the relative absence or ignorance in the West of the Russian literature of the twentieth century—simply because what transpired in our part was indeed untranslatable, not in terms of the language, but in terms of the social reality. Strictly speaking, in terms of the social context, what was transpiring in the United States and in Great Britain and Germany [was also transpiring in the] Russian nineteenth century. In the twentieth century, a completely new society emerged. So translating a sentence from Russian prose depicting life in the communal apartment into English is practically impossible. In the first place, what is the communal apartment? So practically every sentence would require a substantial footnote. The disparity of the reality of life is what is conspiring against being translated successfully into English, not the language itself.

Q: Do you think those same barriers might call into question there being an aesthetic, that perhaps there is a Russian aesthetic, an American aesthetic, an Asian aesthetic?

A: No. I see the sting of that question.[3] (Laughter) Well. No, basically not. And I will tell you why. Now, I will do something interesting now. I will ramble a bit, but try to stay with me because it is going to be quite interesting. (Laughter) Basically if you look at the picture of the species, we have more or less two ideas towards reality, two concepts of how to handle it. One, well, I would call the Western and the other the Eastern. The Western approach is the emphasis on the rational. It puts a great premium on reason . . . the example would be someone like Descartes: *I think therefore I exist.* And that was the emphasis on the value of the individual existence, and that results in the horrendous amounts of laws. . . . That is the premise that while society is organizable, society is rational, that the dominant category in human liberation is rationality, yeah? And that defines our school programs. And there is another approach, which is Eastern, with its emphasis on intuition, on self-negation, on the insignificance of your existence. And it is exemplified best by the figure of Buddha. You have some other goal, presumably reincarnation. So, it is reason versus intuition. These are our attitudes, as a species.

And we continue to go beyond that. In general, when left to their own devices, either the West or the East will generate their own society and their own aesthetics . . . and now I'm getting back to your initial question. The whole point is, in this line of work, in poetry, you know quite well that you're not operating clearly in one or the other fashion. You may begin a poem in a process in delight or in confusion, or it would end in delight, or the other way around. You may begin writing a poem in a state of tremendous excitement and insight or you try to bring it about . . . you work feverishly in the grip of what is called inspiration. That's a fairly intuitive process, yeah? But you've written that, and you're typing it down and you have it on the page, and you pick up the pen and begin to delete and replace the words. And that process is an analytical process. So in poetry, you combine those two aspect, the Oriental approach and the Western approach. In the work of poetry, you always resort to fusion, one way or another. We—poets—are perhaps most accomplished, and that's why we are looked upon by the other disciplines—or by people with no discipline—with such fascination. The aesthetics that emerge from poetry is the aesthetics of fusion—of "Asian" and "Parisian," yeah? (Laughter) So I don't think it's fruitful to speak about an alternative aesthetic existing somewhere in the civilization of Christendom, because one way or another, Russia has been exposed to the poetry of the West, and the West has been exposed to the poetry of the East. I think I have answered your question; there is truth there in something that I've said. There are three methods of cognition: analysis, intuition, or synthesis, yeah? Synthesis is a process absorbing analysis and revelation, and in poetry, in the process of composition, you employ all three in one way or another. And that's what is interesting about poetry simply as a discipline. It is a tremendous mental accelerator. Once you hook up one word, one concept to another, through a rhyme, once you've uncovered that these two things are connected, you get addicted to that linkage, to that ability to create that linkage, to not only the *facility* of the linkage but the *certainty* of that linkage. That's what you do on paper; you uncover the dependencies, the relationships which are built into the language. The general manner in which your mind starts to operate is coupling, coupling, coupling. (Laughter)

Q: How do you see the relation of the image to the sound? Is it incidental, separate?

A: I will give you two answers. Basically, the imagery in a poem should be subordinate to its euphony; however, if you are a relatively old pro, you may forgo the euphonic beauty if you are enamored of the image, but you have to be very dexterous. In general, the reason I insist on euphony is perhaps the primacy of euphony. There, in the sound, we have in some animal way more than we have in our rational, . . . the sound can release a greater energy than the rational insight.

Q: So you think the energy is rational?

A: By and large, yes. Even if it's unrealistic, irrational—I have a question. Does anybody have a ciggy? (He bums another cigarette.)

Q: Yesterday you suggested that Russian is a language of qualifiers. It seems that the Soviet political system was a system of absolutes, and I wonder if you see our political system as one of qualifiers, and if and how it affects your writing?

A: No, no. Language is language, and political systems are political systems. The language of the Communist Party system, when it existed, [was] heavily influenced by the foreign syntax. The language that the state adopted for its newspaper, its official publications, was the language essentially of the polemics between Russia and its European opponents, usually Germany. It was translated from German into the Russian. The Party adopted the language of the victorious argument, so the language bore the imprint of a foreign syntax. I will give you one example: "Communism is the Soviet power plus the identification of the whole country." You wouldn't say this in Russian, though. In Russian you don't say "is." In Russian, you omit the verb "to be" as self-evident. You also wouldn't say "plus"; it's borrowed from the German. Obviously, when you wrote in Russian during the Soviet period, when I did, I would use those patterns simply for the purpose of mockery or some sort of ironic reference, if you will. The language resisted that sort of thing. When I said qualifiers, I meant subtleties. The Russian language is a rather remarkable thing, because the words are polysyllabic. The euphony of the word conveys to you the animal aspect of the word. Also, the Russian language is the language of "although." For instance, you say "I like this gentleman, *although* . . ." and this is where literature starts. (Laughter.) It's not so much the language of qualifiers—I misspoke—it is the language of the nuance, and no manner of violence done to the language by the state or by the commoners, nothing can change it. Hence, now the great weakness of the political process in Russia is that no one can come up with a slogan that will not be immediately ridiculed. Living in this country . . . English is an analytical language, a language of great clarity. You can't be fuzzy in English. The distinction between English and Russian or German or Italian is very simple:

in those languages, when you write, what matters is the combination, the way it sounds. Like playing chess. Writing in English is like playing tennis; the [word] immediately flies back into your face. Demagoguery in English is very difficult. And this, in part, is why you have been saved. It is a language in which it is very difficult to deceive. You can be deceived by an advertisement or by the manual to your refrigerator . . . but not by some great notion of this or that.

Q: It seems, from my perspective, that the only people who read poetry are in academia, and I wanted to know where you stood on this.

A: That's not true, because, as I said to you, had that been the case, were my readership only in academia, I would have to do something else than what I'm doing. I would have to supplement my living in some other fashion. It's not that I'm getting by on my royalties, but I live by my academic salary, so to speak [and he has that job because he is a successful poet read by a comparatively large audience]. But in a sense, I could get by on my royalties if I were single. I am more successful than most—the Nobel Prize and so forth. I count among my readers, in my twenty-three years in this country, people of various walks of life. I haven't seen a farmer . . . but I know doctors . . . okay, they're the educated class, but they're not academia. And they read poetry for consolation or distraction or for all the reasons poetry has been read all along.

The hour is up; the tape ends. Brodsky briefly continues a previous discussion of his "Immodest Proposal" idea of putting a volume of poetry in every hotel nightstand in America. (See the essay "Immodest Proposal" in *On Grief and Reason* [New York: Farrar, Straus and Giroux, 1995].

Notes

1. Brodsky, Joseph, "An Immodest Proposal," *The New Republic,* 11 November 1991, 31–36.

2. Brodsky, Joseph, "On Grief and Reason," *The New Yorker,* September 26, 1994, 70–85. This also appears as an essay in Brodsky's recently published book of the same name.

3. The second questioner, who asks if the "language of the soul could be political or ironic" and who defines "soul" as "a deeper self" is suggesting an individual aesthetic or voice. JB seems to agree when he says translating such realities of life as a communal apartment from Russian to English creates a disparity, but he is challenged by this, the eighth, questioner to recant, therefore "the sting."

Index